D1592598

Fundamentals of Naval Leadership

Titles in the
Fundamentals of Naval Science Series

Seamanship

Marine Navigation 1: Piloting

Marine Navigation 2: Celestial and Electronic

Introduction to Shipboard Weapons

Introduction to Naval Engineering

Fundamentals of Naval Leadership

Fundamentals of Naval Leadership

By the Department of Leadership and Law,
U.S. Naval Academy

Edited by
Professor Karel Montor and
Major Anthony J. Ciotti USMC

With earlier contributions by
Commander Malcolm E. Wolfe, USN
Captain Frank J. Mulholland, USMC
Commander John M. Laudenslager, MSC, USNR
Lieutenant Horace J. Connery, MSC, USN
Rear Admiral Bruce McCandless, USN (Ret.)
Professor Gregory J. Mann

Naval Institute Press
Annapolis, Maryland

Fundamentals of Naval Science Series

Library of Congress Cataloging in Publication Data
Main entry under title:

Fundamentals of naval leadership.

(Fundamentals of naval science series)
Rev. ed. of: Naval leadership. 2nd ed. 1959.
Bibliography: p.
1. Leadership—Addresses, essays, lectures.
2. United States. Navy—Officers—Addresses, essays, lectures. I. Montor, Karel. II. Ciotti, Anthony J. III. Wolfe, Malcolm E. IV. United States Naval Academy. Dept. of Leadership and Law. V. Naval leadership. VI. Series.

VB203.F86 1984 359.3′3041 84-14793
ISBN: 0-87021-419-5

Printed in the United States of America

This new edition of the classic *Naval Leadership* text is dedicated to the following officers, whose command vision and encouragement made it all possible.

Vice Admiral Edward C. Waller, USN Ret.
Commodore Leon Edney, USN
Captain Thomas D. Paulsen, USN
Commander Julius B. Dell, USN

Contents

Acknowledgments

The work of the following officers who so generously gave their time to accomplish the review and editing of the various drafts of this book is most appreciated by the editors. We also wish to thank Mrs. Margaret Seifert for her typing of the final draft, and Mrs. Jackie Wehmueller for her editorial support, which made a significant contribution to the organization and language usage.

CDR J. B. Dell, Jr., USN
CDR D. J. Vellis, USN
LCDR R. F. Stanton, USN
LCDR K. L. Morse, USN
LT E. D. Youngborg, USN
LT P. F. Abel, USN
LT J. L. Smeltzer, USN
LT R. K. Kelly, Jr., USN

This book is based in large part upon *Naval Leadership*, Second Edition, first published by the Naval Institute in 1959, and compiled by the six members of the Department of Naval Leadership of the U.S. Naval Academy listed on the title page of this volume. Their earlier contributions are gratefully acknowledged.

Foreword to the Second Edition of *Naval Leadership*

The Naval profession becomes more complex with each passing year. New scientific discoveries lead to the development of new weapons systems which in turn give new capabilities. These, in turn, introduce the need for new tactics at sea, and new strategic concepts in the employment of naval forces.

Thus naval officers must always remain flexible in their thinking, readily adaptable to change, and imaginative in the application of new developments to the strengthening of naval capabilities.

There is one element in the profession of arms, however, that transcends all others in importance. This is the human element. No matter what the weapons of the future may be, no matter how they are to be employed in war or international diplomacy, man will still be the most important factor in naval operations.

The need for good leadership, therefore, is the constant factor, and in this lies the officer's greatest opportunity for service to his country and to the cause of freedom throughout the world.

As leaders, naval officers are the example to whom others look for guidance, for inspiration, and for standards upon which to base their own conduct and beliefs.

In the eyes of the world, wherever the naval officer may go—indeed in the eyes of his own countrymen as well—the officer represents the finest in the manhood of our great nation.

The badge of naval rank and the insignia of the officers' commission will identify him everywhere with the power of the United States—not only the physical power of military forces, but more importantly the moral power of free men.

This is why it is so important that under the great pressure of our continuing need to develop the finest aircraft, the most modern submarines, the most far-ranging carriers, and the whole complex of nuclear weapons, we keep uppermost in mind that leadership remains our most important task.

No matter what mark an officer may leave in history by his deeds in battle, or in intellectual contributions, or in material inventions, his greatest legacy to his country will be the example he has given as a man and as a leader of men.

Washington, D.C.
2 January 1959

Arleigh Burke
Admiral, U.S. NAVY
Chief of Naval Operations

Fundamentals of Naval Leadership

1

Leadership: A Concept

This book will present the many aspects of leadership—approaches to and styles of leadership, examples of effective leadership, the psychology of leadership, and the factors and traits of the effective leader—to teach its readers to become more effective leaders. Unless leaders clearly understand themselves and the factors that influence the behavior of peers, seniors, and juniors when they are reacting as individuals and as members of a group, they cannot effectively discharge their leadership responsibilities.

Leadership Defined

Leadership can be defined as the art, science, or gift by which a person is enabled and privileged to direct the thoughts, plans, and actions of others in such a manner as to obtain and command their obedience, their confidence, their respect, and their loyal cooperation. Simply stated, leadership is the art of accomplishing the navy's mission through people. This will serve as the definition throughout this text; keep it in mind. The modern concept of leadership embodies a scientific approach; it is not straitjacketed in the philosophy that the ability to lead is an art or a gift with which an individual is endowed from birth.

Leadership concerns human relations, and specifically the relationship between one person and a group, or between leader and followers. It presupposes that there is—indeed there must be—a will, a consuming motivation, that the individual chooses to impose, through command, persuasion, or some other means, on subordinates. It connotes a willingness on the part of the individual to sacrifice personal time and material gain to achieve the capability to lead. Leadership is the profession of the officer in which proficiency can only be obtained through a constant study of leadership principles and practice in applying them in day-by-day relationships with juniors, seniors, and peers. It is not a one-way street that imposes responsibilities only on the follower, but is, rather, a mutual responsibility between follower and leader. A leader must have followers to be successful and must first of all have learned the principles of good "followership."

Consider briefly the four attitudes that leaders desire to instill in their followers: obedience, confidence, respect, and loyal cooperation. Lack of any one of these usually will be sufficient to spell disaster in any situation where naval leadership is involved.

Opinions on Leadership

Many books and papers have been written about leadership, and several different schools of thought and different approaches exist. These opinions range from the view that holds that leaders are born, not made—that either you have it or you don't—to the one that holds that leadership may be reduced to a set of principles that, if mastered, will enable anyone to lead effectively.

Another school of thought takes the stand that leadership is a managerial process, while another considers that it is principally a matter of character, of moral development, and still another holds that leadership can best be learned through a study of the lives and campaigns of great leaders.

Each of these viewpoints has merit, yet none is by itself the solution to the problem of how best to learn naval leadership. There is no denying that some persons are more favorably and more amply endowed than others with a quality that is often called "natural leadership ability." Yet there are instances of persons who were not so happily endowed, even some who were badly handicapped from birth, who nevertheless reached great heights of leadership as the result of arduous study, discipline, and work.

The managerial concept would fit many naval activities. The matter of character and moral development is of primary importance, especially in an age that emphasizes the material and scientific aspect of our civilization. The study of the lives of great people is a fascinating project, but it is time consuming and contains several pitfalls for the uninitiated. Not the least of these pitfalls is the tendency to judge a person in terms of the standards of the student's era rather than the standards of the era in which that great person lived.

The approach of this book. The approach to leadership taken in this book will include tenets of each of these schools of thought. The midshipmen and other young officers for whom this book is intended already have undergone a rigorous physical and academic selection process. Differences in leadership qualities and capabilities exist among these officers, and probably always will exist to some degree, despite the passage of time and the inevitable attrition that accompanies it. However, the leadership abilities a person already possesses can be substantially improved by study. Learning leadership only through experience is sometimes a lengthy and arduous process. To profit through the experience of others not only is good sense, but is mandatory to be an effective leader. Furthermore, there is not enough time in a naval career to learn solely through experience, and oftentimes experience is repetitious, teaching no new values or concepts of leadership.

The psychological principles of human behavior will also be important in this study of leadership. While no great military leader appears to have been a psychologist per se, the most successful military leaders had a keen understanding of human behavior and knew how to get the most from their followers. As a specialist in the study of human behavior, the psychologist has much to offer the naval leader of the present and the future. Regardless of what weapons the future may bring, the human element will remain the most important factor in military service, which is one reason all military officers should study psychology.

The Effect of External Influences

Leadership varies; it is adaptable to meet the requirements of different situations and times. First, different types of leadership are required among the many and varied walks of life, such as the military, the church, politics, industry, and even the underworld. Within each of these we may detect variations in leadership, some occupational or professional and some geographical. In the military area we may distinguish fine differences within the U.S. Navy/Marine Corps team, or Army and Air Force. We may note more distinct ones between, say, the armies of Germany, Japan, and the United States during World War II. Second, as one moves upward in the chain of command, the methods of execution of leadership undergo a gradual change. For example, the approach to leadership required of a commander-in-chief differs from that required of a commanding officer of a cruiser/battalion, which in turn differs from that required of a division officer/

platoon commander. And third, in any particular position of leadership there is a gradual change over the years to conform to the social and technological conditions of the time.

Leadership Is Inspirational

Since leadership is essentially the art of influencing human behavior, the appeal should be charismatic as well as intellectual. Truly great leaders have been able to make an emotional appeal to inspire people. Consciously or unconsciously they were able to use their personalities to inspire the imagination of others, to rally them to a cause, and to lead them to perform seemingly impossible feats. Inspiration is not the whole secret (if there is such a thing) of leadership, but it is a very important part.

Richard the Lion-Hearted was able to inspire men to flock to his cause wherever he fought. Peter the Hermit was largely responsible for the First Crusade. Joan of Arc rallied a dispirited and defeated French people to her cause and won victory after victory. Admiral Halsey was the type of leader needed by the U.S. Navy in the early days of World War II to bolster up sagging morale and instill confidence of victory. General MacArthur, even when driven from the Philippines, was able to inspire millions of Philippine Islanders, both native and American, to continue their resistance with his promise, "I shall return!" During the Korean conflict the 1st Marine Division found itself encircled by the Chinese 9th Army Group (consisting of approximately eight divisions) as it started its breakout from the Chosin Reservoir. When its commanding officer, Major General O. P. Smith, was asked if the division was retreating, he replied: "We are not retreating, we are attacking in another direction."

Inspiration comes in many forms. There are other familiar types of inspirational leadership. A football team is being beaten, for instance. During the half-time period, the coach or the team captain gives an impassioned plea, points out the players' mistakes, exhorts them to go back in and win. During the second half an inspired team turns the tide and wins. Corny? Perhaps—but it happens many times on the football field each fall. Each Saturday there are underdog teams that confound the experts by upsetting a highly favored rival. Navy has done it to Army, and vice versa.

Some emotional appeals seem to be most effective among the red-blooded, virile, youthful, and daring. These appeals may be made by either deeds or words, and the effect may endure not just for the moment, but for ages. Consider, for example, our legacy of Cushing's blowing up of the *Albermarle*, and Winston Churchill's "blood, toil, tears and sweat" speech with which he rallied people of the British Empire during its "darkest hour" in World War II.

But what about heroics? Individual acts of heroism never (in modern times) win wars or campaigns; such unglamorous statistics as tons of steel produced, barrels of oil refined, and miles of copper wire drawn are more significant. However, individual acts of heroism often win battles—but even if they didn't, they inspire acts in other men which do achieve victories. They set new records. The challenge to equal the existing record or set a new one is there, and the overall effect may transcend in importance the original act. Such appeal is inspirational. When you learn to play your job with the same enthusiasm as you do your sport, you will have arrived.

Signals, banners, flags, and other devices rank with deeds and words in inspirational value. All naval officers should recall Nelson's signal before Trafalgar: "England expects every man will do his duty." Banners emblazoned with slogans such as "Don't Give Up the Ship" and "Remember the Alamo" were inspirational. National flags are intended to inspire as well as to identify, and national anthems and bugle calls are part of the emotional appeal. When the ironclad Confederate ship *Virginia* shelled the frigate USS *Cumberland* at Hampton Roads in 1862, its skipper called to the Union ship to strike its colors (to signify surrender). Lieutenant George Morris of the U.S. Navy replied: "We will sink with our colors flying."

It is worth noting that the American people can be aroused and led (or misled) by appeals to the heart rather than the head. In World War I they were more provoked by alleged German atrocities than they were by changes in the map of Europe or statistics. A photograph of a Chinese baby in a bombed-out Shanghai railway station did more to crystallize American feeling against Japan than any of that country's territorial acquisitions. The Pearl Harbor attack united the many diverse and conflicting elements in the United States.

Naval Leadership

Naval Leadership Is Appointive

Some types of leaders are elected by their fellow men and women, some work or fight their way up with entirely selfish motives in mind, and some are appointed.

It is the "appointment" system from which the naval service derives its greatest strength. The military needs of our nation dictate having the capability to move individuals rapidly from one geographical area to another and also from one organization to another efficiently. Efficiency of transfer suggests that an officer be able to move from one organization to another without requiring a long break-in period. For example, in the civilian sector it usually takes a year for individuals to understand fully their new company, for there are both subtle and gross differences between one company and the next in industry. The military system is basically one of building blocks, and thus the division on one guided missile destroyer (DDG) can be expected to function and to be run basically the same as that on another DDG.

This commonality of operating procedures thus makes it possible for an officer to move from one organization to the next without a lengthy learning period. Setting up the requirements for each job and designing commonality into each organization make it possible for the navy to establish a criterion for performance that is expected of all officers, since all officers have primarily the same goals: mission accomplishment and the close second of concern for the welfare of the troops. Commonality of organizations and requirements for the officers who lead the organizations make it possible to create standards that must be met by those who choose the profession of military leadership. Thus with standards the naval service is able to educate and train individuals to become officers, and, on completion of this development program, the officers can be appointed in the officers corps. This is an extremely quick and efficient means of meeting the personnel needs of the service, as opposed to requiring officers to campaign for the leadership role and grapple with the implied necessity of paying back favors to those who contributed to your election—or at least being in a position to be elected out of office when those who you lead no longer want your guidance.

The military is not a democracy. Former Chief of Naval Operations Admiral Arleigh A. Burke stated it well: "Requirements for performance should be reasonable, just, and fair, but an individual in the military cannot decide which requirements will be met and which will be ignored, nor determine under what conditions these requirements will be met." It is the command, higher headquarters, higher authority, which determine direction, and an elected leadership will not survive in the military when a vote has to be taken on whether to follow a leader into battle. With honor as the hallmark of the fine officer and the need to put the organization ahead of oneself it is intolerable to let individuals fight it out for command. The strongest, the cleverest, the most selfish, or the most power hungry might win, and that would not be in the best interests of the service, as these individuals would work toward their own gain rather than putting the organization first. The appointment system is the keystone of military organizations; it is what makes for the smooth transition of officers from one assignment to another and greatly contributes to the variety and enjoyment officers experience in their jobs.

Leadership Styles

"Freedom Isn't Free" proclaims the popular Up with People singing group, and that phrase expresses not only the basis for our profession, but also the willingness of most Americans to pay the price so that our nation may continue to afford our citizens with liberties whose totality exist nowhere else in the world.

The standards of conduct by officers is established by the Congress of the United States, and the president is charged with the responsibility of ensuring that all military men and women meet these requirements. While civilian industry is the backbone of our industrial and economic might, it should also be recognized that outside the military the guarantees of individual rights and liberties are not so strongly defended. Capricious firings in the military are avoided by ensuring that no one individual may have another removed, and to that end highly qualified legal counsel is available to any service personnel who feel that their rights have been violated.

The key word in the foregoing is *rights*. It means for us in the military not only the right to have something done for us but also the right to contribute—to sacrifice—and the right as well as the obligation to take that action necessary to ensure that the mission is accomplished. It must be understood by all members of the military that the mission comes first, though of course the welfare of the troops is a close second. This, however, is no different from the situation in the family. Fathers and mothers and their children, along with close relatives, make up the family as we know it in civilian life. Most of the time the individual within the family is the primary concern of all those in the group, but when economic conditions force a geographic move that none of the individuals wants, the mission of keeping the family alive, together, and functioning may require a subordination of the wants of the members of the group. Thus it is with the military, where the greatest percentage of officer effort is concerned with the smooth functioning of the unit and the welfare of the individual members. To that end the officer must make every effort to ensure that the members of the unit have all the physical and psychological support necessary to do their job. In carrying out this part of the job, the officer will use many of the democratic principles we have learned to cherish in this country: listening, investigating the thoughts of the men and women in his unit, and so forth. Most of the time members of a military unit work together just as members of a family or a corporation do. However, when the mission is imperiled, immediate action and instant obedience of the officer by the group members will be necessary for victory and for lives and materials to be saved. It is at this point that many would say the major difference between civilian and military organizations exists. However, if you will discuss the matter with anyone who has spent a great deal of time in industry you will find that the officers, the executives of the firm, are required to work overtime without pay and, after making their thoughts known, religiously to carry out the orders of the "boss" when and how they are directed or, unlike the military, they will be out of the organization immediately, and without recourse!

Naval leadership, then, should be no more rigorous than necessary, and must not be allowed to become tyrannical, despotic, or dictatorial; nor should it be extended into nonmilitary areas.

Leadership Factors and Traits

Although a wide variety of opinions exist as to what constitutes leadership, there is no set formula as with Energy = MC^2. However, knowledge of the following leadership factors and traits is essential for the practice of leadership.

An effective leader sets the example by adhering to the leadership factors and displaying the leadership traits described here. Possibly the best example a leader sets is being a good follower. A leader knows his job; he establishes objectives and plans for their accomplishment. A leader also knows himself, strives for self-improvement, and takes responsibility for his actions, regardless of their outcome. He is consistent, but not inflexible; he can adapt his leadership to maximize its effectiveness in any given situation.

A leader's responsibilities to those under his command are many, and an effective leader realizes the importance of these responsibilities to the achievement of his organization's goals. Furthermore, an effective leader seeks and develops a sense of responsibility among his subordinates. He maintains their loyalty by treating each of them as an individual, not as a number; by keeping them informed; and by encouraging them to offer suggestions and/or constructive criticism. An effective leader helps his subordinates accomplish a given task by making sure they understand it, they are supervised in undertaking it, and they are trained and operating as a team. A leader knows his unit's capabilities and employs his unit in accordance with them.

The most important trait for a leader is integrity; he is upright, honest, and sincere. He is dependable and cooperative toward his organization and his subordinates, who count on him because he is loyal and unselfish. His sense of humor and his tact carry him through difficult situations. He is a good communicator, both in his speech and in his writing.

To his tasks an effective leader brings initiative, sound judgment, enthusiasm, creativity, and decisiveness. He shows endurance under duress because he is physically and morally self-disciplined and courageous.

On reassignment an effective leader can answer the question "Are the individuals I have just left better men for my having served them?" in the affirmative.

The key leadership factors and traits that have been discussed here are presented in list form below. The repetition of these features in this book is an indication of the importance of them to the naval service.

An effective leader

- sets the example
- has learned to be a good follower
- knows his job
- establishes objectives and plans for their accomplishment
- knows himself and seeks self-improvement
- takes responsibility for his actions, regardless of their outcome
- is consistent, but not inflexible
- seeks responsibility and develops a sense of responsibility among his subordinates
- treats every person as an individual, not as a number
- keeps his subordinates informed

encourages subordinates to offer suggestions and/or constructive criticism
makes sure the task is understood, supervised, and accomplished
trains his subordinates as a team
employs his unit in accordance with its capabilities

The major leadership traits are

integrity
dependability
cooperation
loyalty
unselfishness
sense of humor
tact
ability to write well
ability to speak effectively
initiative
judgment
enthusiasm
creativity
decisiveness
endurance
self-discipline
courage (moral and physical)

Summary

This text has been prepared for midshipmen at the U.S. Naval Academy and other officer candidates or student officers. It is hoped that through a study of this book students will have a better understanding and appreciation of their responsibilities when serving as a junior officer, in their dual roles of follower and leader. Furthermore, more-senior officers, as well as enlisted personnel already engaged in the active role of naval leadership, may find study of this book rewarding in that it can improve their effectiveness as naval leaders. The leadership principles, factors, and traits discussed herein are equally applicable to both arms of the naval service, the U.S. Navy and Marine Corps.

ATKRON 85

2

The Study of Human Behavior

Psychology is the study of human behavior; it is a science that studies the behavior and experience of living organisms in relationship to their environment. Psychology is not some mysterious and remote process that is practiced by and relegated to specialists in the field of human relations. Its principles have to do with people. How the leader controls and directs his interactions with people will determine primarily his success as a naval officer. Because human behavior is complex, there is no single way in which to approach its study. No short course can give the naval officer a complete insight into the interactions between human beings. However, to control and influence other people, the leader must first know himself. Additionally, he should have an understanding of human motives, of the differences between individuals, and of the responses of the individual when functioning alone and in a group.

The study of the principles of psychology in NL200 at the Naval Academy will give the student the knowledge that is considered of importance in a basic study of leadership. How and why individuals differ will be discussed in order to give the prospective leader a background for understanding himself and those with whom he comes in contact.

This book will discuss how motivation influences human behavior, as well as the problems concerned with the learning process, and how people respond when they are confronted with problems involving conflict and frustration. Since most of the actions of people involve other people, it is also necessary to investigate how people respond to one another. This is done in the study of groups: understanding group activities as well as the relation of the individual to the group of which he is a member.

The successful military leader must be a solver of problems. In fact, careful review and analysis will often lead to action that will avoid a problem in the first place. The problems encountered will be of many different kinds, but the most perplexing problems, and the problems that will be the most important to solve, will be those dealing with people. Human behavior has a particular significance for the military leader; it can be understood, and the principles for effectively managing it can be applied, by any intelligent human being. When healthy skepticism, objectivity, and a readiness for change are applied to problems dealing with people, effective leadership will result.

Skepticism

In an emergency situation there is little time for skepticism. To be prepared for an emergency, the leader learns to make accurate observations. In an emergency, there is minimal time to check observations with those of other people. You must be right or you will make a bad decision.

The officer in a nonemergency situation, however, can afford to be skeptical; he is determined not to be taken in by bad answers. One of his outstanding attitudes is a reasonable or healthy skepticism. It is an attitude that keeps a person from believing things until there is good reason to believe. And it is an attitude that is most important when you are seeking answers to problems. It makes you say, "Let's first have a good look," and "Just wait a minute." This attitude is the first step in getting viable answers instead of easy, ready-made answers to daily problems.

Most people hate to be caught not knowing things. When someone asks him a question, a person in a position of leadership or authority hates to admit he doesn't know the answer. It seems like a sign of weakness. But in a scientist or any other intelligent solver of problems, admitting uncertainty is often a sign of strength. It means an honest willingness to look around, an intelligent unwillingness to accept a ready-made answer. A leader must be intelligent enough to admit ignorance and work hard to avoid it.

Skepticism has very practical implications for the problem solver. The Navy or Marine Corps would not have useful tests for selecting and placing naval personnel if someone had not been skeptical about old-fashioned procedures. We would not even know the earth was round unless someone had become skeptical about its flatness. Skepticism leads to looking around; looking around leads to new information; new information leads to progress. Such progress does not come out of the minds of men who are completely satisfied with the intellectual status quo.

Skepticism, however, should not be confused with cynicism. Cynicism carries with it a sourness of outlook, a dissatisfaction with everything. The cynic is in favor of tossing out all the traditional answers, all established procedures. The skeptic is more rational. He wants to accept those answers that are supported by evidence and to modify or reject those that do not stand up under careful examination.

The best way to be a healthy skeptic is to establish the habit of asking yourself—and others—the simple question "What is the evidence?" and "What are the facts?" Asking these questions may not increase your popularity, but it will help to promote clear thinking.

Factual Information Is Vital

Individuals should not base their conclusions on hearsay, opinion, or a meaningless array of high-sounding words. They should demand evidence based on facts. If a person asks for evidence, and then accepts hearsay, opinion, or meaningless words, he is no better off than when he started.

Evidence comes in the form of *facts*. But what is a fact? The answer to this simple-sounding question is not as simple as many people think. It takes a clear-headed man to distinguish between a fact and a lot of other things—such as opinions—that just appear to be facts. If you plan to be a good solver of problems, it is a good idea to think carefully about what a fact is and how it differs from things that so often pass for facts.

This leads to the principle that a scientific fact is based both on observation and on an agreement among observers. In other words, a fact is an agreed-on observation between observers about an *object* or an *event*. How the observation was made, and the point from which it was made, determine the veracity of the observation. This definition has some practical implications. It means, among other things, that the observations of a single person are suspect. It also means that the critical-minded person does not accept his own single observation as foolproof and final. Nor does he accept observations by *any one* person, even though they may be repeated frequently, as solid bases for facts. He remembers that many subtle factors in the overall situation may influence the observation. He demands another look, at another time, under different circumstances.

Opinions, like facts, are often based on observations. An opinion is a personal relation between an observer and what he observes. The alleged fact that results from the single observation or from repeated observations by the single person is really an opinion.

Objectivity

The scientist, in addition to maintaining a skeptical outlook on life and applying the skills that enable him to tell the difference between real and bogus evidence, seeks to maintain an attitude of objectivity toward work. As previously stated, the scientist is skeptical of observations and sometimes goes to considerable lengths to have these observations checked by other people. He has learned that such self-suspicion and precautions are necessary if he is going to establish dependable knowledge.

Objectivity is associated directly with the nature of the observation process. An observation is a relation between a man and some aspect of the world. When, because of emotion or bias or other personal factors, the observation is made peculiar to the observer, the observation is said to be *subjective* rather than *objective*. If the observer has a smoothly functioning and healthy nervous system, he or she will make a clear observation, an objective observation. An important part of observing objectively, then, is observing in such a way that other calm and rational people will agree with the observation. The person who believes too much, who feels too much, who needs too much to have the world conform to a certain pattern, is not the sort of person who registers the clearest impressions of the world.

Both in observing and in interpreting, people are prone to be subjective. Remember the saying that people see the world as they want to, not necessarily as it is? Studies of people disclose a good deal of evidence to support this notion. Bias, prejudices, hopes, fears, likes, and dislikes undeniably serve to create peculiar perceptions. For example, an experiment showed that a fifty-cent piece looks decidedly bigger to a youngster to whom fifty cents represents a small fortune than it does to an adult who is accustomed to dealing with larger denominations of currency.

Nowhere so much as in judging people is observation likely to be biased and subjective. People are objects to like or dislike, to ignore or admire. When the average person observes another human being, he rarely can stifle the distorting influence of his own emotional relation to that person. The objective appraiser tries to get all the facts, and his estimate of the other person's worth is likely to be quite different from that of either that person's friend or enemy.

While the effects of bias are most dramatic when people are judging other people—or judging themselves—bias gets involved in judgments of "impersonal" matters, too. If you are interested in finding out the facts about a destroyer, for instance, you would be skeptical of the observations of the commanding officer if the commanding officer was known to be prejudiced toward the ship. Keep in mind, too, that the person who plans a training program is not always the one best equipped to judge its effectiveness.

The Pitfalls of Subjectivity

One of the basic characteristics of people in our civilization is their need to have answers. The individual grows up feeling that one answer is worth a hundred good problems. When confronted with questions, a person somehow feels inadequate if no answers are available. Embarrassment may be so acute that the person obtains answers without going to the trouble of securing good ones. This is sometimes a very unfortunate thing, for once a person gets an answer, good or bad, he tends to defend it subjectively. It becomes *his* or *her* answer, not the *problem's* answer, and the individual takes personally any attack on it. His ego is invested in the answer and he defends his ego by finding those facts—and only those facts—that support his answer.

This sort of ego-defending bias can be seen very clearly in arguments. The typical argument begins when two people make flat statements on opposite sides of a question. The stage is then set for a showdown in which each person is committed to a stand and is diligently seeking those facts and principles that are in line with his own stand.

Arguments, as a consequence, are rarely productive. They usually end with each participant being even more sure of the rightness of his original stand. Once a human being takes a stand on a question, he may no longer be in a position to observe impartially the facts that have a bearing on the case. He can easily sell himself down the river of subjectivity.

Discussions, on the other hand, sometimes produce satisfying results for the participants. A discussion does not begin with definite statements, but rather with an attitude of wonder, of seeking new evidence. The participants can pool their observations and may reach some tentative conclusions. Because no one has taken a definite stand, because no one has invested his ego in a set of beliefs, the discussion can result in the discovery of new and relevant facts.

The person who wants a good answer never begins his search for solutions to problems by saying "I am convinced . . ." Once he says that, he disqualifies himself as an objective observer. The good problem solver is the one who suspects the objectivity of his own perceptions.

Knowing what to observe and how to observe involves background knowledge. To get the best focus on human problems, the naval officer needs to know how human beings react, and he needs conceptual tools that can help him uncover factors in human performance. One aim of this book is to give the officer enough background to help him pay attention to the right things. It is logical to expect, for example, that the officer who understands the well-established principles of human learning or human frustration will be in a better position to solve training problems or disciplinary problems. He will be inclined to look for, and to see, some of the more subtle factors in human performance.

Readiness for Change

The person with good intellectual health suspects all varieties of ready-made answers, seeks evidence, recognizes evidence when it appears or is found, and strives to ensure objectivity in observations and interpretations. But there is still more to the scientific method than this. The true scientist is characterized by a readiness to act on evidence when it is discovered. This willingness to do something on the basis of evidence implies a good deal about the adequacy of intellectual adjustment. It means a readiness to change. It means a willingness to cast off the status quo if the light of evidence shows it to be out of date or senseless. For example, the naval officer must continually evaluate the current doctrines, standard operating procedures, and tactics to ensure that they have not become obsolete with the introduction of new ships, new aircraft, or new weapons systems.

Life is a process. Things are continually fermenting, continually interacting, continually altering. Some changes are so small that they have little practical significance—like the day-to-day changes in a maple leaf, or a change in one's age between yesterday and today. But changes go on continually. One may have to wait a month or a year or maybe even a decade for a change of practical importance to become apparent. But the person who acts as if yesterday was the same as today, or as if the 1950s were the same as the 1980s, is almost bound to be left holding old answers to new and different problems.

In these days of tremendous technological developments, the modern leader must adjust to change. The instruments of war change. Military problems change. In any group in which a leader may be involved, the social atmosphere, the state of morale, the psychological constitution, will change from day to day and week to week and war to war. The leader who attempts to deal with this pervasive change in terms of set attitudes, crystallized answers, and fixed habits of thought and action is not likely to achieve the pinnacle of success.

A readiness for change, however, does not mean a violent opposition to all aspects of the status quo. The raving radical who opposes all current ways of doing things and the person who would change nothing at all are equally apt to be unhappy, and they will run a close race in uselessness. The leader who recognizes change when it happens is a wise leader. If he accepts change when it is inevitable, he has a better chance of being both a happier and a more effective leader.

Summary

There are skills as well as attitudes involved in successful problem solving. There are skills involved in maintaining objectivity. There are skills involved in recognizing evidence. There are skills involved in bringing about the most profitable sort of relations between the human nervous system and the objects or events it is observing. There are skills involved in asking good questions about significant things. There are skills involved in recognizing and accepting change.

This chapter has described these skills to enable the leader to become intimately familiar with them, to learn them if he chooses, and to use them in wrestling with his own problems.

3

Motivation and Learning

One may refer to motivation as the regulation of behavior that is generated by the needs and drives within the individual and by the influence of the environment. The simplest motivations are generally considered to be physiological in nature, arising from bodily needs. The more complicated motivations are considered to be essentially social in nature, developing from interrelationships among individuals. Learning can result from the need to satisfy either simple or complex needs. This chapter will examine more closely the various factors and influences that account in large measure for the behavior of human beings.

Motivation

The ability to understand and predict man's behavior is increasing. Although they are not in complete accord, scientists generally agree that man will understand better and predict more precisely if he adheres to these scientific principles: (a) behavior is caused and (b) behavior can be accounted for in terms of explainable causes. In other words, behavior happens because things make it happen. Behavior is seldom an accidental, wayward process, and it is generally amenable to cause-and-effect analysis. However, while human motivation is frequently influenced by laws, customs, traditions, and past experiences, actual behavior is the result of choice on the part of each individual. Because the choices made depend on experiences peculiar to the individual, the actions of any given individual are not totally predictable.

The scientist can only see facts; he never sees an explanation. So he observes facts, and he creates explanations, which he calls "constructs." He creates a picture in his mind of the processes going on behind the events he observes. If a man was unable to observe the inner operation of a watch, but he could observe the movement o the hands and the response to winding and hear the watch ticking, he would soon create for himself a picture of what the inside of the watch looked like. If he observed the watch long enough, and under different conditions, he could make a construct—a picture of the dynamics of the watch. The construct, if it accounted for all the behavior of the watch, and if it was the simplest possible explanation, would be accepted as an explanation of the watch's behavior. In explaining human behavior, the psychologist observes what people do and then creates constructs (explanations) to account for the observed events.

Need Constructs

If you closely note the behavior of a shipmate about 1130 or 1200 of a typical day, you will probably observe that the man becomes increasingly restless; that the subject of food comes more and more into his conversation; that incidental things remind him of something to eat; and, sooner or later, that he makes direct movements toward a place where food is available. You can conclude that your shipmate is hungry.

However, you haven't seen this hunger. You have observed only behavior. The man has a need, and you use a construct to explain his behavior. The construct is a mental picture of processes going on behind the behavior you see.

If you observed yourself, you would probably find that at about 1130 your stomach muscles begin to contract. Continued investigation might reveal that elaborate biochemical processes led to this contraction of the muscles of your stomach. Usually, however, you needn't worry about this process working within your body. You need food; and you will satisfy this need.

The need in this case stands for some complicated and unobserved processes within the person observed. The observer creates the notion of "hunger" to explain these inner processes. If he says his friend has a "sex need" or a "need to dominate" or a "need for social status," what he is doing is imagining something to explain behavior. This something that explains behavior is a construct.

Sometimes no detailed information as to what processes motivate behavior is available. In the case of hunger, the internal tensions bring about behavior—which leads to the eating of food. This in turn reduces the internal tensions. In the case of gregariousness, too, a man may behave as if he had a built-in tension. He may become restless if he is not around other people, and he may show evidence of feeling better when his friends are nearby. We say that such a person is endowed with a need to be with others. In other words, his actions indicate that he has a gregarious need. If by composing an explanation, a construct, we can predict this person's behavior, then the construct serves a useful purpose.

The Nature of "Needs"

Psychologists usually agree that the construct of need can be used to account for behavior (some prefer the words *drive* or *motive* to the word *need*, but the basic notion is the same). One can consider a *need* to be a tension that a man carries around with him. It is a tension that will, under the proper circumstances, lead to observable "seeking behavior." Under the influence of a need, a man will keep going until the need is satisfied. He may use behavior patterns he has found to be adequate in the past, he may simply thrash about at random, or he may use recognized, intelligent, problem-solving behavior. When a need is satisfied, then seeking behavior ceases.

Universal needs—needs that are common to people in all cultural environments—include the need for food and drink, the need for rest and sleep, the need for activity, the need for breathing and elimination, and the esthetic need for interesting sights and sounds. All people share these needs; they are a dependable part of human nature. It is necessary to look to other, external, forces, such as the social environment and the state of culture, as determinants of the many other needs individuals develop.

Needs other than these universal ones are a less dependable part of human nature. There is the need for sex, the need to have and love children, the need to acquire property, the need to be successful, the need to be with others, the need to fight. None of these needs is found in every person, but some of them, such as the need to be with others, occur in most people. Some of these needs—the need to fight, for example, or the need to acquire property—are found often, but there are many people who do not have them.

Primary Needs

For our discussion *primary needs* may be defined as those needs that are rooted in physiological necessities and conditions. This category includes the needs described above as universal. More is known about these needs, in a way, than about the more elaborate needs.

Because there is something solid for the constructs of hunger and thirst to rest on, some people are much happier to talk about these needs than about such needs as gregariousness or aggressiveness. They try to explain human behavior almost entirely in terms of these primary tensions. Most psychologists agree, however, that a man's fervent desire to become successful cannot adequately be explained by referring directly to his need for food or love. Life is not that simple.

Primary needs, it is true, must be satisfied if the organism is to survive. Oxygen, food, water, must be taken into the body. The organism must rest, but it can survive for its allotted years without any sexual satisfaction. The organism will often regard itself as unhappy if there is no sexual activity in its life, and sexual deprivation may result in maladjustments, but sex is not necessary for individual survival, though of course it is necessary for the survival of the species.

Derived Needs

Most of the tensions people carry around with them are derived. They are learned needs, presumably derived, through elaborate learning processes, from the primary needs. The derived needs, as we have seen, may be relatively dependable. Gregariousness, for example, is a need found in almost all people. Most people like to be with other people and are vastly unhappy when they are isolated from the company of others. But while the majority of the human race is learning to like the company of others, a minority is learning to dislike being with other people.

There have been many attempts to catalog and classify all human needs, but complete agreement on how needs are best catalogued has never been arrived at, and a satisfactory list has never been made. The variety and complexity of human needs is so great that one can do little better than try to discover the particular needs operating in particular individuals at particular times.

The Influence of Culture on Needs

Man learns many of his needs, and many are dictated by his environment. Each individual is born into a culture. People around him have established patterns of life. They know what is good, what is bad, what is success, and what is failure. They have definite opinions about morality. They work, play, make love, and eat in certain ways. They revere the institutions that they have created to meet common problems and common needs. These habits, values, assumptions, morals, customs, and institutions vary tremendously from one culture to another. The social climate in New York is not the same as that in Tokyo, Tehran, or Belgrade. The individual must live in harmony with the culture into which he is born. For the midshipman this means learning the requirements and operating procedures of the brigade and of the naval service. The process of creating this harmony, this peace of mind, is largely a process of learning the culturally endorsed needs.

The individual's physiological needs are timed and trained by the daily routine of the tribe, class, nation, or culture. Little of the behavior stemming from primary needs is free of drastic cultural influence. In the case of derived needs—social needs—culture is even more influential. Culture determines many of these needs, and it also has a determining influence on the wheres, whens, and hows of the behavior that results from the needs.

Consider, as an example, self-assertiveness: the desire to assert oneself, to obtain standing and position, to achieve superiority. In America this need is likely to be regarded as a basic component of human nature. Perhaps an identifying characteristic of Americans is their need for status, achievement, or excellence. But Americans weren't born that way, they learned to be that way. In our culture, where the pervasive need for self-assertiveness cannot be denied, there are fairly definite rules, known to the majority, about what success or excellence is and what means may legitimately be used to achieve it.

Needs of the Individual

Very little can be assumed about an organism's needs just because it is human. "Universal human nature" is a limited thing. But if you know where an individual has grown up, you can fairly safely make a few additional assumptions regarding his needs. These culturally influenced needs, however, can be pinpointed only if the individual is studied.

A knowledge of general human needs will be somewhat helpful in understanding the individual. But to make real predictions about an individual, it is necessary to find out what needs will account for his behavior. The process of establishing needs for the individual is the same as the process employed in settling on the needs of mankind in general. Observe behavior and create in your mind a construct that will account for the individual's behavior. If the observation is good and the construct is clearheaded, you can predict fairly well what the observed individual will do in a specific situation. Suppose, for example, that on the basis of careful study, the division officer determines that a certain chief petty officer has a strong need to dominate. The wise officer, then, will avoid putting this chief petty officer immediately in charge of a first-class petty officer who violently hates to be dominated, for he can easily predict that this pairing would result in a personality clash.

Emotions of the Individual

Not only do human beings have needs and develop habits, they also become emotional. Men know fear; men get angry. What makes them afraid or what makes them angry varies tremendously from culture to culture and from man to man. Still, the capacity for emotion can be regarded as a basic part of human nature.

Newborn infants will show fear if they are dropped suddenly or if a loud noise is made near their head. And they will show anger if they are restrained so that they cannot move. One might say, then, that it is human nature to fear loud noises and to become angry at physical restraint.

If this is human nature, it is "improved" upon a great deal in the process of growing up. A list of the things that an adult fears or that make him or her angry will be a good deal more elaborate than a list of these things for a newborn baby. Through a process of learning, our emotional life becomes complex. The growing individual learns, perhaps, to fear the dark or snakes or high places or people or airplanes. And he may learn, in a pretty complicated way, to get angry when somebody calls him names or deprecates his home state or belittles his ship. Many of these learned fears and angers make sense—it is sensible to respect rattlesnakes and dynamite, for example—but some emotional responses do not make good sense. An unreasonable fear of high places, for instance, can generate many problems in a person's daily life. So can a morbid fear of dirt—or of fire. Whether our emotions do us service or harm depends mainly on our perceptions.

Emotions are often frowned upon, but sometimes they can be very useful. In times of fear or anger, for example, nature puts the body in an emergency condition. The presence of an enemy who is feared or hated in effect sounds a call to general quarters in the body. The heart works harder, blood leaves the digestive area and concentrates in the arms and legs, ready to carry more energy to the muscles and carry away waste products; the energy-giving sugar in the blood becomes more plentiful; adrenalin is secreted into the blood stream. The net result of these physiological changes is that the emotion-charged individual can work harder, run faster, last longer, and bleed less if wounded. Fear and anger put the body on an emergency footing.

This does not mean, of course, that fear and anger ought to be cultivated. In normal, everyday activities, the body and brain will work much better when they are in a state of harmony. People often "fall apart" under the influence of extreme fear or anger; on the other hand, many battles have been won by the side that most wanted the victory.

It is human nature, then, to have emotions in some situations. Well-balanced individuals learn what to emote about, and also what to do when they are emotional. They learn, for example, that it is gentlemanly to invite an adversary to put on the boxing gloves; that it is "sissy" for a man to cry. They learn that it is irresponsible to panic in an emergency; that uncontrolled anger is counterproductive. The naval leader's responsibility with respect to the emotions of his men includes training them how to react when their emotions become dominant. In a dangerous situation, where the "natural" impulse is to run, the well-trained military person has habits that stifle this impulse and keep him functioning at his duty station.

Learning

Why People Learn

Man is to be understood only as he has been shaped through the interplay of his biological inheritance and the continuous impact of day-to-day living in his social world, the world of other people. Man, in part, is what he has learned to be.

Unfulfilled needs most frequently impel people to learn. As the study of motivation pointed out, unfulfilled needs lead to varied activities in the effort to satisfy them. When a person becomes bored with one way of satisfying a need, he turns to something else. The need to diversify, to learn a new approach, is motivated by boredom. The age-old practices of controlling learning through reward and punishment depend for their successes on the intimacy between motivation and learning. A child is "good" or "bad" (his behavior) to get what he wants (his motivation) depending on which way he has previously learned will produce the best results.

Unfulfilled needs create problems for a person, so another way of stating the basic conditions for learning is to say that the desire to satisfy the need is what brings a person up against the problem and induces him to learn. A problem in this sense covers a great deal: to remove a hatch cover is a problem; to fire a gun is a problem; to operate a radar set, establish a friendship, or complete a term paper—all these are problems, and learning takes place in finding the solutions. In each problem there is something the learner is trying to do and something that delays his doing it. Learning goes on as he seeks to shorten that delay and as he profits by prior experiences in reaching his goals.

An active individual, however, does not wait for problem situations to arise before learning. He creates some of his own needs, and he deliberately seeks problems to solve. Self-created or self-discovered problems provide many occasions for learning: individuals set out on voyages of exploration, or they set up research projects in factories or experimental laboratories. Learning, then, is not merely a way out of difficulties with which the individual happens to be confronted; it is also a way to achieve some of the deep satisfactions that come from productive, self-initiated tasks.

How People Learn

In the learning process, the need comes first. But the need is by no means the whole story. If a man who can't swim is tossed overboard in the middle of the Philippine Sea, there is little doubt of his strong need to swim. There is equally little doubt that the man will drown unless he is immediately retrieved by someone. His natural, unlearned behavior—a wild and desperate thrashing about—will not satisfy the need to stay afloat and breathe. But if the man escapes drowning and resolves to learn to swim, his behavior in the water thereafter will not long remain wild and random. In order to satisfy his need to swim, his behavior gradually changes. Thrashing gradually gives way to more precise and coordinated movements, and the need to get through the water is more efficiently satisfied.

The same sort of process goes on with respect to learning French, calculus, skating, dancing, rowing a boat, or navigating a ship. First comes the need. Then comes a change in behavior so that a person gets his or her need-satisfying job done more efficiently. Actions become more precise, and useless movements are eliminated. Ideas become clearer, and connections between ideas more clear-cut. Useless mental or verbal responses are omitted.

The process of learning any physical or intellectual skill progresses from wasteful, random, and ineffective responses to precise, directed, and effective ones. The skilled swimmer is one who makes no unnecessary motions. The skilled golfer is one who finishes the course in the smallest number of strokes necessary. The competent mathematician manipulates sines and cosines with great precision and without erroneous (wasteful) responses.

Learning, in essence, is the acquisition of more effective ways of behaving. The process will go on, regardless, if needs are there, but it can be made speedier and more adaptive. Learning can be thought of as an observable change in behavior.

Reward and Punishment

Reward and punishment are important aspects of the learning process. When properly used, both reward and punishment can make learning more efficient, but they are often misused, especially punishment. Reward is likely to "stamp in" the response you want the learner to make, but punishment is not so dependable. Punishment not only may fail to erase an incorrect response, it may even ensure that the incorrect response will be learned and repeated at a later time. Punishing an individual for making errors may, instead of erasing the errors, simply make the learner concentrate on them instead of acquiring corrective behaviors. This naturally retards learning.

Calling too much attention to errors is in itself a poor educational practice, but negative instruction takes place when punishment is meted out without the learner knowing what it is for. Perhaps one of the most effective ways to make a man neurotic is to punish him without his knowing what he has done wrong. In response to this disturbing sort of frustration, the learner may fixate on certain responses, right or wrong; he may turn apathetic, go on unauthorized absence, or regress. Punishment is educational dynamite; it must be handled with care.

There is a better way: the system of positive reinforcement. Known to the psychologist as operant conditioning, the principle lets the individual know when he is doing something right. When the recruit properly executes a marching movement you let him know, and if on a limited basis he makes some moves incorrectly, you ignore the errors and then give praise when the right action is taken.

The same principle—the principle of positive reinforcement rather than negativism—can profitably be used to increase the efficiency of almost any process of learning. The teacher must know where the errors are and then take steps to remove them. The best step generally is to call attention to the right response, to find ways the student can make the right response more easily, and then to reward him immediately. This avoids the teaching of errors. An important principle is to praise in public and punish, when necessary, in private.

The best way to learn what not to do is to learn what to do, instead. A teacher with a deflated ego may derive some satisfaction through stressing and punishing his students' errors, but he does not inculcate much learning by such procedures. Negative teaching is ineffective teaching.

In a few situations, and for a few people, reproof or blame for poor performance may, of course, be necessary. But in most situations and for most people, praise for good work gets better results than blame for poor work. Praise doesn't have to take the form of a eulogy. A sincere "well done" and an encouraging smile or an approving nod from an officer is generally rewarding enough.

This discussion of rewards and punishments has been concerned only with those coming from the leader. But often the most powerful rewards or punishments come from the man's satisfaction or dissatisfaction in his own performance. If a man is interested in learning a task, any improvement in performance is stimulating tonic, and failure to learn hurts. No one ever has to reward an addicted golfer to make him want to improve his game. Any adjustment in his swing that keeps him out of the rough and puts him on the green will be pampered, practiced, and perfected. If convinced that he has a bad movement at the end of his backswing, he will spend hours trying to correct it.

In learning anything, whether intellectual or physical, if the learner really wants to achieve proficiency, correct responses are their own reward and incorrect ones are automatically punished. The officer's job then becomes primarily one of helping the junior learn the correct response.

Summary

Learning takes place when a person has a need (or problem) which is not relieved (or solved) by responses already available. If left entirely to their own devices, people may resort to random behavior to solve their problems. But by observation, by the use of transfer, and, to some extent, by the use of mechanical guidance, the period of randomness may be shortened and the efficiency of learning may be increased.

The behavior of an individual is motivated and directed in various ways. In the next chapter, the varieties of adjustment that constitute the "human factor" in man's relationship to his environment will be considered as part of the continued investigation of the basic relationship between psychology and leadership.

4

Conflict and Frustration

This chapter will discuss the factors producing conflict and frustration and the various human responses to conflict and frustration. When a person is caught in a situation where his needs push him in opposite directions—where he wants to have his cake and eat it, too—he is in conflict. The environment we live in is by no means tailored to the needs of any one person. When a complex individual wrestles with a complex life, it is inevitable that he will encounter conflicts. It is also quite certain that many needs will be thwarted. He will have desires that, for one reason or another, cannot be fulfilled. Frustration, in modern life, is frequent and unavoidable. In routine living, a person encounters many things that upset his "normal" adjustment, and he takes steps to regain it.

Adjusting to Unsatisfied Needs

There are many individual differences among members of the human race. These differences make it very difficult to define what is meant by a "proper" or "normal" adjustment for an individual. A person's mental health or adjustment pattern should be seen in terms of not only physical and psychological needs, but also social, moral, and religious needs, along with capacity for self-improvement; and all of these factors should be considered in terms of the individual's daily environment.

Any attempt to define "normal" behavior makes it apparent that the task is not an easy one. Adjustment can be thought of as the satisfaction of needs. But an individual's needs are never completely satisfied. Needs vary from person to person, and even within the same person at different times. Behavior that is quite acceptable under one set of circumstances can be completely out of order under different circumstances. For example, a person's behavior during routine training operations might not be acceptable in combat. "Normal" behavior or adjustment, then, is a matter of degree. The physician is not taken to task because he holds to a rather high definition of health despite the fact that the majority of people suffer from slight or even serious ill health. The concept of normal personality or psychological adjustment requires similar treatment.

In routine living, a person encounters many things which tend to upset his normal adjustment, and he takes steps to maintain his equilibrium.

The human being is a needy organism who is born with a few primary needs and picks up many more in the process of making his way in life. In fact, a person's life is spent in seeking to satisfy needs.

In some situations satisfying a need is a simple process. A person with a strong need for food or rest may almost automatically perform those acts found in the past to be useful in satisfying those needs. In a very simple way the need leads to familiar patterns of behavior that in turn very simply lead to satisfaction. Everything is fine—until the need returns. Then the habitual sequence transpires again, sometimes almost identically, sometimes with negligible variations as a result of minor changes in the environment.

When the individual can give adequate, need-satisfying, responses to stimuli, life is quite simple. However, very rarely is human behavior this simple. At any one time the individual is moved not by a single need, but by plural needs—perhaps a few, but more likely many—and his behavior will be a result of interacting needs. Thus the behavior that grows out of an interacting pattern of needs is always a compromise, because no single need can be fully satisfied.

Conflict

The young seaman recruit or private finds "boot camp" strange, perhaps distasteful. He may come from a home where he had a room to himself, and, although he was required to keep it clean, the placement of his clothes, for example, was not as uniform and exacting as the new situation demands. Perhaps the recruit had a job in civil life and took considerable pride in doing it well. Now he finds that he has a strong urge to return to the things that are more familiar. He would like very much to put his feet under his mother's table, to be free to go dancing with his girlfriend—in short, he is homesick. On the other hand, the recruit feels very strongly the responsibility he assumed when he took the oath of enlistment, and, in those moments when going on unauthorized absence occurs to him, he realizes the full cost of the penalties attached to that action. If he reduced the situation to words he would probably say, "I would give anything to be home tonight, but . . ."

This young person is caught in a highly charged conflict, one that has caused a lot of people a lot of trouble. Conflicts may be highly charged, like this one, where strong needs are involved, or they may be mild, where a choice can be made immediately. A person's pattern of needs is so complicated that resolution is often difficult. Almost everything he or she does or seeks has its advantages and disadvantages.

Types of Conflict

Conflicts can be roughly classified into three types: those that require making a choice between an attractive and an unattractive alternative, between two attractive alternatives, and between two unattractive alternatives.

The problem of the recruit exemplifies the first type of conflict. His motives make going on unauthorized absence both attractive and repulsive at the same time. In our daily life this sort of conflict is frequently encountered. A person may want to succeed—but succeeding in the naval service means hard work. A person wants to marry—but marriage means responsibility. He wants sea duty—but sea duty may mean a long absence from friends. He likes to drink—but drinking may get him into trouble. In many, and perhaps most, life situations, the bad comes with the good. Conflicts become serious only when the pros and cons are strong and of approximately equal strength.

Another type of conflict occurs when the choice is between two equally attractive courses of action. Shall he go to the dance or to the movies? Shall she marry Mark or David, both of whom are ready, willing, and attractive? Having to choose between two equally pleasant courses of action is the most desirable sort of conflict to face, but it still can interfere, at least momentarily, with smooth and effective behavior.

Then, finally, there is the less agreeable conflict where one must choose between two unattractive courses of behavior. Shall she spend her time on mathematics or navigation tonight? Since his uniform hasn't come from the cleaners, shall he get it and report for duty late and pressed, or shall he report on time and unpressed?

Reaction to Conflict

When an individual is caught in a conflict situation, the individual's "normal" pattern of behavior is interrupted.

Paralysis as a response. If the conflict is severe, the individual may simply "freeze." He is unable to do anything. For example, there was a jackass who found himself exactly halfway between two piles of hay. Unable to decide which to eat, he starved to death. This sort of "paralysis" does happen in everyday life, though it is rarely associated with the choice between two equally attractive courses of action. It is more likely to occur when something is both attractive and repulsive at the same time.

Many cases of so-called laziness are probably explainable as "paralytic" reactions to conflict. The "lazy" enlisted man, if studied carefully, often turns out to be the man who has a conflict. He wants to be successful, but the road to success looks extremely difficult or his chances of failure look so great that he is afraid to try. Hard work is good in that it usually leads to success; but it may also lead to failure. In such a conflict a person is likely to continue in a state of dissatisfaction and inaction and to appear to the casual observer to be "lazy."

This sort of conflict often affects the individual's personal efficiency. Most people will work as long as work promises certain rewards; they will not work when work promises to bring failure, punishment, or at most only small rewards. If at any moment the possibility of failure seems equal to or greater than the possibility of success, a person will not wholeheartedly do his work. Of course, he must realize that, with any success, he must take the bad with the good; he must suffer some, and he must run some risk of failure. If the suffering and risk seem greater than the rewards of success, however, a person will make no effort. If the disagreeable aspects of work are too disagreeable, if it looks to the individual as if the reward, instead of being appropriate to the effort and the performance, is a matter of luck, his behavior will be continually uncertain, inefficient, and full of conflicts. On the other hand, if the chances of success are reasonably good, if it appears that success is not accidental but fairly and inevitably dependent on high effort and good performance, personal morale will be high and work will be efficient. The hardships of work will be taken in stride.

The naval leader can place his or her subordinates in either of these situations with little difficulty. It is relatively easy for a division officer to inspire his subordinates—or to make them "lazy." All he has to do is to give reward where reward is due—or, conversely, to reprimand a person who is really trying, or fail to notice when the unit does good work. If the individuals in the division are going to work, they must be assured that hard work pays off, and doing nothing must not be made safer than honest effort.

In many everyday situations where individuals are caught in a paralytic conflict, the pattern of behavior may be only momentarily interrupted. Everyone has experienced a fleeting moment of "freezing" in a small conflict, but generally a decision was reached with little trouble. What happens is that one need becomes stronger than the others—for behavior, as always, will follow the strongest need.

There are those, of course, who will continue to say that the individual in conflict is just "lazy." And they will say that so-and-so, being lazy, needs nothing more than a "bracing up." This diagnosis is never adequate, and while stiff treatment may produce activity of some sort, it will rarely result in enthusiastic work. Good work results when work promises satisfaction of the many needs of the worker. Good work will not materialize if the job promises frustration and unpleasantness. Generally speaking, the more reward-promising the work, the more enthusiastic the worker. If the advantages outweigh the disadvantages, the hardships will be taken in stride. It should be noted that rewards for an officer may well be delayed, and thus military personnel must be educated and trained to perform at their highest level without receiving immediate recognition.

Alternation as a response. A second reaction to conflict is alternation. The person in conflict may try one course of action for a short period of time, then turn to some other course. The hungry rat who can get food only by crossing an electric grill that viciously shocks him will often go toward the food until he gets close to the grill. Then he will retreat, only to approach the food—and retreat from the grill—again. This alternate approaching and retreating may continue until the rat's hunger becomes so strong that he will take the shock in stride to satisfy his hunger. In everyday situations, however, less dramatic instances of alternation are encountered. With respect to work, the individual may alternately work with great zest and loaf with complete ease.

Escape as a response. The person in conflict frequently behaves in such a way as to avoid making a choice. For example, an indecisive officer may consider that if he remains in his billet, he is likely either to get in trouble with his men or to have to be overly strict. Both courses of action are equally distasteful, so he requests a change of duty. This is an easy escape from conflict, but it is a poor demonstration of leadership.

However, sometimes a physical escape from the arena of conflict is very wise. Doctors who recommend a change of scene, such as a trip to Europe, a summer in the mountains, or a winter in Florida, are often simply arranging for the patient to escape temporarily from a situation that throws him into a tense and debilitating conflict.

The only trouble with utilizing physical escape to avoid conflict is that any relief achieved in that way may be only temporary. For instance, the emotionally upset individual who requests sea duty to escape a conflict at home may merely be playing ostrich. He can stick his head in the sand, and perhaps temporarily escape from his conflict, but he has to come up for air sometime. When he does, the conflict confronts him again. He hasn't solved his problem, he has only ignored it temporarily. Perhaps, after some rest and a change of scene, he will be better able to solve it, but the problem still must be solved.

A lot of conflicts, once a choice is made, tend to solve themselves. Suppose a person is fortunate enough to have a choice between two equally attractive alternatives. Unable to reach a decision, he flips a coin. Once he acts on the alternative selected by the coin, the other choice loses its attraction. If the coin had fallen the other way, he ultimately would have been just as happy. Either course of action satisfies the basic needs involved.

Compromise as a response. Much of our lives we live by compromise. We cannot have our cake and eat it, too, so we figure out clever ways to have some and eat some. If we can't eat our cake, we find something else almost as good to substitute for it. It has been said that the difference between the optimist and the pessimist is that the pessimist can always find a difficulty in every opportunity, while the optimist can find an opportunity in every difficulty.

We cannot expect to avoid conflicts completely. Life is full of them. We can only hope to diagnose our conflicts properly and then to go about intelligently finding the best solutions for them. The more difficult conflicts result from our acquiring divergent needs that by their very nature cannot be satisfied at the same time, or, similarly, behavior mechanisms that are inconsistent with the need or with each other.

Frustration

Frustration occurs when need-satisfying behavior is blocked. In the simplest case of human behavior, we have seen how a need arises, how adaptive behavior patterns are turned on, how satisfaction is achieved, and how tension arising from the need disappears. But we have seen, too, that life rarely is so simple. Conflicts interfere with the basic "natural" process. More complications occur if a barrier arises to prevent the individual from going where he wants to go or doing what he wants to do.

When an individual is frustrated, the simple directness of his behavior disappears and he characteristically becomes emotional. His reactions, though they serve a psychological function, may get him nowhere at all. To the casual outside observer, the behavior of a frustrated individual may make no sense whatsoever; but frustrated behavior is human, and the person who is going to work with others will do well to understand something about it.

Causes of Frustration

Inanimate things and intangibles. When an individual wants something he can't get—whether that something is as trivial as a lost pencil or as all-important as reaching the top of his profession—he is frustrated. The man who needs cigarettes and finds the ship's store closed is a good example of frustration. He may try in various ways to get cigarettes and, if he is thwarted, may become agitated and angry. The cancellation of a scheduled airline flight, the changing of a traffic light, physical distance, fences, walls, busy telephones, stopped engines, low tides, and thousands of other impersonal things—all of these interfere with the individual's attainment of his goals.

Human interactions. People, probably more often and more disturbingly than inanimate objects, hem a person in and obstruct the attainment of goals. People, of course, facilitate goal-seeking behavior, too, but because people have their own needs to worry about, it is inevitable that they are going to get in one another's way. The individual can expect almost any human association—even friendship or marriage—to be frustrating at least some of the time. Friends and spouses are people; they have their own needs. When a friend's needs or a spouse's needs run counter to our own, somebody is going to be frustrated.

Being frustrated by a person—whether that person is merely an individual trying to get along, or a symbol of law, order, and property—is generally more disturbing than being blocked by an inanimate object. In the first place, people are more complex than a door that won't open. Secondly, they are supposed to be more sympathetic and understanding than inanimate objects. You expect people to be reasonable and cooperative; when they aren't, your frustration may be increased. Finally, if you resort to aggression under frustrating circumstances and attack the barrier, the human barrier may fight back. You can smash a locker and it won't hit back, but any venting of anger on another person is likely to produce retaliation in kind, as well as a guilt complex in the person who gave way to his feelings in the first place.

Rules and values. When people live together, whether as a culture, a nation, or a crew, certain rules must be established governing their behavior and relationships. These rules are expressed as morals, customs, laws, and regulations. Civilized individuals want to live in the way rules and regulations suggest. Few people, if any, are so completely civilized that rules laid down for the long-term welfare of the many do not seriously interfere with their desires. Rules are enforced by people, and enforcing group rules may deliberately or unintentionally block the personal desires of the members.

Officers of a ship are required to enforce rules and procedures that are not wholly compatible with the personal preferences of individual members of the crew. This inevitably results in the frustration of some crew members. The skillful leader will, of course, present and explain necessary rules and regulations as sensible procedures for achieving satisfaction. The enlisted individual who is interested only in his or her personal welfare will not easily accept discipline. However, if that individual can be made a part of the crew as a whole, can be made to share a stake in the ship and her reputation, the rules will be only temporary frustrations, of no importance in comparison to the long-term satisfaction that conformity to them can bring.

Closely related to the barriers of external social pressures—rules—are moral value barriers. When any highly desired course of action conflicts with an officer's code, or with the role he pictures for himself, frustration is likely. In any society, the rules, regulations, disciplines, and institutions established to make it possible for people to live together with a minimum of friction will often block the personal needs of the individual. When these rules and regulations become part of an officer's code of values, his individual needs are still blocked. But if his code is sufficiently strong, he will experience no conscious conflict or frustration.

Personal limitations. Sometimes a person appears to be his own worst enemy. His desires are repeatedly blocked by factors he cannot control. For example, the healthy individual who loses the use of an arm or a leg is bound to experience frustration. A boy who wants to be a football fullback but who cannot get his weight up to more than 125 pounds, or a girl who dreams of being an artist but who does not possess artistic talent, is likely to suffer considerable frustration and defeat. Mental incapacity also produces frustration. Every year hundreds of young people enter American universities, optimistically seeking a degree in law, medicine, or engineering, only to discover after a few months of realistic exposure to life and higher education that they just do not have the ability to reach these professional goals.

In many situations the individual's plans and expectations exceed his abilities. When an individual's level of aspiration is too far above his level of achievement or abilities, frustration results.

Conflict as a Source of Frustration

As noted earlier in the chapter, it often happens that in situations involving conflict the individual must choose one course of action and deny another; as a result, there is partial gratification of some needs and denial of others. The partially or wholly denied need will not always disappear. It may linger with great insistence. If a course of action that satisfies the first need makes gratification of the second impossible, the second need is frustrated and proceeds to influence the individual's behavior accordingly. On the other hand, when a person makes a choice between two equally attractive courses of action, the basic needs involved can be satisfied equally well by either of them.

Often the negative needs in positive-negative conflicts are needs involving fear—the fear of what people will say, the fear of being caught and punished, the fear of failure. These fears often can frustrate positive needs more effectively and more disturbingly than any impersonal or external barriers yet encountered.

The individual who wants to be a success but who is locked in inactivity because of fear of failure, unfairness of competition, or his own inabilities is a frustrated person whose behavior is probably characterized by a tense, dissatisfied, and unstable disposition.

Reaction to Frustration

When an individual confronts a barrier, whether impersonal or personal, his initial behavior will normally resort to a problem-solving mode. He will search to find some way to circumvent the obstruction. If attempts at problem solving lead to failure, behavior soon ceases to be of an intelligent, problem-solving character and becomes emotional.

Probably the most frequent response to frustration is anger and attack. Frustration toward an object may lead to a physical or verbal attack on the object or to a transferral of the anger felt toward the object to a person or persons. If the frustration is produced by a person, the attack may be directed at that person, or it may be transferred to an object. If the frustration is due to an individual's own incapacity, the aggression is usually, but not always, directed inward. The person may think and say derogatory things about himself and may devise ways to make himself suffer for his shortcomings. Aggression can take several forms, and people can draw from a collection of subtle devices to make their fellow humans suffer for frustrating them.

The scapegoat phenomenon. Often a person will resort to misplaced aggression. He may go home and go on a rampage, verbally or even physically attacking family and surroundings, thus relieving some of his pent-up aggression. This misdirected aggression may be the result of an inability to diagnose and understand what is causing the frustration, or it may result from being unable to vent anger on the person or object actually responsible.

Misdirected aggression not only is frequent, it often has serious social consequences. Any sane seaman knows that he cannot resort to physical violence against the skipper who has berated him, but he may take it out on a shipmate who, understandably, will resent the unprovoked attack.

The well-known phenomenon of the "scapegoat" is accounted for in terms of misplaced aggressions. When frustration is extreme and the source of frustration is unknown, unavailable, or unsafe to attack, there is a tendency to pick a scapegoat. The best scapegoat is one who is convenient, easily recognizable, and in a social position that makes the venting of frustration in the form of aggression safe.

Some situations seem naturally to produce the scapegoat phenomenon. If members of a unit are frustrated, they may pick one of their own members or even a junior officer to focus their aggression on. Military units must be trained to withstand frustration without reacting negatively. If the group is continually denied satisfactions such as liberty and is not provided opportunities to build esprit de corps and has the feeling that rewards and punishments are inconsistent—then aggressive behavior from members of the crew can be expected.

Aggression as a response. Conversely, when the group or any of its members become embroiled in group or private aggression, frustration is usually the cause. The aggressions of a frustrated team may take the form of surliness in the presence of officers, choosing a scapegoat, outbursts of fighting on board ship or ashore, or general unwillingness and laxity in work.

Evidence indicates that aggressive behavior usually results from frustration. While frustration may produce behavior other than aggression, aggression can almost always be traced back to frustration. This generalization can be most helpful to a leader, and will guide him in the diagnosis and control of human behavior, including his own.

Dependence as a response. Sometimes when adults are unable to face the complexities of a frustrating life, they regressively adopt a childlike dependence on a powerful individual who substitutes for an all-wise, all-sufficient father. This tendency is fairly marked in time of emergency or great insecurity. This is one reason why the leader, in emergency situations, not only can act in a more dominant manner, but also must lead with strength and paternity if the group is not to disintegrate.

Fixation as a response. Sometimes the individual reacts to frustration by falling into repetitive, stereotyped patterns of behavior. This sort of reaction is known as fixation, a compulsive continuation of behavior that apparently does not get the individual anywhere. A rat, if put into a problem situation where no answer is required, may resort to such maladaptive fixations as bumping his head repeatedly against a cage door without ever trying the adjoining door, which may lead him out of his dilemma.

Human beings at times resort to the same sort of behavior. We have all known someone who was fixated on—who continued to pine away for—a man or woman who would never return his or her affection. A person in this situation would do better to transfer his or her attachment to someone more receptive, but often is unable to do so.

Substitution as a response. The frustrated individual, denied one goal, may cast about for something almost as good. The man who wants to be a naval aviator but fails in flight training may request other assignments and thus at least partially satisfy his needs. The man who wants to play football may, after a season of sitting on the bench, turn his energy to soccer or lacrosse, where his abilities are more suited. Taking an alternative course in such situations generally makes good sense. It is surely better to turn energy into sensible and useful paths than to resort to aggression or apathetic resignation.

Substitution does not always lead to action that can be called "good." For example, people who are frustrated in their attempts to gain status in a group by doing work may turn to horseplay, shirking duty, or worse in order to show other shipmates that they are smart enough to get away with it.

Where the frustration is due to some physical or mental disability, the energy that is released in an approach to a substitute goal sometimes appears greatly increased and leads to regular compensation. Teddy Roosevelt is a superb example of this reaction to frustration. A puny child, he conditioned himself unmercifully until he became the rough-riding picture of virility. Demosthenes, a stutterer, engaged in long compensatory practice with pebbles under his tongue until he achieved great oratorical skill. Helen Keller overcame incredible handicaps and became world renowned for her courage and her insight.

Escape as a response. The individual who meets with failure in his attempts to satisfy his needs may, as in the case of conflict, seek to escape. Escapist activity can be physical or it can be mental. The person may take himself away physically from the frustrating situation, or he may do the same thing psychologically by creating for himself an imaginary world where all is calm and he reigns supreme.

Physiological response to frustration. A drawn-out emotional battle with frustration sometimes simply exhausts the individual. He develops chronic fatigue, insomnia, restlessness, and irritability, and he completely lacks enthusiasm. This sort of reaction may in extreme cases develop into a complete physical and psychological collapse. It then becomes a "nervous breakdown." In the military services, one form of this exhaustion is combat fatigue.

Prolonged emotional stress has definite effects on the physiological workings of the body. The emotional factor in stomach ulcers is well recognized. But the severely frustrated or conflict-ridden individual may also develop symptoms that appear physical in nature but for which the medical profession is unable to prescribe. These symptoms are called "functional" or "hysterical" symptoms. The aviator with an aversion to flying on a particular day may unconsciously attempt to solve his problem by coming down with diarrhea or severe stomach upsets before flying. A combat marine may escape the fear of fighting by developing a paralysis or a functional blindness. "Shellshock" patients often display these symptoms. To the individual the symptoms are very real, but no physiological basis can be found for them.

Frustration Tolerance

Individuals differ in their capacity for withstanding frustration. In the face of frustration, some almost immediately will resort to one or more of the negative responses that lead nowhere. Others have great resistance; they can tolerate frustration and can apparently marshall their energies more successfully in the effort to overcome the frustrating situation.

In the process of "growing up," most people learn that all needs cannot be satisfied immediately. Learning almost always takes place before achievement. A person learns to deny himself today so he can enjoy himself tomorrow and next year. Most people learn to delay gratification of their needs. And, with the inevitability of frustration in daily life, this is a very handy lesson.

Some people, however, never learn to tolerate frustration. The inability to delay gratification may be due to long practice at being a "spoiled brat." A person who was not frustrated enough as a child, whose every wish has been gratified easily by overly lenient parents, may go through life expecting good things to come his way if he merely acts cute or pleasant. On the other hand, a person who was unduly frustrated as a child may have more than a healthy amount of practice at responses such as indulging in fantasy, aggression, repression, or regression. He, too, may be unable to sustain realistic effort in the face of frustration.

Frustration tolerance is essential for anyone who must absorb extensive training before he can assume the responsibilities and rewards of an established position in life. The individual who hopes to be an officer in the naval service, for example, who strongly wants the status, advantages, and responsibility of rank, must be able to tolerate frustration. After formal training is completed he will be able to gratify his needs.

Recognizing Symptoms and Causes of Frustration

The doctor who treats the fever and ignores the virus, who cures the cough while the lungs disintegrate, will soon find himself without many patients. The naval leader who prides himself in his "common sense," and who treats the symptoms of conflict and frustration while remaining insensitive to the causes, will not achieve the utmost as a handler of personnel. He will punish "laziness" and expect it to disappear, and he will call aggressive behavior "meanness" and deal with it as if the aggressive person is deliberately being mean. He will diagnose regression as stupidity, fixation as stubbornness, escape as a "yellow streak," and he will attack these symptoms; and sometimes he will succed in making them disappear—temporarily. Often attacking the symptoms will seriously aggravate the disease behind the symptoms.

The line officer will not be called on, of course, to diagnose or treat any behavior that is extremely deviant. But he should be able to recognize abnormal behavior when it occurs in a unit. Since the abnormal is almost always an extreme form of the normal, the study of everyday behavior should aid in recognizing the serious departures from the everyday. The officer's job with respect to abnormal behavior is to recognize it and to see that it receives treatment by the medical department.

Summary

Life is full of conflicts. These conflicts may involve reacting to a situation that is both attractive and repulsive at the same time, or choosing between two attractive or two unattractive things. When caught in a conflict situation, the individual may come down with a paralytic inactivity, often confused with laziness. He may alternate between the two horns of a dilemma, or he may escape, sometimes physically, sometimes mentally, from the conflict; he may also figure out a way to have his cake and eat it, too; he may solve his problem.

The naval leader will have many occasions to manage conflicts, both in himself and in the personnel he leads. A frequent conflict he will meet is that between duty and pleasure. His success as a leader will depend at least in some degree on his ability to guide the behavior of his subordinates toward duty. He can do this by making work pay off.

In a complex life in a complex culture, people are also bound to encounter frustration. An understanding of the causes and results of frustration can take us a long way toward understanding human behavior. The individual's desires can be thwarted—he can become frustrated—by impersonal barriers, by people, by rules of society and those who enforce them, by his own conscience or code, by his own conflicting motives. An individual can respond to frustration in many ways, too, and he can learn to develop a tolerance for it.

To understand and control human behavior, normal or abnormal, we need to have a basic understanding that all actions can be traced to causes.

5

Selection and Performance Evaluation

Every individual—and the military officer is certainly no exception—is actively involved in both selection and performance evaluation from the time he starts developing his reasoning intelligence. As a teenager he selects friends and evaluates their performance, perhaps rather basically, on the basis of whether they satisfy his immediate wants. As an individual matures, selection and performance become increasingly important to his daily functions.

On assuming initial responsibilities, the junior officer becomes immediately concerned with selection and performance. He will be selecting instructors, who will obtain school nominations, who will advance in rating, who will fill billets in his organization, and who will carry out specific assignments and details requiring special talents and personality factors. To a large extent, the overall performance of a naval officer depends on his ability to select individuals and to appraise objectively their future capabilities in more responsible assignments. The performance evaluation sheets that the junior officer completes on petty officers or noncommissioned officers affect their immediate promotional opportunities for achieving higher rating. In case of war or other periods of national stress requiring an accelerated expansion of the naval service, these performance evaluation sheets determine to a large extent those select enlisted men and women who will be advanced to warrant and commissioned rank.

Selection

Every time it is necessary for an individual to be selected from among others, whether for a decoration or a special assignment, someone has to judge the personnel, size them up, and make a selection. That someone is the leader, who must be a good judge of human nature.

Every person has his own unique pattern of abilities, aptitudes, and traits. Some individuals oppose a job selection process that is based on this premise. They would argue that all people are pretty much alike, that the leader can take any average person, give him the proper training, and make him into almost anything he wants: gunner, mechanic, baker, teletype operator, or yeoman. But every person can do some assignments better than he can do others.

Just as personnel differ, so do assignments.

The modern naval service is a highly technical, highly specialized organization. It entails hundreds of different jobs, each more or less special in the sort of demands it makes. Perhaps any person can be taught any one of these jobs. Perhaps any person can learn to operate sonar; make precise judgments about the time, pitch, and loudness of sounds; tell the differences between whales and enemy submarines. But when one person is gifted with unusual hearing, and a job requires unusual hearing, it is wasteful not to join that person and that job. The individual who has quality hearing will likely learn sonar skills sooner and outperform those who lack special auditory abilities.

Matching Abilities to Requirements

Selection, then, involves (a) knowing the demands of the job, (b) knowing the abilities of the men, and (c) arranging for the best possible fit between the two.

It is wasteful personnel policy to use first-rate individuals on less demanding jobs. It always works out that the more demanding the job, the fewer individuals there are who have the inherent ability to do it. If those who have the capacity to perform a tough and complicated job are detailed to less demanding work, the complicated job may have to be filled by someone who can perform creditably but not outstandingly.

The young officer will do well to bear in mind that any individual "worth his salt" will serve a period of apprenticeship to the best of his ability as long as he has assurance that it is only temporary. However, there are a few "prima donnas" who consider it below their dignity and talents to perform less glamorous assignments (mess duty, etc.), though they consider it quite acceptable for other men to do these less desirable jobs.

Good selection involves consideration of not only the type of personnel required but also the nature of the assignment to be completed. Other things being equal, maximum efficiency will be achieved when the best possible fit between ability and assignment is made. It must be remembered, however, that "other things" are never equal; that human beings are more than a mere pattern of abilities. Achieving compatibility between jobs and aptitudes does not ensure that personnel will have job satisfaction or will produce efficiently. Efficiency depends on many things. Aptitude, though certainly important, is only one of the prerequisites.

Performance Evaluation

Definitions of Terms

The following definitions of terms used in personnel selection are provided for clarification purposes. Knowing the meaning of these terms is essential for the selection and performance evaluation of personnel.

Performance: Behavior that can be evaluated and sometimes predicted.

Ability: The capacity to perform or to achieve specific desired results.

Aptitude: Specific learned and innate qualities that an individual can bring to an assignment.

Achievement: The extent to which an individual or organization meets its goals.

Methods of Evaluating Performance

Context and guidelines are important. Frequently people talk about an individual's performance, ability, aptitude, or achievement without tying these terms to specific jobs. A discussion on these grounds is too vague because people do not merely have great aptitude or great ability; they have aptitude or ability *for* something. When you say, "Smith demonstrates above average performance in navigation, in seamanship, or in personnel administration," you are approaching a statement of verifiable fact.

If you want to make good judgments about people, you will find valid guidelines to follow. These guidelines should apply whether you are judging specific performance, intellect, or honesty, and whether the person deserves praise or a reprimand for his performance.

Don't depend on cliches. Many people have their own means of judging character. Some "study the eyes—they really tell all about a man," and others never hire a man who has a weak handshake. Other superstitions prove equally fallacious in judging people: all redheads have hot tempers; all fat people are jolly; intellectually gifted people are physically weak; and big muscles accompany little brains.

There are individuals who supposedly can tell all about people by studying the length of their noses or the shape of their heads. While there is some evidence that keen judges of people can make shrewd guesses about personality from studying facial expression, handwriting, or manner of speech, the connection between these surface things and personality is vastly overrated and lacks scientific validity. The wise leader avoids basing evaluations on this sort of evidence.

Look at behavior. One way to judge people is to look at what they do. A good way to describe an individual is to study what he does and then find words to fit his behavior. As a cautionary note, the officer is reminded that first impressions are lasting impressions. Thus a maximum effort should be made at all times: this should be a guiding principle.

Be suspicious of prejudices. Everyone has certain preferences and prejudices about others. There are people you automatically dislike at your first meeting, and there are people you automatically like. There are many people who are "our own," such as friends, family, or team. Most humans are biased. Almost everyone looks at other people through colored glasses: the rosy ones of friendship and favor, the jade ones of envy, and so on. So, what you see is not people as they really are, but as you have pictured them to be.

To form an unbiased judgment of people requires skills and an awareness on the part of the judge of his own likes and dislikes. You must always take these biases into account. A good procedure to use in making judgments of people is to put yourself in the mental shoes of an "umpire." You should ask yourself, "What would a completely fair-minded, impartial observer say in this case?" Only then can a judgment be formed that is free of bias.

Use fair standards and announce what they are. Almost any judgment made of another person is bound to be a comparison. For instance, if you say that Seaman Jones is a good man, you are unconsciously comparing him with other men you have known. Relative to these men, Jones is a good man. There is nothing wrong with making a relative judgment, provided you realize what you are using as a comparison. You should be sure, too, that the yardstick being used is a fair one, and you should announce what it is.

When talking or writing about the qualities of an individual it is a good idea to tell the listener or reader what standards are being used. Just saying "Jones is a good man" does not tell the listener anything except that Jones is more or less good by some vague standard never mentioned. And that sort of appraisal is anything but helpful if the listener, for instance, is trying to determine Jones's fitness for a particular job. Instead of saying "Jones is a good man," it is better to say "Compared to the other men aboard ship, Jones is a good man," but even that is not as informative as it ought to be. Standards of evaluation should be made explicit.

Avoid the halo effect. Sometimes people are judged favorably on many traits because they are particularly and obviously gifted in some traits. These are the well-known "fair-haired boys." They are given a halo such as angels wear. They can do no wrong.

Other people are just as hastily given negative halos, and because they are outstandingly poor with respect to some traits or some activities, they are relegated to the doghouse. What good qualities they may have are overshadowed by their bad qualities.

In judging people, it is a common error to let an overall favorable impression, or an overall unfavorable impression, carry the entire verdict. To avoid this, a person must be judged on one trait at a time. No one is likely to have either an overabundance or an absence of good traits. A viable description of what Jones is like can be made if you take one trait, such as "energy," and compare him on that trait with other members of the ship. Let's say that he is extremely energetic compared to the other men. Then as far as that one trait is concerned, Jones is outstanding.

But how does he rate on intelligence? That is a tough question because in judging intelligence, you must bear in mind that intelligent behavior and energetic behavior are not the same thing. Now how does Jones compare in practical intelligence with other men?

The good judge puts neither positive nor negative halos on people.

Avoid generalities and abstractions. It has been noted that the good judge of people observes behavior—and a large sample of it—before making a judgment. But almost all evaluations of people come in abstract terms.

If ten people, all familiar with Ensign Smith, were asked to judge how often he goes to ship's service or how often he puts one of his men on report, there would probably be close agreement. All ten people know what they are judging, and they all judge the same thing. But if they were asked to rate Ensign Smith on "leadership quality," trouble and disagreement would set in. One rater may think that the maintenance of discipline is very important for leadership. Ensign Smith maintains good discipline, so that observer gives him a leadership rating of 3.7. Another may think that ability to handle a group in an emergency situation is the cardinal quality in leadership. Ensign Smith seems moderately good at that sort of thing, and therefore this observer gives him a leadership rating of 3.0. A third, perhaps, thinks that the true leader, above all else, must maintain a formal, dignified relation with his men. Ensign Smith seems too familiar, so he gets a low leadership rating, a 2.3, say, from this last observer.

The fitness report. The fitness report, by specifically listing the items to be judged, makes it possible to equate performance of officers and of enlisted personnel. The fitness report recognizes that behavior is not an end in itself. An individual's behavior may be above reproach, but the results achieved may be below standard. Performance must be evaluated. Furthermore, experienced seniors, in marking a subordinate's fitness report, not only look at the standards of his behavior in the current billet, but call attention to the junior's potential in future billets.

For the more-senior officer, the fitness reports made on junior officers largely determine their promotion to higher rank as well as their assignment to positions requiring special qualifications and capacity for greater responsibilities. The preparation of performance evaluation sheets and fitness reports should never become routine or perfunctory; it requires special knowledge of the individual on the part of the evaluator, as well as a knowledge of human nature and an objective performance evaluation, both current and potential, of the individual concerned. The officer is responsible for writing well, for the performance evaluation is one of the few ways of fully rewarding troops for their performance.

The officer must be prepared to discuss, in private interviews with senior enlisted personnel, the performance evaluations submitted on them. They cannot improve if they are left unaware of their shortcomings as seen by their division officer/platoon commander. Perhaps the enlisted person experienced problems that caused his performance to drop off during the reporting period—problems that he was reluctant to bring to his officer's attention.

The officer also must have the moral courage to inform personnel of their deficiencies. Nothing is more damning to officer or enlisted personnel than a performance evaluation or fitness report that is cloaked in generalities and gives no specific data. It is much better, if the individual is considered unsatisfactory in performance, to mark him that way, so that he has an opportunity to make a rebuttal if he so desires.

The rating scale. A slightly more objective procedure for evaluating a man's present or past involves the use of the rating scale. The rating scale, a device for improving the objectivity of impressions, is more and more widely used in industry and in the services. In industry the rating scale is called a merit scale. In the naval service rating scales form a large part of the fitness report.

The aptitude test. As has previously been emphasized, the personal approach to the judging and selection of men for specific duties and assignments is all important, but there are other aids that have been introduced to make this selection process more precise. The naval service has introduced a series of tests to determine a man's aptitudes, and the results of these tests are to be found in the service record.

Summary

Selecting the right person for a specific task involves evaluating the performance of each person who is being considered for it. Periodically the senior must judge the performance of each subordinate in his unit. The reporting senior is instructed to consider each person separately and to judge him as compared with other individuals of the same rank and similar duties. The reporting senior is asked to remember that on any human trait or factor one can always expect most members of a population to be at or close to "average," with a minority falling at both extremes.

6

The Structure and Functioning of Groups

Perhaps a majority of the human relation situations that confront the naval officer will be those in which individuals are the crucial factor. Competent though he may be in professional knowledge, ability, and technical specialty, his success for the most part will be determined by his effectiveness in directing the efforts of individuals. But the leader will encounter groups, too, and his ability to understand and direct groups is bound to be an important factor in his worth to the organization. Groups are composed of individuals, but individuals who are assembled in a group take on group properties.

The study of groups demands an approach considerably different, in some respects, from the approach to the study of the individual. Groups have properties of their own which are not apparent if you concentrate on the individual members. Group structure and behavior and the relation of one group to another can often be understood by backing away from the group and studying it as a whole.

In this chapter we will look at the individual's relationship to the group. We will find out why individuals join groups and why they are more enthusiastic about some groups than about others by analyzing the individual's needs and the ways in which group membership satisfies these needs. In this way groups can be studied as a unit rather than in their component parts. The objective is to give the leader a general background that will be useful to him in his encounters with groups.

The Definition of a Group

There are many definitions of the word *group* just as there are many types of groups and group activities. It is not the intent here to settle on a specific definition, but, instead, to consider some of the basic elements of group activity in general. However defined, or of whatever type, the group that is organized for, and that directs its collective behavior toward, the accomplishment of specific goals and missions begins to assume many characteristics. From the beginning, the group assumes structure and organization, and adopts organizational principles, in order to facilitate attainment of its goals. The group must be welded into a cohesive unit in order to be poised for action, with its activity directed toward its goals.

In both organized and informal groups, the members of the group have something psychological to do with one another; they interact with one another. The reactions of members are influenced by other members. The term *group* as it will be used in the following pages means a number of people who, in some way, are interacting with one another.

Interactions within Groups

There are, of course, various sorts and degrees of interaction among members of any group. Take, for example, one hundred new recruits arriving at basic training. As they pass through the main gate, these recruits constitute a group mainly because they happen to be in the same place at the same time. At this point they can more appropriately be described as a *bunch*. Now look at the members of a company. Here is a recognized organization, with leaders at various levels playing their proper roles. There is a systematic division of labor. The men know one another and refer to themselves by the name of their unit. This is not a bunch: now the term *group* is a more adequate description.

In both of these collections of people, individuals interact with one another. However, the bunch becomes a group when the members identify themselves as a group, when structure begins to take place, when the members begin to use the word *we* to refer to themselves, and when individuals pool their combined efforts toward the accomplishment of specific goals. Spontaneous organizations—informal groups or cliques—also begin to appear within the regular organization. When directed properly, these informal groups and cliques can be of great aid in the group's progress toward its goals. On the other hand, where individual identification with the total group is minimal or nil, these spontaneous organizations can retard the overall group accomplishment.

Group Dimensions

In dealing with groups, both explanatory and descriptive terms are used. Customarily groups are talked about in terms of function; that is, what they do or seek to attain. Groups are also discussed in reference to the membership: who and what the members are. Groups can also be discussed in terms of dimensions. These dimensions can be relatively appraised, and in most instances they can be measured. Knowledge of these dimensions and, when applicable, of their measurements is advantageous to the leaders who direct the efforts of their groups.

Size. Groups obviously vary with respect to the number of people who are members. The larger the size of a group, the more potentially complex it becomes. This complexity increases much more rapidly proportionally than numerically. For example, the addition of one member to a group of three increases the interpersonal relationships between individuals from six to twenty-four within that group. It is obvious that procedures employed in directing the efforts of a small group will differ from those used in directing a large one.

Structure. Groups have structure, and they are capable of maintaining their structure. The organizational structure of the group provides status, recognition, and a role for each of its members. It also defines relationships.

Structure may be formal or informal. It may be objective and concrete, as in organizational charts, rules and regulations, rank and rate, and billet descriptions; or it may be informal, as in suborganization and "unwritten codes." In either case, structure serves to maintain organizational integrity.

Density. The notion of density refers to the number of people per unit of space in an operating group. A group with high density is clearly different from one of low density.

Face-to-face relationships with a few individuals are rewarding in a way that impersonal relationships with a large number of people rarely are. Militarily, this is important. Studies in both World War II and the Korean War have reached the conclusion that the individual fighting man's relation to his immediate unit was much more important psychologically than his relation to his branch of service or his nation.

Unit cohesion. Groups differ in the relations that exist between the individual members. A study of one group may show that each member of it is closely and cooperatively tied to every other member. All members are important, all equally belong, all will stick together. In contrast, the members of another group may be very loosely bound together, or may even have negative, hostile relations with one another. The first group is high in cohesion, the second low. Some groups lack cohesion because of the existence of small subgroups or cliques within them that go their own ways. It is the rare group, indeed, that does not have at least one informal group or clique. Subgroups can be powerful assets, or they can be liabilities to the overall group, depending on the leader's success in channeling membership efforts in a uniform direction.

Stability. Some groups change very little over time. Tomorrow, next week, or next year, they will be essentially the same. The same members are there, the goals are essentially the same, and the leaders are the same. With a view to maintaining high group stability, the armed forces make a conscious effort to keep the group intact by arranging for rotation of an entire unit at the same time. While individual rotation of selected persons also takes place, the recognition of the importance of stability in the home has led to a significant increase in accompanied tours, and thus while an entire group may shift from one part of the country to another, the basic friendship groups, mission, and leader-subordinate relationships are kept essentially the same. Where individual rotation is dictated by the needs of the service, compensation is achieved by shortening the length of the unaccompanied tour.

The Individual and the Group

Identification with the Group

An individual may become strongly motivated toward a group to which he belongs, or he may treat it with complete indifference. A person may lose himself in the group or sacrifice himself for its welfare. He may take very personally the group's success or failure and feel ashamed if the group is let down. In such a case the individual is said to be closely identified with the group. On the other hand, if a person doesn't care much about what happens to the group, is not inclined to make sacrifices for it, feels no need to carry a part of the load, then his identification with the group is weak. You should react to the group as if it were an extension of yourself: group welfare is your welfare and the group's goals are your goals.

Participation in the Group

Another aspect of the individual's relation to the group is the extent to which he participates in the group's activities. In almost every group there are those who work actively to advance the group's goals and there are those who "just belong." Every member could be placed somewhere on a line from "most participation" to "least participation."

The amount of participation is closely related to the member's degree of identification. If it is "his group," he will find ways of participating. If he "just belongs," he will not inconvenience himself in working for the group. Forced participation may get the job done, but when ways are found and used to permit extensive, willing participation by each member, such participation ensures higher member identification as well as higher quantity and quality of group output.

Dependence on the Leader

In some group situations the follower may be completely dependent on the leader. The leader's acts, the leader's decisions, even the leader's whims, may decide whether the follower will rise or fall, live or die. In other group situations the follower is almost completely independent of the leader. Probably a study of any leader-follower relations to determine degree of dependency would result in followers being placed on a line somewhere between total dependence and total independence.

Ego Status

Within the Group

The individual not only needs a structured, meaningful, and secure relationship with those in the unit, he also needs to "be somebody." The individual needs to feel important, have a good opinion of himself, and have social status among his comrades. If a group promises status and the opportunity to feel like an important member or an important cog in an important wheel, then the individual will most likely join that group. Being treated as a very nonessential, unimportant hanger-on will probably result in a person wanting to leave a group.

It is a mistake to assume that a person's particular position within a group guarantees that he will feel important and secure in his group relationships. Such a feeling will depend primarily on how the individual feels about his position in relation to himself and the others. What is felt depends in part on how success is defined. It is not always true that the lowest-ranked individual in a unit feels like a nobody, for success must always be partly judged in terms of the aspirations of the individual, patience to learn the job from the ground up, and the realization that, in time, the efficient individual will move up the chain of command.

Because of the Group

The strong and ever-present need of each individual for high ego status arises in another way. The individual's self-impression may be elevated simply because he is a member of a particular group. If the military, for example, is well thought of and accomplishes a great deal, the individual who wears the military uniform will derive a great deal of ego satisfaction. The exclusive country club does more for its members than furnish them with a place to play golf, it provides them with status. The naval service also gives its members much more than an opportunity to see the world.

On the other hand, if membership in a group is unrestricted, there may be little, if any, ego satisfaction derived from it. There is little social value or status attached to belonging to a group where membership is not prized by both group and nongroup members. The individual's personal goals and aspirations must always be kept in mind. Pride in membership depends on what an individual wants to attain and whether participation will enable goals to be accomplished.

The Needs of Group Members

Security of Group Relationships

Man is generally a gregarious being. He likes to be around people if for no other reason than to avoid the feeling of being alone. Balance suffers when this feeling of being alone constitutes feeling "left out" or isolated from participation and communication with others. An individual depends on effective interactions with others in order to survive, to obtain goals, and to satisfy needs. In the formation and maintenance of groups, man acknowledges by behavior that goals can best be obtained through an organized, collective effort. Participation in group activity not only serves to satisfy particular needs, it also tends to satisfy miscellaneous needs as well.

Sheer gregariousness is not enough, however, to account for the formation of groups; it is more likely to account for "bunches." Highly rewarding groups involve more than mere physical proximity, or being in the same place at the same time with others. The individual elects group activity when it gives the feeling of secure "belongingness." People join groups and contribute to their activity to obtain the feeling of security. Whether membership status in the group is high or low, an individual derives a great comfort from occupying a definite and defined place in a group.

On the other hand, if the roles of the group are inconsistent, and if the individual has difficulty in determining the rules by which the group operates, then he suffers a feeling of insecurity that is likely to drive him from the group. In the military, such a feeling of insecurity may lead to lowered morale and inefficiencies which may culminate in excessive disciplinary cases and unauthorized absences.

The individual needs to know how the group operates; needs to know its leaders and what its standards and objectives are; needs to know how long he can count on being a member of the group, and how he can rise in its ranks and become a necessary and effective member in it. When people know these things, their lives in the group take on a more desirable stability and meaning. An individual who knows these things tends to accept change, even though he will momentarily rebel when there are aspects of change that he can neither accept nor understand. When, due to constant shifting and changing in the individual's interpersonal relationships, stability and meaning are lacking, then the group will be a source of frustration and bother.

Reward from Group Participation

Reward may be of many types and of many degrees. It involves much more than money. Many individuals rank other factors above money in their requirements for personal satisfaction.

Reward involves the multitude of psychological satisfactions represented by real or intangible things that are important to the individual. One person's reward might be considered trivial by another. This is psychic income. It is composed of those factors that enable the individual to feel fulfilled; that is, his needs are satisfied, and he can see his goals being obtained through participation within the group.

When an individual invests time in a group, the rewards or psychic income for that participation must be equal to, or greater than, the investment. This determination of reward involves making a personal evaluation. When reward or psychic income is consistently insufficient, a person begins to evaluate the group in a "this isn't for me" fashion, with the recognizable rewards "not being worth" participation. At this point the group has most likely lost another member and a potential contributor to the organization.

Thus, anything that the organization can provide that tends to enable the individual members to feel that their participation is worthwhile helps to cement the relationships between the individuals and their group.

High Morale from Group Functioning

High morale occurs when the members of a group are progressing toward a goal with an expectation of success. However, no leader will be able to rally enthusiastic group effort toward a group goal that is strictly unimportant to the individual members. Morale of either the individual or the group must relate to the individual's or to the group's goals. The most enthusiastic group is the one that is looking forward to success—and this means a definition of success that the group has adopted as its own.

The greatest and most enthusiastic effort appears to result when the goal is defined so that success is reasonably possible, and known action is required to avoid failure. Realistic goal setting is a first prerequisite for developing a military plan.

Group Leadership

Much of the discussion about morale, the individual, and willing participation in effective groups is centered around group leadership. How so? What does all this have to do with leadership? Generally, it may be said that leadership is behavior that the leader exhibits when placed in various leadership roles.

Volumes have been written on leadership, but very little attention has been given to consideration of the equally important "followers." This is not to oversimplify, for you might have every leadership trait in the book, yet if you had no followers and you were placed in no leadership roles that permitted behavior to be designated as leadership by others, you would not be considered a leader.

Leadership Is Behavior

However it is described or defined, leadership is behavior. To be acknowledged as leadership, this behavior must be communicated socially in terms of interpersonal relationships with other people. Thus behavior designated as leadership is relative and situational as to time, place, and person, for not everything that a leader does becomes classified or designated as leadership.

When an individual exhibits behavior that is instrumental and successful in directing the activity of others, he is said to exhibit leadership, and he is called a leader. In the interaction between this leader and the others, called "followers," many apparent and meaningful relationships may be seen. Although some of these relationships may be unique to a particular group, may be due to the particular individuals involved, many of them are common to groups in general. The following quote from a World War I hero helps to put this matter in perspective.

> In a social order in which one person
> is officially subordinate to another,
> the superior if he is a gentleman
> never thinks of it
> and the subordinate if he is a gentleman
> never forgets it.
>
> General John J. Pershing

It must be remembered that leadership may be defined as the art, science, or gift by which a person is enabled and privileged to direct the thoughts, plans, and actions of others in such a manner as to command their obedience, their confidence, their respect, and their loyal cooperation.

The individual who exhibits behavior that others accept and designate as good leadership relies heavily on personal attitudes and values relative to human nature and how people will best work together to do a job. The leader utilizes knowledge and experience gained to determine the best way to get the group going and get the job done.

Whatever the leader does or however the task is done, when the followers work together effectively toward group goal accomplishments, the individual is by definition a leader in that situation. On the other hand, individuals who omit valid appreciation, knowledge, and understanding of the nature of individuals and groups from their "leadership tactics" do not usually find themselves in leadership roles.

In evaluating leadership, the important factor is what the leader does. The leader's behavior may affect the group in a desirable way so that success is attained; this is good leadership. Conversely, when behavior affects the group in an undesirable way, that is, when the group is unsuccessful, this is poor leadership. The good leader is the individual who has a rich variety of social skills, skills that enable evaluation of individuals, groups, and situations and then produce reactions to them in a way that gets results.

Military leadership is a challenging task. The leader must satisfy his own command duty responsibilities as well as present the official goals of the unit as a way of meeting individual needs. This is not easy; but it is a good bet that if any naval leader is keen in sizing up his men and in diagnosing the needs of the moment, overall effectiveness will increase.

Summary

The leader and the group members gain psychic income in terms of, first, a secure and satisfying set of social relations in the group; second, a feeling of status both within the group and because of their membership in it; and, third, the satisfaction by the group of various individual needs—security, reward, morale—that are important at the moment. The leader can help make the group's goals meaningful, concrete, and immediate, and he can help create a feeling of progress and an expectation of success. The leader can adjust his own behavior to the varying demands of the many situations the group encounters.

7

Moral Leadership

The following quote sets the standards that must be achieved by the officers and enlisted personnel of the U.S. Navy and Marine Corps, and indeed by all of this country's citizens, if the United States is to meet the challenges of its position in the world.

> America's most important role in the world, almost from the day our country was born, has been the role of moral leadership. . . . Teach our young people to believe in the responsibility of one to another; in their responsibility to God and to the peoples of the world. Teach them to believe in themselves; to believe in their place in leading the world out of the darkness of oppression. Teach them to believe that no one owes us a living, but that we owe so much to others. Teach them to believe in their priceless heritage of freedom, and that it must be won anew by every generation. And teach them to believe in the United States of America. The hope of the world has been in our physical power, our moral strength, our integrity, and our will to assume the responsibilities that history plainly intends us to bear.

The Responsibilities of Freedom

The United States is the leader of the free world, but its citizens are still not completely adjusted to the responsibilities that go with this position, and many would prefer to ignore them or encourage and allow others to become involved. To the people of the United States falls the moral duty of supporting freedom as well as those who are trying to gain it or regain it for themselves and their people. This support will take many forms, all involving a certain amount of sacrifice. Sometimes food must be supplied, sometimes arms and equipment, sometimes troops. All of these will divert energy and money from the increase of the American standard of living. This is the price that must be paid for the privilege of exercising the duty that Americans have to their fellow men and women. The stabilization of the standard of living may be adequate compensation for the sacrifices, for history has demonstrated that civilizations usually begin to decay when the way of life of their people becomes too soft; that is, when the standard of living becomes too high.

The young people of the United States must be taught to accept as their own the moral values that were the guiding force of the leaders of earlier American generations. These young people must believe in their responsibility to God, to their country and their countrymen, and to the world. They must be taught not to desire only material goods, but to have as an ideal a life of service, or at least the giving of a portion of their lives in the service of those things in which they believe.

They must be taught to appreciate the freedom that their country and its form of government gives them. They must not merely accept this freedom, they must earn it for themselves by fighting any force that is trying to curtail their freedom and democratic ideals. The American people must feel a debt of gratitude to others who have gone before them and established a government climate of freedom and democracy in which technology has been permitted to flower. They must feel a debt of gratitude to God for providing the great natural resources that have contributed to the overwhelming power and force that can be mustered by the United States in support of righteousness and freedom. These debts must be repaid by the acceptance of the responsibilities that go hand in hand with the gifts. America has no choice but to become the protector of right in the world. Its people must grasp the principle that honor, integrity, and loyalty are not things to be bought and sold, that, indeed, they are more valuable than life itself. Without them there is nothing, and this country will wither and die like the Roman Empire, leaving the great principles that this nation represents to mold in the pages of history.

Moral Leadership in the Naval Service

The United States Navy and Marine Corps must accept the challenge to be even more diligent in teaching their members to maintain the high standards and ideals so necessary to the success of this country in its world leadership position. If they are to meet their obligation to the country, the navy and marines must continually reemphasize the assumption of moral responsibility and leadership. The type of leadership practiced and taught in the naval service must always have a moral foundation, or it will not survive.

The Dual Aspects of Moral Leadership

Moral leadership involves two practical aspects: first, the naval leader must develop the high standards of moral character so necessary for his own integrity, and, second, he must impart these moral values to subordinates through example and, more directly, through personal interviews, organized group instructions, and discussions.

Moral character of the leader. To be able to establish positive discipline within the unit that he commands, the naval leader must exercise moral leadership and must exemplify a personal character that is above reproach. Admiral Burke, in his article "Naval Leadership in Action," examines this concept.

> The word "leadership" is usually associated with one who possesses admirable traits—one who espouses benevolent doctrines. Almost all treatises on leadership, particularly those written in recent years, emphasize such words as "integrity," "steadfastness," "understanding," "honesty," "faith," and "high principles"—all these which connote the "good" that is in man.

Burke points out that not all successful leaders have possessed these moral attributes, but that these attributes are essential to the American naval officer if he is to discharge properly his duties and responsibilities to an enlightened people under the present democratic system of government.

Moral character of the personnel. The naval leader must feel the importance and responsibility of developing high moral standards in navy personnel. The word *moral* as used here embraces far more than what is often brought to mind by the word. It includes honesty, integrity, and a sense of duty and obligation to serve the country and defend it and its ideals against all enemies. It includes the obligation of personnel in the armed forces to work at maximum capacity in any task assigned them, whether they are being supervised or not.

Young people entering the service are at a very formative stage of their lives. Many are away from parental control for the first time. Some of these young people have a properly developed character, while others do not. It is the obligation of the leaders to whom their lives are entrusted to develop uniformly high moral standards in all their personnel.

Background and Mission of Moral Leadership

The concept of moral leadership is not new. It has been practiced and taught by leaders of the Navy and the Marine Corps from the issue of the first American regulations for the naval service to the present. Moral responsibility for the unit has traditionally been placed on the commanding officer. Article I of the *Rules for the Regulation of the Navy of the United Colonies of North America*, written in 1775, stated:

> The Commanders of all ships and vessels belonging to the thirteen United Colonies are strictly required to show in themselves a good example of honor and virtue to their officers and men, and to be very vigilant in inspecting the behavior of all such under them, and to discountenance and suppress all dissolute, unmoral, and disorderly practices; and also such as are contrary to the rules of discipline and obedience, and to correct those who are guilty of the same according to the usage of the sea.

The responsibility for the protection of moral standards was reemphasized when the following memorandum (quoted in part) was sent to the military departments by the secretary of defense:

> It is in the national interest that personnel serving in the Armed Forces be protected in the realization and development of moral, spiritual, and religious values consistent with the religious beliefs of the individuals concerned. To this end it is the duty of Commanding Officers in every echelon to develop, to the highest possible degree, the conditions and influences calculated to promote the health, morals, and spiritual values of the personnel under their command.

This memorandum was implemented in the naval service by a directive to all commanding officers "to strengthen by every means available, the moral, spiritual, and religious lives of the officers and men of the naval establishment."

Responsibility of the Military for Moral Character

These directives recognize the fact that the military organization is responsible to the people of the United States for the conduct and character of its personnel while they serve in the military establishments. The responsibility for accomplishment of this mission rests with every officer and noncommissioned officer in each echelon of command. This responsibility cannot be delegated to the chaplain, the legal officer, the personnel officer, or the information and education officer. It is a command function. At the heart of the program is the junior officer, and, more specifically, the division or company grade officer. Unless officers appreciate and assume this responsibility, the effort toward moral leadership is doomed to failure from the start. The junior officer will find that each command approaches moral leadership in a different manner; some will have very extensive organizations for the accomplishment of the mission, while others will have very simple organizations. Rest assured, however, that unless this mission is integrated effectively into each organization, there will exist only a hollow shell, a military organization that is primarily concerned with accomplishment of paper missions rather than the spontaneous participation by unit personnel in a program that actually promotes strong character, good leadership, and high ideals.

Summary

For the professional naval officer, leadership consists of many facets. Command leadership can exist effectively only if it is based on a strong and dynamic code of character, integrity, and moral conduct, and only if moral leadership is intimately enjoined with military leadership. Moral leadership is ineffective unless it is supported by command concepts of positive discipline, enlightened administration of military justice, and sound practices of administration and organization in the daily functioning of command. All officers are charged by navy regulations with the responsibility of keeping themselves informed of the capabilities and needs of their subordinates, and taking such action as is within their authority to promote efficiency, welfare, and morale.

Any attempt to separate command leadership into two distinct facets—military leadership and moral leadership—is tantamount to separating the aircraft carrier from its primary weapon, the airplane. In either case, one cannot perform its mission without the other. Command leadership is the responsibility of every officer, petty officer, and noncommissioned officer. Officers cannot perform their military leadership responsibilities in such a manner as to gain the wholehearted cooperation, obedience, and respect of the men and women over whom they have been given command responsibility unless their personality is built on firm moral character. Such moral character must in turn be built on the officers' personal integrity, honor, and loyalty to their country and its basic laws and institutions, to the service of which they are a part, and to the personnel over whom they are assigned command.

To be an effective leader, the individual must above all want to be an officer. He must appreciate and understand the role of an officer and must realize the value of customs and traditions as well as the demands that will be made on him in discharging command responsibility. The basic philosophy of leadership must be based on an impeccable foundation of high moral values and integrity. This must be accompanied by a fine sense of obligation, responsibility, and personal relations with subordinates, peers, and seniors alike. It is necessary to understand and appreciate the value of efficient and reasonable administrative practices in carrying out command leadership functions so that the result will be a highly trained and well-organized unit imbued with a positive spirit of discipline.

8

Role of the Naval Officer

In this investigation of the leadership process, the student has been given a basic concept of naval leadership and a brief introduction to some of the basic principles of psychology. Before continuing this investigation by examining the personal characteristics of the leader and other aspects of naval leadership in action, the student should look at his future as a naval officer.

This chapter will discuss the role of the naval officer and the ways in which a naval officer's career is fundamentally different from a civilian career. It will point out some of the requirements placed on the naval leader as well as some of the naval inheritances that have made the naval service great in the past and more able to withstand the stresses of the impact of science and technology.

Components of the Leadership Role

Admiral William V. Pratt set the stage for the naval officer in this way:

> The greatest problem facing the career naval officer is leadership. Yet this most important factor in a man's life frequently is allowed to grow like a choice flower in a garden surrounded by rank weeds. So many feel that if they follow the average course of naval life, experience will finally give them the qualities of the great leader, and opportunity may reward them with a high command. Few realize that the growth to sound leadership is a life's work. Ambition alone will not encompass it, and if ambition alone be a man's sole qualification, he is indeed a sorry reed to lean upon in time of stress. The path of qualification for leadership is a long, hard road to travel. It is a path of life. It envisages all of a man's character, his thoughts, aims, and conduct of life. It requires the wisdom and judgment of the statesman, the keen perception of the strategist and tactician, the executive ability of the seaman; but above all, it requires sterling worth of character and great human understanding and sympathy.

The Naval Service Is a Way of Life

The naval service is more than just a business, profession, or trade; it is a way of life. It considers its members to be in a duty status twenty-four hours a day, month after month, except when they are on authorized leave—and even then they are subject to military regulations and recall. The naval service demands much, but it also gives much.

The wise leader will see to it that subordinates not only give their most to the Navy and Marine Corps but also get all that they are entitled to from it. It behooves the leader to keep up to date on such matters as benefits, rights, privileges, and other opportunities for those under him.

Admiral Carney, while he was serving as chief of naval operations, said this regarding the role of the navy and its people:

> The Naval Service is a remarkably integrated and complex human system that constitutes a great national asset. The Naval Service is actually founded on a system of education and indoctrination which is designed to give young men and women selected early in life the attributes of mind and character which history and experience have indicated will make them good Sailors or Marines. Of course, the first thing which has to be developed in a Navy or Marine Corps recruit is a latent strength of character. They must be taught to understand the concept of service in the best meaning of the word, and must be imbued with sound ideals and convictions before proceeding with their basic career development.
>
> The Naval Service is an organization for training people to train people. Its ultimate objective is to prepare and to ready fleet forces for combat operations. As a corollary, its personnel must be trained to do a disciplined, resolute, and successful job under the stress of combat. This calls for a high order of leadership that will, through study, practice, and experience, acquire knowledge and skillfully impart that knowledge to others; a leadership that will inspire the confidence and voluntary obedience of others; a leadership built on the foundation stones of firmness and justice, where the harsh voice is the exception rather than the rule; a leadership that lives in accordance with the code that it enforces.
>
> People today are passing through an unprecedented technological phase of human existence in which scientific and engineering improvements have a tremendous effect on the outcome of all activities. Naval personnel must be practical and capable of understanding the transfer of thoughts and ideas into hardware; they must understand the fundamental importance of national solvency, the intricacies of technical design,

and the realities of industrial production. They must understand that teamwork is the key to success. They must be in full partnership with the scientist, the engineer, the industrialist, and the imaginative contributor.

Self-motivation. For an officer to have a satisfying naval career, he or she must first of all have a genuine desire to be not just a naval officer but an outstanding naval officer, one deserving of the special trust and confidence imposed by the government and seniors, peers, and juniors. This motivation for a service career is the difference between a person who is trying to improve professionally and one who is merely "putting in time" before seeking greener pastures.

Flexibility. Now, more than ever before, the duties that a naval officer may be called on to perform are diverse in nature and often complex. Initially, a young officer probably will be given experience in several different positions, such as an aviator, submariner, or platoon commander. Whatever the line of endeavor, he or she will be shifted from one position to another every two or three years—and perhaps more often—and will have to cope with many new and challenging situations. If you remain in the naval service long enough, you may be assured of thirty years' experience, not one year's experience multiplied thirty times. There is a great difference between the two, and the officer of today must be able to adapt rapidly to changing circumstances. Regardless of the predictions you care to make about the future, flexibility of mind appears to be a major requirement for future success.

Prestige

Everyone likes to have the feeling that he is playing on the first team, that the person for whom he is working is one of the very best, and that the unit is a crack outfit. A leader with an impressive series of wins and few, if any, losses soon acquires the reputation of being a winner, and thereby gains prestige. The U.S. Navy and Marine Corps, with their history and tradition of victory, provide a background of prestige for their officers. The intelligent officer can make use of that prestige to add authority to words and actions which is overwhelming when compared to the authority available in nonmilitary organizations.

The uniform, insignia of rank, decorations and campaign ribbons, warfare specialty devices—all these are items of prestige. They should be worn proudly, not only for the prestige that accrues to the wearer, but also for the prestige that is reflected indirectly down on his subordinates.

Service Reputation

When the naval service was much smaller, an officer's "service reputation" became well known and was an important factor in evaluating him. A "service reputation" is still important, but the large size of the modern military has made it more difficult to establish one. Hence it is desirable for the first impression you make on others to be a favorable one, and for you quickly to build up a local equivalent of "service reputation" and prestige.

The following special order (quoted in part) issued at the U.S. Naval Academy covers this aspect of the role of the naval officer most adequately:

> A fine service reputation is a matter of deep personal pride to all naval officers. It is founded upon the positive character, moral integrity, and potential value of an individual to the service. Aggressive leadership, reliability, initiative, loyalty, and the respect for obedience to constituted authority . . . these are the very essence of those qualities which develop a moral fiber and contribute to fitness evaluation and service reputation. They are essentially attributes of character developed here at the Naval Academy as a by-product of the daily way of life, and are directly reflected in attitude, performance of duty, military bearing, and service desirability. It can not be overemphasized that utmost attention must be given to the development of these characteristics, so essential to aggressive and resolute naval leadership, early in an officer's career. Your character must be your closely guarded possession.

The elements of character and ability inherent to the "service reputation" are unchanged by time. In a special order issued in 1922, then Superintendent Admiral Henry B. Wilson defined "Service Reputation" as follows.

> 1. "The service reputation" of an officer means the reputation for character and ability, either good, bad or indifferent, that an officer has among his brother officers.
>
> 2. "Service reputation" is a gradual development. While a young officer's character and ability is well known to only a few, as his work

increases it spreads throughout the service, until by the time he has reached the grade of lieutenant commander or commander, his ability is well known to the majority of officers. This unofficial seal of approval or disapproval by his comrades is often the deciding factor in making assignments to important duty; in influencing promotion, either favorably or adversely; and in lightening—if the reputation is good—the punishment consequent upon some unintentional dereliction or neglect. The surest guarantee of selection for important duty is a knowledge by the senior that the officer selected has the necessary characteristics for success.

The surest amelioration of serious punishment for some heedless infraction is a sufficiently good reputation to ensure a belief in the mind of the responsible senior that the dereliction was heedless rather than willful.

3. The common service knowledge of an officer's capabilities, while not wholly dependent on his official record, is a reflection from it.

Leading by Example

An officer who sets the example, who gets out in front and does what he wants those following him to do, will be far better obeyed than an officer who takes a position to the rear and makes signals to his men or sends dispatches to them. For many years it has been doctrine in the U.S. Navy and other navies for a division flagship to be first in column; in that way the others can follow their division commander with a minimum of signals merely by staying in the flagship's wake and doing what it does. Signals and messages take time, they don't always get through, and they often are misunderstood. A leader who is in the middle or rear must rely on communications alone, for by taking such a position he has deprived himself of leading by example—the best, and often the quickest, method of all.

The Royal Navy was at one of its periods of peak proficiency when it fought by divisions against the Dutch. Then came the Duke of York's fighting instructions, which were to deprive the Royal Navy of its positional asset: the three divisions were arranged in column, with the division commander in the center of each, and the commander in chief in the center division. Signals were slow and poor, and they were hard to read, as they were obscured by dense clouds of powder smoke. The result was a long (eighty to one hundred ships) column that came under one man's rigid control. He could not lead by example, and the ships blazed away lustily and accomplished little, except wasting ammunition. It remained for a later generation of British naval officers—Rodney and Nelson, in particular—to break this pattern and restore to the Royal Navy its original greatness. At Trafalgar the two British division commanders, Nelson and Collingwood, raced each other into action. The captains who followed had been well briefed, to be sure, but they also had example to fortify precept (a rule).

Pros and Cons of Leadership

There are many advantages to being a leader, most of them either well known or easily inferred. The leader has increased authority, higher rank, increased pay, and great prestige. He or she is in a position to have his or her work more easily recognized and rewarded instead of submerged in a mass enterprise. All these are quite normal and legitimate assets when leadership is audited.

It would be less than straightforward not to mention some of the liabilities of leadership. While rank has its privileges (RHIP), it also has its responsibilities (RHIR). The two are inseparable. One of the responsibilities of leadership is ensuring that work ordered done not only gets done, but is entirely satisfactory when it is done. It may be necessary for the leader to recommend someone for trial by court-martial or that someone be relieved for incompetence. Neither of these actions is pleasant, but it is absolutely necessary for those in a position of responsibility to ensure the maintenance of discipline.

Then there is what the late James V. Forrestal of honored memory called "the loneliness of leadership." It is regrettable, but nonetheless necessary, that a leader remain a little aloof from his subordinates, especially in a military organization. This does not mean that he should be haughty and unapproachable; far from it. He should be affable and accessible. It does mean that he cannot be on intimate terms with any of his followers without giving rise to suspicions of partiality, favoritism, unfairness, and perhaps a bit of espionage. No matter how unfounded such suspicions may be, they play havoc with discipline, morale, and esprit de corps. It also is quite likely that the followers would prefer their leader to consort with his organizational equals and not intrude in their affairs except on special occasions.

There will be times when a unit has to work harder and longer than usual. The personnel will work harder, better, and more cheerfully if they know that the leader is sharing the burden with them.

Characteristics of Enlisted Personnel

Enlisted Naval Personnel

The size and demographic parameters of the navy's enlisted ranks are fairly stable. Little change is expected in the remainder of the decade. Characteristics of a sampling of the enlisted ranks in March 1981 can be seen in Table 8.1.

Table 8.1. Grades and ages of enlisted personnel, U.S. Navy, 1981*

Grade	*Approximate Number*	*Age*	*Approximate Number*
E-9	3,100	20 and younger	130,000
E-8	8,300	21–25	172,000
E-7	30,600	26–30	72,000
E-6	65,200	31–35	47,000
E-5	79,500	36–40	32,000
E-4	101,300	41–45	10,000
E-3	81,500	46–50	3,000
E-2	54,600	over 50	1,000
E-1	42,900		
Total	467,000	Total	467,000

*Adapted from VAdm. William P. Mack USN (Ret) and Capt. Thomas D. Paulsen USN, *The Naval Officers Guide*, 9th ed. (Annapolis, 1983), p. 193, by permission of Naval Institute Press.

These men and women (29,800, or 6.4 percent of the total in the table, were women) came from all states of the union. Seventy-five percent had high school diplomas when they entered the navy. The navy worked hard to recruit them, and in 1980 and 1981 it achieved 100 percent of its recruiting goals.

In 1983, 50 percent of first-term men and women reenlisted and, in the career category, 60 percent reenlisted. In the 1983 group, approximately 12 percent were black; 3 percent were Hispanic; and 6 percent were members of other minorities. Half of the 40 percent who had spouses also had children.

The picture that can be drawn from the foregoing demographic data is of a navy that is young, not as well educated as it should be, short in middle-grade petty officers, and partially staffed with women, who are limited by law from serving in combatant ships and aircraft.

Some of these factors have changed in recent years. Raises in navy pay and the economic troubles of our country have increasingly encouraged better-educated men and women of the civilian community to enlist. The navy can expect some petty officers who left in recent years to return. The result may be an older, more experienced Navy. The percentages of minorities and women probably will not change much; nor will the numbers of dependents.

Enlisted Marine Personnel

There are approximately 196,000 enlisted marines; 188,000 of them are men, and 8,000 of them are women. Seventy-one percent of the men and 61 percent of the women are Caucasian, and 22 percent of the men and 23 percent of the women are black. Hispanics constitute 5 percent of male and 4 percent of female enlisted marines. Other ethnic groups have enlisted at the rate of 2-1/2 percent for males and almost 3 percent for females. In recent years almost all recruits have been high school graduates or have been eligible for a general education diploma. Minimum age for enlistment for males is seventeen and for females, eighteen.

Male recruits go to bootcamp at either Parris Island, South Carolina, or San Diego, California, for basic training. All women recruits are trained at Parris Island. Recruit training stresses physical fitness, orientation to the corps, and developing combat skills, particularly learning to use the rifle effectively.

After they complete recruit training, marines may elect, if they qualify, to train in one of forty-one occupational fields. These range from basic infantry, artillery, and armor to public affairs, weather forecasting, aviation, and administration.

Unlike the Navy, the Marine Corps does not have promotional examinations. Regular quarterly tests are given to privates, lance corporals, and corporals (E-1 through E-4) on basic military subjects. These quarterly scores, along with a score for physical fitness, conduct, and job performance, are compiled into a multiple. An annual minimum multiple for various occupational fields is formulated, and those marines who meet that standard form the pool from which those who are promoted are drawn. Those ranked sergeant (E-5) and above are promoted on the basis of a regular fitness report filed by their commanding officers. The four groups of marine enlisted ranks can be seen in Table 8.2.

Table 8.2. Marine Corps enlisted ranks and grades

	Rank	*Grade*
Enlisted	Private	E–1
	Private First Class	E–2
	Lance Corporal	E–3
Noncommissioned officers	Corporal	E–4
	Sergeant	E–5
Staff noncommissioned officers	Staff Sergeant	E–6
	Gunnery Sergeant	E–7
Senior staff noncommissioned officers	Master Sergeant	E–8
	First Sergeant	E–8
	Master Gunnery Sergeant	E–9
	Sergeant Major (senior enlisted person)	E–9

NOTE: Use of pay grades is inappropriate in discussions of a person's rank.

The Enlisted Person of the 1980s

We can draw some conclusions regarding the general character of these men and women, but first we should remember that there is one key trait of American men and women which is at once a handicap and a great advantage, and that is the tendency of Americans to be individuals. No person is totally like any other person. A key point in leadership is to treat each person, where possible, as an individual.

The average bluejacket or marine will be fairly well educated: about 90 percent of naval service personnel will be high school graduates. Many will want additional formal education, and most will want vocational training. You will encounter many enlisted persons with a quick, native intelligence and a mechanical bent who will want to solve problems with their hands and avoid manuals and instructions. Positive leadership will be required to make many people under your command adhere to safety precautions and sign check-off lists.

Enlisted personnel will need adequate explanation as to why a course of action is to be followed, but they will carry out orders promptly and wait for a later explanation if their leader is respected.

Many enlisted persons will be strongly controlled by the welfare, interests, and feelings of their dependents, including parents, spouses, and children. Those who are married are often more easily led, since they have made a commitment to their families which requires that they succeed in order to provide support.

Some of your personnel will be highly motivated, and you should encourage them to achieve rating and commission. Many will see the naval service as a satisfying career, will put up with the hardships and separations that come with it, and will go on to become the backbone of the naval service. At the other end of the spectrum, some will never do well, and they should be marked early and discharged as soon as possible. Early discharge procedures and better recruiting now make this possible.

These men and women will be of various ethnic and social origins. They will be willing to accept deprivations and to work hard and long if they know why they are making these sacrifices, but they will resist dictatorial leadership. Many will be too independent to be driven or regimented but, given proper leadership, they will be the world's best. At a change-of-command ceremony for one of his commissioned officers, Rear Admiral Richard K. Fontaine, a service group commander, said, "Treat the American bluejacket well, for with proper leadership and guidance, there is nothing they can't or won't do for you, and they will do it well."

Naval Customs, Usage, Ceremony, and Traditions

It has been often said that the faith, creed, and ways of the seagoing man are not clearly seen or understood by the landsman. Moreover, it may be said that tested tradition and dignified and time-hallowed ceremonies, together with customs that are linked with the lore of the sea, are not always fully recognized or adequately appreciated by the seaman himself. To some extent he is a product of a materialistic and machine age. It has taken all the time and intellect that the officer could muster to keep abreast of the naval profession as it has progressed rapidly along with advancements in science and technology.

The service should find worth and inspiration in a review of its naval inheritance. To evaluate properly the attitudes and inner feelings for the service, every naval officer must for a short time forget science and the machine and must consider the effect of tradition on morale, and of customs on naval law and regulations, as well as the unusual distinction that ceremony lends to a military organization. Inasmuch as the principles of honor, loyalty, and devotion to cause are immutable, it follows that any study that will intensify these qualities in the individual is worthy of particular attention.

Shipboard Traditions and Customs

The traditions of shipboard life differ from those of life in a shore operation. Some shipboard traditions might seem meaningless and unnecessary to the superficial observer: from time to time we hear criticism of the spit and polish that is required on board ship. But important thinking underlies these rigid demands. In the first place, spit and polish is a small but important manifestation of the perfectionism that is carried out in every minute detail. The significance is this: if all the details are perfect, the machine itself will function perfectly. The insistence and the stress that is placed on perfection is not stuffy adherence to something that is obsolete; rather, there is a deep, underlying necessity for a set of standards that will assure that things will work properly when they are needed. Also, it is well to remember that there is a vast difference from operating installations ashore and ships at sea. Many a mistake at sea can be fatal.

Customs aboard ship are not enforced for the pleasure of some martinet in command; virtually every rule and regulation aboard ship has evolved as a safety measure. Sailors are the greatest safety engineers in the world. They must take precautions against falling overboard or being electrocuted; of necessity, they have devised ways to prevent boiler explosions, gun explosions, and collisions. Safety of the ship is the primary reason command must never be diluted. It is a continuing responsibility, both when people are awake and when they are asleep. It is a twenty-four-hour-a-day proposition. A ship commander knows that in his densely populated community there are certain rules that must be followed, both for the safety and security of the ship and her people and to prevent the irritations that can undermine morale.

Many of these precautionary measures now appear as traditions rooted in obscurity, but people who have been exposed to shipboard life have come to understand and respect those rules and the standard of discipline which to the uninitiated might seem like regimentation. This philosophy is an inherited tradition that deserves perpetuation.

Customs and Usage

National customs existed before statutes; observances of customs come imperceptibly to control the conduct of a circle of nations. Emerson once remarked, "We all live according to custom." Bacon, in recognition of the influence of customs in the Elizabethan Age, wrote, "Since custom is the principal magistrate of men's lives, let men by all means obtain good customs."

Customs have always played an important role in the administration of a military organization. The naval service is bound by customs of the sea as well as by customs of the service. In fact, there is a brotherhood that has from man's first venture upon great waters been characteristic of men of the sea, whether sailor or marine.

The role that customs played in the formulation of naval regulations is an example of the effect of sound usage. Usage is a long-continued or established practice that, often, becomes custom. Customs of the service have the full effect of law when they fulfill a naval legal definition. The principal conditions that must be fulfilled in order to establish a valid custom, in order for usage to become custom, are:

The usage must be long continued. This means that it must have been that way for so long that no one can remember when it was different—for so long that the mind does not run to the contrary.

It must be certain and uniform. A thing is "certain" when it permits of no doubt. It is "uniform" when it has always the same form and is unvarying when applied to all people in the same way.

It must be compulsory. That is, it is obligatory. It is enforced, if by no other force than that of public opinion. "Square your hat" is a command frequently used by the shore patrol and platoon commanders.

It must be consistent. It must be harmonious with other customs and regulations. For example, the custom of wearing the hat square is consistent with the customary procedure of rendering the hand salute. The finger tips shall touch the lower edge of the hat, just above the eye. Wearing the hat on the back of the head cannot satisfy the element of consistency as long as the salute is fashioned in the present custom.

It must be general. That is, it must pertain to all of a class, section, nation, etc. All officers exchange salutes, but it is the junior who initiates it, and this applies to all juniors.

It must be known. This does not require that each individual affected must know or be familiar with the particular usage. It simply must be so generally known that knowledge may be presumed. Hence, ignorance of the law is no excuse.

It must not be in opposition to the terms of a statute or lawful regulation or order. While usage may operate to cause a written law to be repealed, usage by itself can never render a written law null and void. Only a duly constituted law-making body is so empowered. This point may be illustrated by the following incident:

> In one of our large New England cities there was an old law which required that any public house which provides board and lodging for a wayfarer must also provide food and shelter for his horse. That law, rendered useless by the advent and development of the automobile, was still on the books, when a "Hollywood Cowboy," seeking publicity, registered in a prominent hotel of the city and demanded food and shelter for his horse, and got it. The horse had to be put up in the freight elevator. (The legislature then removed the law from the books.)

Custom, on the other hand, may be nullified by usage. Research in the development of regulation and law clearly shows that, in general, usage led to custom and custom led to regulations and established ceremony.

Ceremony

Ceremony is valuable mainly because it binds us to the past and fills a persistent need. At the same time, it lends an air of dignity and respect to all official relations, whether these occur at home or abroad.

Ceremony may be defined as "formalities observed on some solemn or important occasion in order to render it more imposing or impressive." Examples of ceremony are the changing of commanding officers and the inauguration of a president of the United States. In addition, ceremony can merely be a usage of politeness or formality. The simplest ceremonies of politeness are the customs of friends shaking hands on greeting, a gentleman raising his hat to a lady, and a junior saluting a senior. An introduction is a simple ceremony of formality.

Today ceremonies, in contrast to their servility of the past, are accepted in military organizations as the observance of regulations or dignified respect to the symbols of the state and the state's officials. Naval personnel, in the service of a democratic republic, entered the navy voluntarily, or in compliance with laws that, as citizens, they had a voice in making. They thereby embraced a system of ceremonial institutions. The navy values its ceremonies because they are *a function of discipline*, and they have definitive regulations for important occasions. They are tributes to worthy traditions and an acceptance of law and order.

Ceremony always has been a factor in the maintenance of discipline. However, only the impractical man places ceremony above common sense; likewise, a person who hasn't the common sense to value and to use dignified ceremony is impractical. A man may be taught to feel pride in uniform, pride in service, and pride in his respect to the flag through ceremonial deference to them. The ceremony of religious worship, whether it be one of utter simplicity or of gorgeous ritual, has, dependent on the worshiper's personality, ever been a factor that has given religious institutions their coherence and their discipline. In fact, it is impossible to join in worship without the use of form, however simple. It is also impossible to maintain and conduct with order and dignity a military organization without form and ceremony. Naval leaders should refrain from lightly relinquishing any dignified ceremony or custom which the test of time has proved to be conducive to good discipline.

Tradition

Tradition, when it is coupled with courage and pride, gives to the officer corps its highest incentive to carry on. The value of tradition to a military service is recognized best by those who know something of the deeds in the service's history.

Tradition contributes a background to the service. To appreciate the value of naval tradition is to know the country's naval history. Time may add or subtract from the original facts of tradition, but in practically all cases, the deed, the action, the gesture, the veritable essence, remain. "Surrender be damned, I haven't yet begun to fight" was echoed by McAuliffe at the Battle of the Bulge when he responded, "Aw, nuts." "Don't give up the ship" was modernized by Commander Gilmore's calm order, "Take her down," as he lay wounded on the deck of his submarine, which was in danger of being destroyed on the surface. Lieutenant John J. "Jo-Jo" Powers and dozens of other naval aviator heroes gave added life to the tradition of courage expressed in "Damn the torpedoes, full speed ahead" by pressing home their attacks through devastating antiaircraft fire.

Tradition is important in some measure to all people—even to those who would destroy it because it is a symbol of the past. To the military, correct understanding of tradition is of special importance, for if it is wisely used, tradition is inspirational; if it is blindly adhered to, it can be both shackle and dry rot.

The service cannot be a slave to tradition. If tradition was interpreted to mean that today's soldier should defend himself with the weapons of yesteryear, the nation's safety would soon be endangered. Yet if today's soldier carries his weapons with the boundless spirit, the courage, and the faith of David, the Goliath of today will not prevail.

If upholding tradition meant supporting the out-of-date tactical battle plan so successfully employed by John Paul Jones, our national safety would not be well served. On the other hand, if those in the service discriminate wisely, and pattern their thoughts after that tough, courageous sea captain who, after his ship was a shambles, after most of his nine-pounders were out of action, after both rudder and rigging had been shot away, and after most of his crew had been either killed or wounded, thundered he had not yet begun to fight, then they are on pretty solid ground, indeed.

There must, forever, be the nicest discrimination made in terms of military tradition. Tradition does not mean shackling yourself to the ironclad concepts of the past, emulating yesterday's tactical doctrine today, or blinding yourself to the trends of the future. Real military traditions are those that recognize and enshrine those immutable elements that are of lasting importance, whether the war is being fought by bow and arrow or by ballistic missile.

Both the United States and its armed forces can derive everlasting benefit by continuing to revere the tradition that carries on the spirit of this nation's patriotic predecessors; and, conversely, irreparable damage could be done if the military became hidebound in the name of tradition, adhering to those things that are no longer militarily practicable and useful.

Now, it must also be realized that military safety is not always achieved by adherence to proven practices; it can best be attained by continuous and candid reappraisal of the total situation; by remaining receptive to new concepts and techniques; by being first to conceive, design, build, and operate new systems better suited to counter those weapons the enemy might develop.

The value of tradition in a military and naval service is incalculable—a fact that has always been recognized by the outstanding officers of yesterday and today. In the desire to emulate the progenitors of tradition, an individual becomes imbued with some of the spirit that prompted tradition's birth. In fact, the greatest homage that can be paid an officer after he leaves the naval service is for people to say that he lived and acted according to the best traditions of the service.

Naval Manners and Conduct

Manners

Manners are the outward manifestation of the individual's breeding. The young naval officer's manners, more than anything else, will be the basis on which others will form their early opinions. It is true that there are certain customs considered good manners in the naval society that are not generally practiced in civilian society; nevertheless, a well-mannered person is acceptable in either. The officer is on parade for public appraisal each time he comes in contact with civilians, especially when he is in uniform. The public attitude toward and support of the naval service is determined in great measure by the composite impression formed through appraisal of individual naval personnel in uniform.

An officer has a position to maintain, and most people will be proud to see a dignified determination to do credit to the uniform.

Military Conduct

In the following paragraphs are outlined some of the accepted customs in general military conduct that each officer should practice and become familiar with.

1. The procedure for getting into and out of automobiles is the same as that for boats: juniors first in, last out. But the opposite is true for boarding or leaving a ship: senior first on, last off. In entering buildings, the junior opens the door and enters last.

2. The junior always walks on the left. Those to be honored should be placed on the right side.

3. When passing through the halls of a building, if there are no rules to the contrary, you may remove your hat or leave it on, as you choose. The hat is removed, of course, on entering an office.

4. On entering the office of a senior, or on greeting him, an officer should announce his name unless he is certain that the senior knows it and will be able to recall it. It is embarrassing to the senior to be greeted by someone he knows, or should know, and whose name he cannot recall.

5. A junior officer approaching a senior for the purpose of making an official report or request should maintain an attitude of military attention. He does not take a seat, or smoke, until he is invited to do so.

6. A junior should never offer to shake hands with a senior; he should allow the senior to make the first gesture. It is considered good manners, however, to offer to shake hands with juniors, both officers and enlisted men, on being introduced.

7. At parties where the captain is present, it is not considered good taste to leave before he does. If it becomes necessary to do so, pay your respects to him before departing.

8. There is only one proper response to an order: "Aye, aye, Sir" or "Aye, aye, Ma'am" (or the appropriate rank). This response means "I understand and will obey." Responses such as "OK, Sir" or "All right, Sir" are improper. And, of course, a junior never says "Very well, Sir" to a senior. This response is reserved for the use of seniors when they are acknowledging the report of a junior.

9. The word *sir* should be employed as a prefix to an official report, statement, or question addressed orally to a senior. It should also be used when addressing any official representing a senior. For example, the officer of the deck is addressed as "Sir," regardless of his rank.

10. There are certain differences in phrasing which should be noted: a senior sends his "compliments" to a junior, whereas a junior sends "respects." In written correspondence, the senior may "direct" the attention of the junior to something, while the junior "invites" the senior's attention. A junior writes a memorandum for a senior, while the senior writes a memorandum to a junior. A junior would subscribe his memo "Very respectfully," but the senior would subscribe his "Respectfully."

11. It should be pointed out that the relation between officers and

subordinates is founded on the same mutual respect as that between fellow officers. Some inexperienced officers feel that they promote friendliness between themselves and their men by calling them by their first names or, worse, by their nicknames. Nothing could be further from the truth. Familiarity breeds contempt within the service as well as without.

12. Navy, marine, air force, and army officers are addressed by their military titles. Doctors of any grade may prefer to be called "Doctor." The chaplain is always addressed as "Chaplain," regardless of his grade. Commanding officers of ships are called "Captain," irrespective of rank, and the executive officer is referred to as "the commander" when he is of the rank of commander, without the concurrent use of his name. There can be only one "captain" on a ship and only one "commander."

Other officers of the rank of captain or commander on board should be addressed as "Captain" Brown or "Commander" Brown. The habit of calling lieutenant commanders "Commander" is without foundation in naval custom and should be avoided. On the other hand, lieutenant colonels are quite properly addressed orally as "Colonel."

Wardroom Manners

The wardroom and quarters on board ship and ashore should be treated as the naval officer's home and made a pleasant place to live. It is also a club, where he may gather with shipmates for moments of relaxation or for a discussion of the daily problems over a cup of coffee. The quiet of a public reading room or a morgue need not be maintained. One commanding officer, in welcoming a new ensign on board, made the statement that his criterion of a happy wardroom country was based on the amount of noise which filtered up to his cabin, and that his outfit was the "noisiest damned bunch he had ever heard." His, incidentally, was a happy ship.

The executive officer is the president of the mess. Navy regulations prescribe the seating arrangement of the mess table. Common courtesy and respect require each officer to be in the mess prior to meal times so that all may be seated when the executive officer takes his seat.

Every officer is a member of the mess. His vote carries equal weight with all others. Considerable rivalry usually develops in the election of mess treasurer (or caterer). The officer so honored should endeavor to turn in a first-class job. There is no excuse for poor food indifferently served on board any ship or station of the naval service. Nothing will increase morale quicker than appetizing meals, properly prepared and served. The steward will cooperate when he knows that his services are appreciated.

The wardroom country is out of bounds to enlisted men except in special circumstances. An officer should not use his stateroom as an office unless he is forced by circumstances to do so. He should handle his business with the men in their parts of the ship or in the regular ship's offices.

The following instructions on wardroom manners quoted from a navy instruction pamphlet contain excellent advice.

1. Do not enter or lounge in the wardroom out of uniform. On some destroyers and small ships some latitude is allowed in this, but you should be certain the commanding officer sanctions any variance. You may rest assured that the commanding officer of a smart ship will never relax this requirement for any reason less than hardheaded practicality. Be on guard against following the example of the careless or slovenly individual under the impression that he is "salty." Do not wear your hat in the wardroom.

2. Never sit down to meals before the executive officer and/or the commanding officer—or, in his absence, the senior member—sits down.

3. If it is necessary to leave before the end of the meal, excuse yourself to the senior member at your table.

4. Always introduce your guests to those at your table and to the other wardroom officers if practicable.

5. All guests are guests of all wardroom officers. Be friendly and sociable to guests. Do not talk shop continuously. It gives the appearance that you know nothing else, or that you are showing off. In addition, you may accidentally reveal security information.

6. Whenever an officer from another ship enters the wardroom, introduce yourself, extend all courtesies, and ask to help him in any way possible.

7. Never be late for meals. If you are unavoidably late, make your apologies to the senior member.

8. When you are bringing guests, be on time. If you see that you

are going to be late, notify your messmates if it is practicable to do so. The arrival of guests after the mess has begun is awkward.

9. Only those on the sick list have the privilege of eating in their rooms.

10. Do not be boisterous or otherwise noisy in the wardroom. This is the home of all the officers, and their rights and privileges must be respected.

11. Pay your mess bills and all other personal ship's bills promptly. Your wardroom mess bill and mess entrance fee are payable in advance. It is proper to ask the mess treasurer within the first twenty-four hours the amount of the mess bill and entrance fee and to pay them at that time.

12. Be civil and just in all your dealings with mess personnel. If you have a complaint, make it to the mess caterer.

13. Do not abuse the use of the messman of the watch by sending him off on long errands.

14. Remember that gambling and drinking, or even possessing alcoholic beverages, aboard ship is prohibited by regulations.

Marine Corps Tradition

The most comprehensive treatment of this subject can be found in "Naval Ceremonies, Customs, and Traditions," "The Marine Officer's Guide," and "The Naval Officer's Guide." All three books are published by the Naval Institute, Annapolis, Maryland.

The traditions of the Marine Corps, its history, its flags, its uniforms, its insignia—the Marine Corps way of doing things—make the corps what it is and set it distinctly apart from other military organizations and services.

These traditions give the Marine Corps its flavor and are the reason why the corps cherishes its past, its ways of acting and speaking, and its uniforms. These things foster the discipline, valor, loyalty, aggressiveness, and readiness which make the term *marine* ". . . signify all that is highest in military efficiency and soldierly virtue."

One writer on marine traditions nailed down their importance in the following way: "As our traditions, our institutions, and even our eccentricities—like live coral—develop and toughen, so the Corps itself develops and toughens."

And remember: Whenever the Marine Corps is impoverished by the death of a tradition, you are generally to blame. Traditions are not preserved by books and museums, but by faithful adherence on the part of all hands—you *especially*.

Symbols

Globe and anchor. When the late Major General Smedley Butler (winner of two Medals of Honor) was a lieutenant in the Philippines in 1899, he decided to get himself tattooed.

> I selected an enormous Marine Corps Emblem (wrote Butler) to be tattooed across my chest. It required several sittings and hurt me like the devil, but the finished product was worth the pain. I blazed triumphantly forth, a Marine from throat to waist. The emblem is still with me. Nothing on earth but skinning will remove it.

Butler's last sentence was somewhat premature. Within less than a year, during the storming of the Tartar Wall in Peking, a Chinese bullet struck him in the chest and gouged off part of his emblem. The rest of it accompanied him to the grave forty years later.

Whether you are a private or general is secondary compared to the privilege you share of wearing the emblem. The globe and anchor is the most important insignia you have.

The globe had been conferred on the Royal Marines in 1827 by King George IV. Because it was impossible to recite all the achievements of marines on the corps color, said the king, "the Great Globe itself" was to be their emblem, for marines had won honor everywhere.

General Zeilin's U.S. Marine globe displayed the Western hemisphere, since the "Royals" had the Eastern hemisphere on theirs. Eagle and fouled anchor were added to leave no doubt that the corps was both American and maritime.

Marine Corps colors. The colors of the corps are scarlet and gold. Although they have been associated with U.S. Marines for many years, these colors were not officially recognized until General Lejeune became thirteenth commandant. Today you will see scarlet and gold throughout marine posts, on signboards; auto tags; bandsmen's drums, pouches, and trumpet slings; military police brassards; officers' hat cords and aiguillettes. Sometimes it seems the colors are everywhere in sight.

In addition to scarlet and gold, forest green enjoys at least semiofficial standing as a marine color. During the years since 1912, when forest green was adopted for the winter service uniform, it has become standard for such equipment as vehicles, weapons, armor, and organizational chests and baggage. In addition, forest green is today virtually the distinguishing color of marines throughout the world, being worn as a service uniform by the British, Dutch, Korean, and other corps.

Forest green originates from the same source as the light infantry bugle that was once part of the corps badge. The costume of eighteenth-century huntsmen was forest green. The riflemen recruited from that calling wore green uniforms—a green that survives not only among marines but also in the uniforms of Britain's Rifle Brigade (the "Greenjackets") and India's Ghurkhas.

The three colors of the corps—scarlet, gold, and forest (or rifle) green—are the colors of the corps necktie, designed for wear with civilian clothes.

"The Marines' Hymn" and the Marine Corps march. "The Marines' Hymn" is what its name implies, the hymn of the Marine Corps. "Semper Fidelis," one of John Philip Sousa's best known works, is the corps march.

"The Marines' Hymn" is the oldest of the official songs of the armed services. Every marine knows those words and will sing them at the drop of a field hat. The origin of the hymn is obscure. Its words date back to the nineteenth century, and its author remains unknown. The music comes from an air, "Gendarmes of the Queen," in Jacques Offenbach's opera *Genevieve de Brabant*, first performed in November 1859. Regardless of its origin, however, *all marines get to their feet whenever "The Marines' Hymn" is played or sung.*

"Semper Fidelis" was composed by Sousa in 1888 during his tour as leader of the Marine Band. "Semper Fi," as the troops know it, is habitually rendered for parades, reviews, and march-pasts of marines.

Birthday of the corps. The Marine Corps was founded by the Continental Congress on 10 November 1775. The resolution which created our corps reads as follows:

> *Resolved.* That two Battalions of Marines be raised consisting of one Colonel, two lieutenant Colonels, two Majors, & Officers as usual in other battalions; that particular care be taken that no persons be appointed to office, or enlisted into said Battalions, but such as are good seamen, or so acquainted with maritime affairs as to be able to serve to advantage by sea, when required. That they be enlisted and commissioned for and during the present war with Great Britain and the colo-

nies, unless dismissed by order of Congress. That they be distinguished by the names of the first and second battalions of American Marines, and that they be considered as part of the number, which the Continental Army before Boston is ordered to consist of.

Motto, Slogan, and Nickname

The Marine Corps motto. "Semper Fidelis" ("Always Faithful") is the motto of the corps. That marines have lived up to this motto is proved by the fact that there has never been a mutiny, or even the thought of one, among U.S. Marines.

Semper Fidelis was adopted about 1883 as the motto of the corps. Before that there had been three mottoes, all of them traditional rather than official. The first, antedating the War of 1812, was "Fortitudine" ("With Fortitude"). The second, "By Sea and by Land," was obviously a translation of the Royal Marines' "Per Mare, per Terram." Until 1848, after the return to Washington of the marine battalion that took part in the capture of Mexico City, this motto was revised to: "From the Halls of the Montezumas to the Shores of Tripoli," a line now familiar to all Americans. This revision of the corps motto has encouraged speculation that the first stanza of "The Marines' Hymn" was composed by members of the marine battalion who stormed Chapultepec Castle.

The Marine Corps shares its motto with England's Devonshire Regiment, the Eleventh Foot, one of the senior infantry regiments of the British Army, whose sobriquet is "the Bloody Eleventh" and whose motto is also Semper Fidelis.

"Tell it to the Marines." In his book *Fix Bayonets*, Captain John W. Thomason, Jr., gives the generally accepted version of the origin of "Tell it to the Marines":

> They relate of Charles II that at Whitehall a certain seacaptain, newly returned from the Western Ocean, told the King of flying fish, a thing never heard in old England. The King and court were vastly amused. But, the naval fellow persisting, the Merry Monarch beckoned to a lean, dry colonel of the sea regiment, with seamed mahogany face, and said, in effect: "Colonel, this tarry-breeks here makes sport with us stay-at-homes. He tells of a miraculous fish that foresakes its element and flies like a bird over water." "Sire," said the colonel of Marines, "he tells a true thing. I myself have often seen those fish in your Majesty's seas around Barbados—" "Well," decided Charles, "such evidence cannot be

disputed. And hereafter, when we hear a strange thing, we will tell it to the Marines, for the Marines go everywhere and see everything, and if they say it is so, we will believe it."

This yarn (for such it is) was for many years credited to Samuel Pepys, although scholars disclaimed it. On the other hand, the phrase "Tell it to the Marines" is an old one—it can be found in print as early as 1726.

"Leathernecks." The marines' longstanding nickname, "Leathernecks," goes back to the leather stock, or neckpiece, that was part of the marine uniform from 1775 to 1875. One historian has written:

> Government contracts usually contained a specification that the stock be of such height that the "chin could turn freely over it," a rather indefinite regulation, and, as one Marine put it, one which the "taylors must have interpreted to mean with the nose pointing straight up."

Although many justifications have been adduced for the leather stock, the truth seems to be that it was intended to ensure that marines kept their heads erect ("up and locked," the aviators would say), a laudable aim in any military organization at any time.

Descended from the stock is the standing collar, hallmark of marine blues, whites, and evening dress. Like its leather ancestor, the standing collar regulates stance and posture and thus proclaims the wearer as a modern "Leatherneck."

"The President's Own"

Founded in 1798 (more than a century before the bands of the other three services), the Marine Band has performed at White House functions for every president except George Washington; it was especially sponsored by Thomas Jefferson. Because of its traditional privilege of performing at the White House, the band is spoken of as "The President's Own." President Kennedy epitomized the band's special position when he remarked in 1962, "I find that the only forces which cannot be transferred from Washington without my express permission are the members of the Marine Band, and I want it announced that we propose to hold the White House against all odds, at least for some time to come."

The Marine Band has been present at many of the most memorable and cherished moments in our nation's history, including the dedication of the National Cemetery at Gettysburg when Lincoln gave his immortal address (his aide-de-camp was Second Lieutenant H. C. Cochrane, USMC). The band was led for twelve years by John Philip Sousa. Among the band's many traditions is its scarlet, full-dress blouse, the only red coat worn by American forces since the Revolutionary War. (In 1956, the Marine Corps Drum and Bugle Corps was likewise granted the privilege of wearing red coats.)

The Marine Band tours the country each fall and has done so ever since Sousa commenced the practice in 1891, although one section of the band always remains in Washington to fulfill its traditional primary mission "to provide music when directed by the President of the United States, the Congress of the United States, or the Commandant of the Marine Corps."

The Mameluke Sword

The Mameluke sword gets its name from the cross-hilt and ivory grip, both of which were used for centuries by the Moslems of North Africa and Arabia. The Marine Corps tradition of carrying this type of sword dates from Lieutenant O'Bannon's assault on Derna, Tripoli, in 1805, when he is said to have won the sword of the governor of the town.

In addition to being used on parade, the sword is the center of many Marine Corps rituals. You wear your sword when you get married, and you cut your wedding cake with it. At many posts, you wear it while you serve as officer of the day. Should you ever be unlucky enough to be placed under arrest, you must surrender your sword.

Never unsheathe your sword inside a mess or wardroom. If you do, custom decrees that you must stand drinks for all present. This tradition goes back to stringent rules against dueling in the early days of the Navy and the Marine Corps.

The Naval Officer as a Gentleman

The expression "an officer and a gentleman by an act of Congress" is heard frequently. In actuality, the terms *officer* and *gentleman* should be synonymous. Robert E. Lee's test of a gentleman in today's service is fully applicable to officers of both sexes. Since the term *gentleman* arises so often, it perhaps would be enlightening to discuss its meaning in relation to the role of a naval officer.

An anonymous author has given the following splendid definition of a gentleman:

> A man that is clean inside and outside, who neither looks up to the rich nor down on the poor; who can lose without squealing; who can win without bragging; who is considerate of others; who is too brave to lie, too generous to cheat, and too sensible to loaf; who takes only his share of the world's goods and lets other people have theirs—this is a real gentleman.

Any individual, regardless of rank or ranking, wealth or poverty, social position, race, color, or creed, can be a gentleman. On the other hand, no amount of fanfare, no amount of lawmaking, no amount of money, can make a gentleman out of a boor. If a person is well educated and has been born into a good social position, he probably has learned more of the requirements for a gentleman than someone not so favored, but many of the finest gentlemen in the world never had the advantage of an education and never realized the meaning of social position.

Every person has the right to determine for himself whether another is, or is not, a gentleman, but it is interesting to observe the almost unanimous agreement that is usually reached whenever opinions are exchanged as to whether or not a certain person is a gentleman. It is safe to assume that, if an individual is a gentleman, all those coming into contact with him will realize that fact; and if he is not a gentleman, all those meeting him will be just as unanimous in their opinion.

Nimitz Personified a Gentleman

Fleet Admiral Chester W. Nimitz personified the ideal concept of an officer and a gentleman. No difference ever existed in his relations as a gentleman with juniors, peers, or seniors. He never was offensive to others, even in the performance of the most unpleasant duties. He was well mannered, and he never stopped learning. He fulfilled all of the qualifications in the quotation above. In his conduct of the Pacific War, even his dispatches were phrased in such a manner that the recipient, whether a tugboat skipper or an adjacent theatre commander, could not help feeling the gentlemanly spirit of his words. The most arduous tasks were eased by his words and manner. Captain Eugene B. Fluckey, who was aide and flag lieutenant to Fleet Admiral Nimitz while the latter was chief of naval operations, had this to say:

> The dictionary defines the word "gentleman" as a well-bred man of fine feeling, good education, and social position—a man of refined manners.

> However, the word "gentlemen" as applied to Fleet Admiral Nimitz connotes much more than this. To properly define the word is to describe him—a man of honor, a man of his word, a man of undoubted integrity and scrupulous fairness.

True to his ideals, Nimitz believed that all men have much in common and that misunderstanding is the basis for much of the suspicion and hatred in the world. A spirit of friendship and mutual respect marked his every contact with others. In his mind there was an understanding sympathy and neighborly tolerance of such depth that he never offended anyone.

No matter how heavy his responsibilities in the Pacific were, Admiral Nimitz showed the same courtesy and consideration to the seamen with whom he might be playing horseshoes as he showed to the admirals and the generals. On his return to the United States he signed many pictures and shook many hands, offering the same cordiality to schoolchildren as to the leaders of our country.

With him, courtesy was real. He habituated himself to thinking of others first. On long and tiresome trips he was as thoughtful of those who looked after his safety as they were in looking after him.

At all times the complete master of his every thought and action, he won the respect, confidence, and the admiration of millions throughout the world.

Lee's Test of a Gentleman

Since Robert E. Lee, a true aristocrat with a long line of distinguished gentlemen in his ancestry, was probably one of the most perfect gentlemen this nation has ever produced, his words on the subject of what constitutes a true gentleman are worth pondering.

> The forbearing use of power does not only form a touchstone [test or criterion for determining genuineness or value], but the manner in which an individual enjoys certain advantages over others is the test of a true gentleman.
>
> The power which the strong have over the weak, the magistrate over the citizen, the employer over the employed, the educated over the unlettered, the experienced over the confiding, even the clever over the silly—the forbearing or inoffensive use of all this power or authority, or a total absence from it when the case admits it, will show the gentleman in a plain light. The gentleman does not needlessly or unnecessarily remind an offender of a wrong he may have committed

> against him. He can not only forgive, he can forget; and he strives for that nobleness of self and mildness of character which impart sufficient strength to let the past be the past.

Ironically, when Lee met with Grant at Appomattox to arrange terms of surrender, Grant, a man of quite different cultural antecedents, revealed himself as a personification of Lee's specifications for a true gentleman. Bruce Catton described the meeting.

> It [the new society of the West] could speak with a soft voice, and it could even be abashed by its own moment of triumph, as if that moment were not a thing to be savored and enjoyed. Grant seems to have been almost embarrassed when he and Lee came together in this parlor, yet it was definitely not the embarrassment of an underling ill at ease in a superior's presence. Rather it was simply the diffidence of a sensitive man who had another man in his power and wished to hurt him as little as possible. So Grant made small talk and recalled the old days in the Mexican War, when Lee had been the polished staff officer in the commanding general's tent and Grant had been an acting regimental quartermaster, slouching about like the hired man who looked after the teams. Perhaps the oddest thing about this meeting at Appomattox was that it was Grant, the nobody from nowhere, who played the part of the gracious host, trying to put the aristocrat at his ease and, as far as might be, to soften the weight of the blow that was about to come. In the end it was Lee who, so to speak, had to call the meeting to order, remarking (and the remark must have wrenched him almost beyond endurance) that they both knew what they were there for, and that perhaps they had better get down to business. So Grant opened his orderly book and got out his pencil. He confessed afterward that when he did so he had no idea what words he was going to write down.

Summary

The role of the officer in the naval service is based on a tradition of pride in the organization: its history, symbols, and purpose. Certainly the Marine Corps is one of the finest examples of a tradition-driven organization. The naval officer knows that he can best lead through example; through adhering to rules and regulations; and through gentlemanly conduct and manners. The leadership role is one of direction and authority, but the effective leader realizes that authority must never be abused.

9

Personal Qualities for Effective Leadership

In this chapter and the one following, certain personal character traits considered important to the development of the naval leader are discussed in detail. In studying these chapters, the student must remember that the study of personal character traits can be meaningful to the student only if he performs a critical self-analysis of his own character with a determination to correct deficiencies that this self-analysis reveals. The student must be willing to recognize certain character trait deficiencies, and he must be determined to correct them. The self-analysis of the individual's character traits should not be limited to a personal self-searching, but should also involve an analysis of the individual by others.

Determining Personal Qualities for Successful Naval Leaders

The personal character of some prominent world leaders lacked qualities that are considered essential and necessary for a naval leader under our democratic form of government. Hitler, certainly, was a leader who had rather glaring moral and spiritual inadequacies; in fact, many scholars question whether Hitler was a successful leader.

Admiral Arleigh A. Burke, in his article "Naval Leadership in Action," outlines certain personal qualities that he considers common to all leaders, whether they are good or bad. Burke believes all leaders have

self-confidence
knowledge
enthusiasm
the ability to express themselves forcefully and clearly (both orally and in writing)
the moral courage to eliminate incompetent subordinates
the willingness to do something about a cause

These principles can be practiced by an individual who does not possess a great deal of personal integrity, but it is certain that if all leaders possess all of the above characteristics, then all successful naval leaders must possess these and a great deal more.

Inevitably, we must determine what qualities are essential to effective naval leadership and which of the many human attributes an individual should strive to develop in order to become a competent naval officer, an effective leader of men. The need to select personal qualities for leadership is not new; indeed, generations of naval and Marine Corps officers have sought to determine these necessary qualities. The following discussion sets forth the qualities considered essential to effective naval leadership today.

Loyalty

Loyalty may be defined as "a quality, state, or instance of being faithful or faithful adherence to a person, government, cause, duty, etc." Since there are several varieties of loyalty, it is desirable to specify the kind of loyalty that is being considered in a discussion.

Most important is loyalty to country. Each military officer takes an oath to support and defend the Constitution of the United States against all enemies, foreign or domestic. This oath should be renewed with each promotion.

A second loyalty is to your seniors: loyalty up. Briefly, this means wholeheartedly serving them efficiently and well, not in any way undermining their authority or prestige by any word or action of your own. The acid test of loyalty in an officer is the ability to pass on to his personnel orders from the commanding officer of which he disapproves and which he knows will be unpopular with the men. Once the commanding officer has listened to input from others and has made a decision, it is the duty of the subordinate officer to support the senior as if that decision had originally been his own. There is great danger in the tendency of some officers to take an attitude of sympathy toward their subordinates because of an order or regulation issued by the commanding officer. To do so is disloyal. The personnel will detect it at once, and the guilty officer will lose much of their respect as well as his own.

In some officers there is a strong inclination to examine the orders of superiors. If these agree with the junior's own ideas, he will be intensely loyal. If they do not, he will take them ungracefully. In other words, an officer's loyalty must not only ring true when the plan laid down agrees with his own ideas. It is a very poor and unreliable subordinate who can be depended on to carry out energetically only those plans of which he himself approves. No commander in the service would care to have such a subordinate on his ship or battalion in time of war.

There is also loyalty down, which is essentially having consideration for the welfare of juniors, a willingness to look out for their legitimate interests, and a readiness to "go to bat" for them when necessary. "Loyalty down begets loyalty up." Loyalty up and loyalty down are both absolutely essential to the success of any undertaking. Unless loyalty is a mutual feeling between the senior and the junior, it degenerates into blind obedience, on the part of the best people, and disloyalty—or at best indifference—on the part of the remaining personnel. As soon as an officer discovers disloyalty among his subordinates, he should look first to himself to find the cause. If he has been disloyal to them, it is almost certain that they will be disloyal to him. Nor can they be blamed for this. You cannot refer to officers or other personnel as a "lot of worthless bums" and expect loyalty in return from them. This runs against human nature. On the contrary, the junior officer must improve his subordinates by setting high standards for them through precept and example in every facet of his professional and personal life.

There are other forms of loyalty: loyalty to relatives, to friends, to beliefs, and, finally, to oneself. The last, frequently overlooked, is the key to the others: "To thine own self be true, and it must follow as the night the day, thou canst not then be false to any man."

It would be beneficial to all officers to become students of Admiral Nelson, to learn about his life and, especially, his professional career. There has never been such an exponent of loyalty as Nelson. His whole career was a demonstration of loyalty—loyalty up and loyalty down. Never was he known to speak ill of his subordinates. When, on one occasion, a captain under his command complained of a certain young officer who had been sent to his ship, Nelson replied, "Send him to my ship; I can make an officer of any decent man." Loyalty, to a great extent, was the keynote of his success, but to this, of course, was coupled a thorough mastery of his profession.

Finally, loyalty allows no differences in degree. There is no such thing as a little bit of it; either you are loyal or you are not!

Courage, Physical and Moral

The most ancient and most time-honored requirement of a leader—of any fighting person—is courage. Originally the emphasis was almost entirely on physical courage, and so highly was it esteemed that deeds of reckless daring, even to the point of foolhardiness, were performed to impress the multitude and win respect. Today an individual's physical courage will be assumed; in fact, it would be well that it never be questioned, as there are few things that people—Americans, in particular—care less for in a leader than a lack of courage.

Moral courage means simply having the courage of your convictions, the fortitude to call things as you see them, and the readiness to admit a mistake (to yourself as well as to others) when it is made instead of trying to "bull it through." It requires a high degree of moral courage to report to a senior that you have made a mistake when perhaps the mistake has not even been noticed by others. However, a junior officer's prompt action in reporting his own mistake may enable his senior to take corrective measures before too much damage is done. Any young officer will be pardoned an occasional mistake, for infallibility is not a characteristic of junior officers, but he will not soon or easily be forgiven for an attempt to "cover up."

Disinclination to assume responsibility is an indication of lack of moral courage. An ever present fear of being blamed does much to cramp an officer's initiative and is the most potent reason for causing a petty or noncommissioned officer to "await orders." The particular form of fear which is most common in the service is fear not of physical injury, but rather of condemnation. Few personnel do their best work with the sword of condemnation swinging over their heads.

Overcoming fear. Closely allied with courage is bravery, as both involve the conquest of fear. Fear is one of the most powerful of human emotions, and if it is not controlled it can cause a person seized by it to seek safety in headlong flight, which in turn may cause other persons to do the same. It is highly doubtful whether a completely fearless person ever lived, song and story to the contrary. At birth all human beings are without fear simply because they have not *learned* that some things—fire, for instance—can harm them. As people grow older, they learn, often the hard way, that some things can hurt or kill them. In growing up, an individual learns to avoid these hazards, to overcome or minimize their menace, and even to utilize the very elements that at first caused terror.

Generally speaking, humans fear the unknown, the untried, the untested. It may even be argued that the more intelligent a person is, the more dangers he may conjure up in an unknown or hostile situation, often magnifying them out of all proportion. History shows that estimates of the size and composition of enemy forces almost invariably have been far too high. A bold attitude therefore would seem to require a greater amount of courage on the part of a more intelligent person than of one who is less intelligent.

Even a well-tested combat veteran is nervous, somewhat apprehensive, when he first goes into action. Indeed, he would have to be extremely dull witted not to experience some trepidation. Yet equipped with confidence in your leaders, weapons, and self, and faced with some task to perform, you can muster the courage to subdue fears and turn in a creditable performance. Having successfully conquered fear on a first occasion, it becomes progressively easier on subsequent ones. Through familiarity in coping with danger, therefore, a person may become contemptuous and even careless of it.

Courage, then, is not being without fear; it is suppressing fear and carrying out assigned duties despite the recognition of manifest danger.

Honor, Honesty, and Truthfulness

These characteristics are closely allied, but they are not synonymous.

Honor, as used here, means an acute sense of right and wrong and adherence to actions or principles considered right. It constitutes the personal integrity of the individual. For centuries and in all lands an officer has been expected to be a person of honor, one whose integrity is above reproach. Personal integrity has always been demanded of U.S. officers, and in an age of rapid scientific and technological development, the leader must never forget that this is still the prime ingredient of the naval officer.

Honesty implies the refusal to lie, steal, defraud, or deceive under any circumstances. An honest person recognizes and adheres to virtues such as truthfulness, candor, respect for the possessions of others, sincerity, and fairness. There are no degrees of honesty. As in loyalty, either you are honest or you are not.

Truthfulness is the essence of nobility of character. It is utterly impossible for a liar to be a gentleman. There is no virtue that any school dedicated to training junior officers, such as the Naval Academy, tries harder to instill than truthfulness.

Aside from the importance of these virtues from the standpoint of personal integrity, there are some compelling reasons for stressing them from a purely practical point of view. In a military organization, people work and live together in close proximity, often for months at a time. They must rely heavily, perhaps exclusively, on each other, not just for day-to-day companionship, but for their very lives. It is necessary to put the greatest confidence and trust in your shipmates, and this would hardly be possible if they were other than men of honor, honesty, and truthfulness.

If it is conceded that an individual's fellow officers, shipmates, and messmates need to have these qualities instilled in them, consider how even more important it is for the leader to possess them. Furthermore, if the leader is to command the respect, confidence, unhesitating obedience, and loyal co-operation of others, he must have honor, honesty, and truthfulness in full measure. While possessing these qualities will not of itself make a person a leader, failure to have them will almost certainly preclude his being one.

Faith

Faith, as used here, merely means confidence. There are three kinds of faith: faith in yourself, faith in mankind, faith in the cause for which you are striving. Faith is much like enthusiasm in that it is contagious. Faith begets faith. Faith in yourself—or self-confidence—increases the respect others have for you. Faith in yourself adds to your control over others.

"As a man thinketh in his own heart, so is he." If an individual loses faith in himself, he becomes weak, submissive, apologetic; he lacks initiative, energy, and drive; and he loses respect for others. If an individual loses faith in his fellow humans, he becomes cynical, a doubter, and he trusts no one and is loyal to no one. He becomes crabbed and suspicious and loses the trust and loyalty of seniors and juniors alike. Faith in a cause is essential to victory; the absence of it borders closely on disloyalty. The weakening of faith or confidence in a campaign invariably is followed by a lowering of morale, demoralization, disintegration, and defeat.

Officers who believe with all their hearts in the naval service, their unit, and their commanding officer see their attitude reflected in the bearing of their personnel. Officers who, for reasons best known to themselves, develop a dislike for naval life, should, in loyalty to the service that has trained and supported them for years, keep the fact to themselves lest it cause subordinates to lose faith.

Faith is a strong factor in an officer's ability to handle delinquents. If an officer tells subordinates forcibly that they are too good to be misbehaving, that they have it in them to reform, to snap out of it, to come back, and to show up some of the others, they presently will think so too, and the results will be amazing. Faith will be aroused in them because of the officer's own convincing belief in them.

Religious Faith

Anyone who aspires to leadership in a military organization should reflect on the strongest and greatest motivating force of all time, religious faith. The leader who sincerely believes and has faith in a Creator, regardless of the particular denomination to which he belongs, is endowed with a fortitude and a serenity which will sustain him during periods of stress and misfortune.

The buoyant force of religious faith is evident in the well-known story of Washington praying in the snows of Valley Forge. This force has sustained lesser persons in their darkest hours in enemy prisoner-of-war camps: some of those held by Communist captors were not affected, even under Communist "brainwashing" techniques.

A student of history is aware of how many great military movements had a strong religious impetus: the Crusades, the Wars of Religion that plagued Christendom, the dynamic sweep of Islam across northern Africa and into Europe from both East and West, Cromwell's psalm-singing New Model Army ("God made them as stubble to our swords"). In more recent times, the standards of Kaiser Wilhelm II, emblazoned with "Gott mit Uns," and the kamikaze pilots splattering themselves against American warships for their God-Emperor, are examples.

The world today is still faced with the menace of world communism, which, although it denies God and all his works, has all the fervor and dynamism of a religious movement. It is, in essence, a religious fanaticism whose god is materialism. If our way of life is to prevail, this antithesis of religious belief must be countered by an even greater belief in God.

While the individual is strongly urged as a leader to have religious faith, it is his own affair whether he does so. However, as a leader he is under obligation to his followers to see to it that their spiritual needs are met.

Sense of Humor

An ability to see the humor in a situation—when it exists—is a valuable asset. This does not mean that you should attempt to play the part of a clown; on the contrary, the individual is cautioned against this activity. But there are situations where a well-phrased humorous remark is most appropriate and will ease and even obliterate mental and physical tension. Long hours in foxholes, on watch, or working overtime have been made less dreary by some humorous anecdote, and sagging morale has been thereby restored. In some particularly tense situations an apparently inane remark will cause everyone to laugh, and the tension will disappear. Laughter is like medicine: use it—but do so with caution. And be sure that people know you are laughing with them, not at them, for ridicule is fraught with danger.

Modesty

A truly great person can afford to be modest, and anyone who is not great cannot afford to be otherwise. It is proper for a person to have a moderate opinion of his own value, abilities, and achievements, but you must constantly guard against acquiring too good an opinion of yourself and your work. Give credit to those to whom it is due. It is better to give too much than too little. The generous spirit gains more in the long run than does the selfish one.

Nothing so surely ruins the success of a young officer as the suggestion of pomp and egotism in his demeanor. A case of swollen ego has wrecked many careers. It is quickly noted by enlisted personnel as evidence of smallness of character and limited experience. Modesty, quiet dignity, even humility, are characteristic of greatness of character and broad experience. It is dangerous for the leader to admit self-importance, even to himself. Magnifying your own importance is likely to make you consider your own welfare when you should consider others.

It is good for the soul of any man to travel to a great height, like the top of the Empire State Building, and from there to view humanity on the earth below him, hurrying to and fro on its self-important business. From a height, humans appear to be about the size of ants, and the spectator is led to realize the unimportance of any one individual in comparison with the world about him, and to wonder just how big he himself appears to the distant Eye of Omnipotence.

Self-Confidence

Naval Officers do not begin their careers overly endowed with the quality of self-confidence. The acquisition of self-confidence occurs through the years and is accelerated by the individual's personal experiences and increase in professional knowledge. Self-confidence comes with the eradication of the fear that you will fail in an assigned task. To develop his self-confidence, the naval officer must be willing to accept responsibility for and perform those tasks that may appear personally beyond his capability. You may be tempted to bypass certain assignments that present the fear of failure, but you must suppress any impulse to "leave it to Joe." "Joe" may not be around the next time that task comes up. In essence, building self-confidence means doing each job to the best of your ability. Seek out responsibility, and never pass the buck to someone else because of fear of failure. If you do fail on occasion, remember that failure has happened to everyone at one time or another. The ability to bounce back, to profit by sad experience, and to do the next job better than the last will establish your stature as a naval officer.

Common Sense and Good Judgment

Sense, common sense, good sense, horse sense, gumption, judgment, and wisdom—all these mean the quality of mind or character which enables a person to make intelligent choices or decisions or to reach intelligent conclusions. Common sense implies a learned capacity for seeing things as they are, without illusion or emotional bias. Common sense is the ability an individual possesses to make practical choices or decisions that are sane, prudent, fair, and reasonable. Judgment, on the other hand, seldom applies to a native quality, though it does suggest a foundation in common sense. It also suggests intellectual qualities that are usually the result of training and discipline, such as discernment of facts or conditions that are ascertained—including the ability to comprehend the significance of those facts and conditions and to draw correct, unbiased conclusions from them.

The common sense a person is endowed with can be developed. When it has been fully developed, the exercise of good judgment can be expected. The more knowledge that an officer gains, the better qualified he becomes to exercise judgment. If an individual's common sense and judgment become acutely accurate, then he is said to have wisdom, and he has attained the acme of mental achievement.

The common-sense thing to do is usually the simplest, and often it is the most obvious. It is not common sense, for instance, to punish a hopeless, mentally inferior enlisted man over and over for repeated infractions of discipline. A misfit should be discharged from the service for inaptitude reasons, making room for a better man. It is common sense, however, to investigate the case thoroughly and to make every effort to ascertain the cause of his derelictions before taking such drastic action.

Health, Energy, Optimism

These three attributes of character are clearly interwoven, and one can hardly exist separately from the others. Good health is a priceless asset that few appreciate until it is lost. Good health cannot always be controlled by the individual, but in some instances the Navy and Marine Corps lose the services of outstanding leaders because these officers neglect their health. There are times, it is true, when the naval officer must work around the clock and perhaps sacrifice his immediate health to perform the "job of the moment," but in some instances leaders have not learned the principle of delegating some of their responsibilities to capable juniors. On the other hand, the many duties of an on-board or in-the-field officer often require after-hours work; remember, an officer is part of the naval service twenty-four hours each day.

To preserve the energy that will carry the commanding officer through long periods of fleet operations, an officer must plan his daily routine to provide for such emergencies. An individual must have a planned program of daily exercise and, above all, must know when it is more important to get away from the job, and participate in recreational activities, than it is to read the operation orders or to perform routine paper work.

And what is optimism? Without energy and health, it is often very difficult to be optimistic. Someone said, "The world loves an optimist." The optimistic person is a person who looks at the brighter side of the problem, who expresses that "can do" attitude and imbues seniors and juniors alike with the enthusiasm that the job "can be done" and is worth doing. This is the opposite of the "pessimistic grouch" who always looks for the reasons a job can't be done rather than at the reasons it can be done. An officer who tries to be optimistic in daily contacts with juniors and seniors will be surprised at how infectious optimism can be.

Summary

To be a successful naval officer, an individual must, among other things, be willing to analyze his own character and to accept constructive criticism from other people and to work to rectify any shortcomings that are revealed. The naval officer must possess many fine personal qualities. The individual who possesses—and works to improve—these qualities will find that his personal integrity carries him far in his naval career and in his life.

JOOD

10

Dynamic Qualities of Leadership

The preceding chapter described the personal qualities necessary for leadership which grow with experience and environment. But there are other leadership qualities, ones that must be practiced each hour of the day and each day of the week to achieve the results required and desired by an effective leader. Naval leadership is institutional, it is true, and not all officers will be as famous—or as effective—as Nelson, Farragut, Dewey, Nimitz, Burke, or Lejeune. In the practice and development of leadership qualities, each naval officer must prepare himself for the "role of the leader" so that he can be ready to assume that responsibility if opportunity and privilege permit.

Planning for the Future

Appraising the Career Choice

Keep in mind that the naval profession is a way of life, and that much of that life will follow an established route. However, an analysis of his attitude toward several variables can help guide the young officer in determining the prospects of his future role as a naval leader.

If his choice of a career as a naval officer is right and is rewarding personally, he should be able to make positive, affirmative answers to the following questions.

1. Have I charted a course and established a long-range goal for achievement in my role as a Navy or Marine Corps officer?
2. Do I believe in the naval service—both its mission and its indispensability to the country's security?
3. Do I obtain a great deal of personal satisfaction from my role as an officer?
4. Is my work just a forty-hour-a-week affair, or do I think of it at times other than when I am on duty?

5. Do I feel the necessity to improve my knowledge of the naval profession?

6. Do I have a little "blue/scarlet and gold" in my outlook, and am I motivated by other than the materialistic viewpoint of "What's in it for me?"

If the officer has any doubts whatsoever as to his attitude concerning these six points, then it would be well for him to make a reappraisal of his original decision to choose the naval profession as a career.

Setting a Goal

First and foremost, the newly commissioned naval officer must set a goal—or, in nautical terms, chart a course from his present location to where he wants to go. Few successful people—civilians or naval officers—become successful through mere luck or "happenstance," and those who ride the tide and lack the courage or ambition to go against it from time to time will be those who normally fall by the way.

Setting an ambitious goal is fine, but it may be necessary to set several intermediate, more attainable, goals. Once each of the intermediate goals has been attained, a reappraisal should be made in the light of current events and present circumstances. If the short-range goals appear not to have been the wisest, the earnest officer will not sit back and speculate about lost opportunities. Instead, he will rechart his course and take advantage of the knowledge and experience accumulated to date—whereupon he will generally discover that some of his lost short-range goals were not as important as they had originally appeared to be.

Practicing Leadership Qualities

The young naval officer who has affirmed his commitment to his career and has set a career goal for himself must develop and strengthen through daily practice the leadership qualities described in this chapter.

Enthusiasm, Cheerfulness

Emerson said, "Nothing great was ever done without enthusiasm." Enthusiasm is contagious; it builds enthusiastic supporters. And enthusiastic supporters are just what Admiral Burke has said every naval leader must have in order to be successful. An officer's enthusiasm for the profession determines to a great extent how important his job becomes to himself, and, in turn, how important his job becomes to his seniors and juniors. Along with enthusiasm and zest for the job, every naval officer should try a little cheerfulness in his day-to-day relations. It is rather difficult after long hours of operations, loss of sleep, or other unpleasant experiences, to display a cheerful attitude to your juniors and seniors, but cheerfulness begets cheerfulness, just as a sharp answer to a peer usually produces a sharp answer in return. The officer who tries a double dose of enthusiasm and cheerfulness for a three-month period may be surprised at the results.

Cooperation

Naval personnel may forget the importance of cooperation, but a little reflection will place cooperation in its true relation to other leadership principles. Naval personnel should observe those who practice the fine art of cooperation in daily relations with their seniors, juniors, and peers, and then observe those who rely solely on the prestige of their job or rank to accomplish a mission. The difference between an outstanding and an average officer is easy to detect.

Cooperation, like loyalty, must be practiced up and down, and in an equally important direction: horizontally. Consider the following from Admiral Pratt's article on leadership:

> It was not without reason that this fundamental principle (cooperation) was accepted as the foundation stone upon which to build the organization of the Fleet, to embody into our methods of training, and into our plans governing the Fleet's use. In the highest technical officer of the Navy, that of Chief of Naval Operations, this principle carries with it even greater weight than almost does any other, for the success or conduct of any war in which we might be engaged depends upon the celebrity, smoothness, and efficiency with which our great national war machine gets under way. Its contemplation furnishes a first lesson for the young officer, and one for him to follow through his entire career, if he wishes to glean some conception of what is required as one of the elements of sound leadership in this country.

In today's operations, which involve joint exercises and organizations based on unified commands, the principle of cooperation is all important; it is also the most frequently violated principle at each echelon of command.

Promptness, Reliability

The "kiss of death" on the career of any naval officer occurs when he is tagged "unreliable." Reliability's first requirement is promptness—and promptness is largely a matter of habit. The naval officer must be prompt in carrying out his social engagements, his obligations, and all aspects of his work. Being prompt and reliable should be one of the attributes most sought after by the junior officer. Nothing is more comforting to the captain of a ship at sea than the feeling that the officer of the deck is one on whom he can depend if an emergency arises.

Tact

Tact is the skill and grace with which a well-bred person conducts relations with others. It is one characteristic that everyone can—but few take the trouble to—develop. You can develop tact by practicing it daily on all those with whom you come into contact.

Tact is the lubricating oil of human relationships. The individual who considers tact unnecessary in dealing with others is probably the same person who hammers the sextant with a monkey wrench to make it work.

Tact is not displayed, as many people think, by being pleasant, by bowing and scraping, or by merely being polite. A tactful person may be polite, but many polite people lack subtlety of feeling, and as a result, they are tactless. Thus tact goes much deeper than politeness. It is a quick or intuitive appreciation of what is proper or right. It might also be described as the practice of the Golden Rule: putting yourself in the other person's place. It involves sensitivity of feelings, knowledge of the consequences of conduct, and an insight into what disturbs or offends others. Tact can be cultivated by experience and by observation of others.

An essential of tact is an intimate knowledge of human nature. The tactful person knows how to deal with others. In the military services today there are some officers with experience and ability whose military usefulness is seriously marred because of their lack of tact. Just a little knowledge of when and how to do things sometimes accomplishes the desired results, while the lack of such knowledge results in failure: there is no telling how many good ideas have been lost because the originator of the idea was so carried away with enthusiasm that he burst in on the commanding officer when the latter was deeply involved in a different problem.

Oftentimes, tact is what is *not* said or implied. No person is infallible, but alluding to a mistake someone else has made, or to a reverse someone else has experienced—unless it is necessary to do so in the line of duty—is not being tactful. Withholding a remark that would be made at another's expense, or an unkind word, or an expression or gesture of exasperation or weariness—repeatedly glancing at a watch while someone is speaking, for instance—is not exercising tact. An officer cannot possibly agree with everyone all the time, but at least he can learn how to disagree without being disagreeable. A person can say just about anything if he chooses the right time, the right place, and the right words.

Consideration

A workman who was careless with tools, who used them indiscriminately, who did not keep them cleaned, sharpened, and polished, or who left them lying around, could not be expected to produce work of very high quality. A leader who shows no consideration for subordinates, who keeps them waiting unnecessarily, will be poorly served. People will endure great hardships when there is a reason for them, or when they cannot be helped, but they will become quite restive and bitter when hardships stem from a lack of consideration on the part of someone in authority.

Fairness

A leader cannot afford to play favorites. He must be eminently scrupulous and fair in dealing with subordinates, in making awards and assigning punishments, and in granting favorable assignments and dispensing onerous ones.

Self-Control

Before an officer can control others he must first learn self-control. "It is the man who is master over his countenance, his voice, his actions, his gestures, of every part," wrote the French philosopher Diderot, "who can work upon others at his pleasure." An ungovernable temper indicates not a high spirit, but a lack of mental balance.

The officer who loses his temper, who "flies off the handle," who blames subordinates in a torrent of personal abuse, merely betrays personal emotions and proves his incompetence to assume control over other personnel. Good officers never shout, nag, taunt, or are vindictive. When an officer screams at the troops he loses not only their respect but also real authority over them.

An officer who possesses self-control is an officer who is always calm and collected in an emergency, who never lacks presence of mind or loses his head. He is not affected by the contagion of wild excitement among those about him.

Professional Knowledge, Preparation, Using Spare Time

Each year the naval service becomes more complex; there is more to know about it, both historically and technically. Good advice for the young naval officer is that he should acquire a thorough general knowledge of a particular part of the naval service: gunnery, engineering, administration—whatever he is most interested in and best suited for. Professional knowledge is of the greatest importance in commanding the obedience, confidence, respect, and loyal cooperation of juniors; in fact, subordinates simply will not follow—not far, anyway—if they feel that their commander does not know "the score."

Professional knowledge involves more than technical knowledge; it encompasses all of the knowledge of the military services necessary for the naval officer to function effectively in any billet assigned. Acquiring this knowledge requires effort on the part of the officer which surpasses the training and education offered to him by the service.

There is no doubt that an individual does not obtain this knowledge by merely going to postgraduate school. The naval profession is competitive, and it requires constant preparation and study on the part of the individual. Douglas Southall Freeman stated the problem very succinctly to students of the Naval War College:

> Young man, make the most of the scraps of time. If you want to know your stuff—and know it better than the other men—you have got to spend more time on it. And if you are going to spend more time on it, you have to make the most of the scraps of time. The difference between mediocrity and distinction in many a professional career is the organization of your time.

An enterprising officer will develop the habit of reading good literature early in his career, and he will devote at least one hour each day to this, when possible. This hour can probably be put together out of the "scraps of time" which otherwise would be wasted.

Initiative, Ability to Plan Ahead, Imagination

The characteristics of initiative, the ability to plan ahead, and imagination are so closely interwoven in practice that one can scarcely be discussed without bringing in aspects of the others.

Initiative probably will mean many things to the junior officer, but, generally, it is a quality that prompts a person to do what he ought to do without being told to do so. The practice of initiative will be closely related to the development of the young officers' professional knowledge; it has aptly been stated that "a combination of ignorance and initiative in the character of an officer can lead to disaster."

In addition to developing his professional knowledge so that his initiative can be exercised intelligently, there are many ways in which the junior can develop his initiative. A person with initiative does the right thing if he has been told how to do it. The capable officer never puts off until tomorrow work that a few extra minutes will permit him to do today. He attempts to do something each day which he should do without being told, and he instructs and impresses subordinates with the importance of their doing the same in carrying out their duties.

No job to which the junior officer will be assigned will have been run so efficiently that some improvement cannot be accomplished. Imagination is a necessary ingredient, and once the officer is sure he is doing the job to the best of his ability, he must try to visualize or think of new ideas and plans which improve the job—or perhaps someone else's job that he has had occasion to observe.

Imagination and the ability to plan and think ahead are inseparable. You can probably recall individuals in your own experience who seemed to work from one crisis to the next—they never seemed to get organized. Also, no doubt you have observed others who seemed always to have the right answers and an orderly plan of procedure, and you should realize that this is not usually by luck or pure happenstance. The junior officer must develop the capacity to project the present job into the future, to study what can be done to improve it, and, above all, to determine what will be the requirements for carrying out the job efficiently.

Many a battle has been won by a subordinate acting on his own initiative—seeing what needed to be done, and then doing it without having to be told to do it. An officer's responsibilities prevent him from seeing everything, and he often is unable to communicate with all subordinate units; in every such case, the occasion becomes what Nelson called "a captain's fight," with the day going to the side that had the best captains, the ones who took the initiative. It could well be, as some persons have prophesied, that any war of the future will see smaller groups of men, under the command of junior officers, more widely dispersed than in any previous war. This will make the proper use of initiative of even greater importance. Remember, however, that initiative is a sword that cuts both ways; in the hands of a person who does not know how and when to use it, it can be more damaging to friend than foe.

Decisiveness

A young officer should not be misled into the belief that he must at once, and without due consideration, express his orders in precise and unmistakable language. Such a course would inevitably lead to "snap judgment" and, probably, unhappy results. The point is that, in matters involving weighty decisions, where time is available, the officer should consult with others whose opinions are valued; then, after mature consideration, he should issue orders in such a manner that they cannot fail to be clearly and decisively impressed on the minds of those who are to receive and act on them.

On the other hand, there will be times when an immediate decision and command are not only necessary, but also vital. In such cases an officer must rely on his own intelligence, on his own good judgment, and, sometimes, on mere instinct; but in any case, he must issue his orders with courage, resolution, clarity, and decision.

If an officer is assailed by doubts, he can remember this: there are usually several ways of doing anything, and a poor plan vigorously executed is better than the best plan carried out in a lackadaisical manner. If the leader gives an order and then modifies it, countermands it, and issues another one, his men cannot help wondering if he knows what he wants, or is sure of the course he has chosen.

Related to this indecision is the matter of consistency. Juniors always appreciate a senior who is fairly consistent, one who does not alternately blow hot and cold as the mood strikes him. The most difficult person in the world to work for or with is one who is perpetually shifting from one extreme to the other. During World War II the U.S. Navy, by alternating Admirals Halsey and Spruance—two truly great naval officers of dissimilar but steadfast methods—was able to keep Japan off balance most of the war.

Try this on your enemies—but not on your friends.

The Will to Win

A quality that is essential to effective naval leadership is the will to win. St. Paul phrased it thus: "Whatsoever thou doeth, do it with all thy might." John Paul Jones, when asked if he surrendered the battered and sinking ex-Indiaman called the *Bon Homme Richard*, called back, "No. I have not yet begun to fight." And the less fortunate Lawrence's dying words were, "Don't give up the ship. Fight her till she sinks." The story of the Civil War may be found in Lincoln's search for a general who had the necessary combative disposition, one who had the will to fight and to win.

In peacetime contests, athletic or otherwise, an officer should strive to win, but he should still abide by the rules; he should play hard but clean, as a gentleman. If he wins, he should not "crow"; if he loses, he should accept the fact with good grace. Poor sportsmanship is unpardonable.

War, however, is not a game. It is fervently to be hoped that there never will be another war. But there is only one thing that would be more tragic than having another war, and that would be losing it. In war there is no prize for second place, there are only varying degrees of defeat. In wartime, even more than in peacetime, the will to win means more in a leader than any other quality.

Summary

Having decided that a career as an officer in the naval service is what he wants in life, and seizing every opportunity to strengthen the qualities and skills needed to reach this goal, the dedicated naval officer must practice every day the leadership qualities outlined here.

11

Other Success Factors

The preceding two chapters discussed qualities that are considered essential to effective naval leadership. But consideration must be given to other qualities, traits, practices, or attributes—call them what you will, while they may not be essential, they certainly are important in that they enhance the leadership ability of a person who possesses and practices them.

The Ability to Call People by Name

There is nothing quite so flattering to a person's ego as to be called correctly by name by someone—especially a senior—after a prolonged absence. It makes the junior feel that he has made a favorable impression on the senior, who not only remembers him but will continue to do so. Knowing that he has been noticed and will be remembered makes almost every individual strive for more approval and recognition.

Some people seem to have this ability to associate names and faces to a high degree. Julius Caesar reportedly could call every man in his legions by name. Since a legion usually consisted of 6,000 men, and Caesar commanded several, the story has probably been exaggerated, but it boils down to this: Caesar had a remarkable ability to identify people. There is no doubt that his men put a bit more effort into their work and their battles because they believed that the all-seeing, all-remembering Caesar was looking their way.

Napoleon, too, appreciated the value of calling people by their names; while inspecting his troops, he would stop for a moment in front of one veteran, call him by name—say something like, "Ah, yes . . . you were with me at Austerlitz"—and then inquire after the soldier's wife and children and make other personal comments. Of course Napoleon had been well briefed in advance by his adjutant; nevertheless, an incident of this sort left all who witnessed it deeply impressed and all the more loyal to Napoleon.

Tolerance

An individual who appreciates the meaning of tolerance has progressed far on the road to success in relations with others. There is no room for intolerance or prejudice in the personality of a naval officer, who must control subordinates of different races, sexes, and creeds. Tolerance also connotes many other things. A wise person will keep an open mind and try to understand the viewpoint of others. A wise person will be tolerant of their point of view, and will try to find out what they really think rather than try to impose his own personal philosophy as "the only" solution. Tolerance implies a willingness to put up with unpleasant situations and conditions which will improve with time, and which may have originated through no fault of any one individual. Tolerance, in essence, means a true respect for the other's viewpoint and a realization that as long as there are individual personalities there will also be divergencies of opinion. Only under a dictatorial form of government is it otherwise.

Being a Good Listener

Few people appear to realize how much more can be learned from listening than from talking. The human being is by nature gregarious; thus most people must conscientiously curb their inclination to do all the talking. There is no greater bore than an individual who monopolizes all conversation, unless the others present make it clear that they are extremely interested in what he is saying. A person learns little from his own conversation—but much wisdom and understanding can be obtained from listening to someone else.

Communications, to be effective, must work both ways—they must be both sent and received. The Naval or Marine Corps officer must carefully avoid being merely the transmitter.

Temperance

Most people think of temperance as the control of drinking. Actually, temperance applies to all daily habits, and especially to those that affect physical and mental well-being, such as sleeping and eating.

Responsibilities Concerning Alcohol

One of the factors that will shape the young officer's future career in the naval service is how he will handle alcohol-related problems. What does he know of the practical aspects of this problem as it exists in the naval service? Well, for one thing the officer knows—or should know—that to drink, to induce others to drink, or to tolerate drinking in others aboard ship is the quickest and surest road to disaster.

One salty old admiral once gave the sound advice, "Never take a drink because another man is thirsty." No officer should fear being criticized for refusing to drink. Even though his friends may complain that he is not a good sport if he refuses to drink with them, actually they will admire the officer as an individual who has the courage of his convictions, so long as the convictions are honorable. So, if an individual is a teetotaler, he should not start to drink just because he thinks that a naval officer "should." By keeping the courage of his honorable convictions, he will be off to a headstart in any walk of life.

If an individual does choose to drink, he must guard against becoming a habitual drinker or an alcoholic. An individual can become an alcoholic so gradually that he may be unaware of what is happening. Someone has compiled the following basic common-sense rules for keeping out of trouble.

Never drink alone.
Never drink before or during working hours.
Never drink on an empty stomach.
Be particularly careful of that extra drink when you are tired.
Never drink rapidly.
Never allow yourself to get into the habit of having a drink every day.
If you are feeling the drinks too much, keep moving, dancing, eating, talking—and take one drink fewer the next time.

Alcohol is an evil only when the individual becomes a slave to the habit of drinking. If that happens, the person has indeed become as much a slave as if he were chained in a medieval galley—and his naval career is doomed to early termination.

Responsibilities Concerning Marijuana, Narcotics, and Other Controlled Substances

The term *controlled substance* means a drug or other substance included in Schedule I, II, III, IV, or V established by section 202 of the Comprehensive Drug Abuse Prevention and Control Act of 1970 (84 Stat. 1236), as updated and republished under the provisions of that act.

All personnel shall endeavor to prevent and eliminate the unauthorized use of marijuana, narcotics, and other controlled substances within the naval service.

Except for authorized medicinal purposes, the introduction, possession, use, sale, or other transfer of marijuana, narcotic substances, or other controlled substances on board any ship, craft, or aircraft of the Department of the Navy or within any naval station or other place under the jurisdiction of the Department of the Navy, or the possession, use, sale, or other transfer of marijuana, narcotic substances, or other controlled substances by persons in the naval service, is prohibited.

The Power of Speech

Speech is the primary means of communication between people. Every naval officer speaks thousands of words for every word he writes, and, in the matter of giving instructions, orders, and commands to enlisted personnel, he generally relies on speech almost entirely. Therefore, it is incumbent on the officer to ensure effective speech.

Manner of Speaking

A frequently used expression regarding speech goes like this: "It isn't so much what he said as the way he said it that made me angry." In other words, our manner of speaking—of presenting information—influences to a great extent the way others receive and react to our words.

No one would think of breaking bad news, such as the death of a loved one, to another person in a lighthearted or flippant manner. The unfortunate individual who received the news in this way would never forget it, and probably never forgive it, either. This is an extreme case, it is true, but frequently the naval officer is called on to be the bearer of other unfortunate tidings, such as disapproval of a request or report of a failure. Such information should always be delivered with sincere regret and the appropriate expressions of sympathy or encouragement. Whatever you do, you should never give the impression that you are enjoying another person's misfortune or are callous and indifferent to it.

Conversely, you should congratulate a person wholeheartedly, not grudgingly. A good example of the way *not* to congratulate a peer is to say, "I see you were selected—but don't let it go to your head. Ninety-seven percent of your classmates were selected. From here on in it gets tough." When an officer finds it necessary to reprove a person or otherwise take him to task for something inadequately done, the officer's attitude should stress correction and instruction; he should not try to humiliate or "bawl out" the other. If a more lengthy explanation is required, it should be saved for another time.

Verbal Orders

The means most often employed to issue directives is the verbal order. An order, while it is a directive to a junior to perform a certain task, does not necessarily specify the means for accomplishing the task. The methods of accomplishment are normally left to the junior's discretion if the senior feels that the junior is qualified to carry out the order in a satisfactory manner.

Every order must satisfy two requirements: it must state the objective, and it must be understandable to the person receiving it. The officer of the deck might give this order to the coxswain of a motor boat: "Coxswain, make the Officer's Landing at Old Point Comfort; pick up the first lieutenant and return to the ship. If he is not there when you arrive, leave the landing not later than sixteen hundred and return to the ship." In this example the objective, returning the first lieutenant to the ship, is clearly indicated. In addition, the details are made clear to the coxswain, for he knows not only exactly where he is to go, but also when he must start his return trip.

The careless officer of the deck might phrase this same directive as follows: "Coxswain, go to Old Point Comfort and pick up the first lieutenant." In this case the objective is not clearly stated in that the coxswain has not been directed what to do with the first lieutenant after he picks him up. The situation as a whole will be confusing to the coxswain because he has not been given a definite landing point at Old Point Comfort and he has not been informed how long he should wait in case the first lieutenant has been delayed.

From the above example, the necessity of perfect clarity in giving orders should be understood. The officer issuing the orders should make sure that they are given loudly enough to be clearly audible to the recipient. He should watch the face of the recipient for any indication that he has not been clearly understood. Good officers develop the habit of asking the junior if the order just given to them is understood. And it is a wise officer who, when a junior fails to carry out orders correctly, does not jump to the conclusion that the junior is making the mistake. He should verify that the orders given were completely clear.

Talking before a Group

The naval officer spends almost his entire career instructing and training other officers and enlisted personnel. Most of this instruction and training is accomplished verbally and under circumstances that vary from the loud commands and exhortations of loading exercises to the calm atmosphere of the classroom. Hence proper knowledge and use of the English language become necessities for good naval leadership.

The officer must learn to speak in a clear and concise manner, and he must strive to attain the ability to speak in language that all can understand. He must take the time beforehand to prepare even a simple speech. Sometimes it is necessary to speak extemporaneously, but even under these circumstances it is possible to think through what you are going to say before you say it.

A cardinal principle to observe in speaking is to get the point across quickly. Fifty words should never be used if ten will suffice. Also, you must guard against wandering from the subject at hand. Nothing will spoil a speaker's effectiveness more quickly than if he starts out with a good train of thought and then interrupts it with digressions. Pausing a second to think before speaking is a practice that pays off. The pause that you take to think of what you wish to say next will never be as embarrassing as the stupid things you might blurt out just to keep talking.

The following points are set forth to assist the amateur in the matter of getting ideas across.

1. Be sure you can be heard by everyone present.
2. Talk slowly enough so that your audience can understand.
3. Look directly at your audience while you talk to them, and move your gaze from one section to another. The experienced speaker can determine whether his audience is interested and whether his

message is being understood by watching the faces of the people before him.

4. Make your voice as colorful and effective as your personality will permit without becoming too theatrical.

5. Use body movements and hand gestures to emphasize your points. However, too much movement can detract from the effectiveness of your speech.

6. Make sure that no outside interference will distract the audience during the talk.

7. Plan the talk carefully, but above everything else do not read it, unless it is planned that way and unless you have practiced a great deal to give the reading a natural delivery.

8. Limit the length of your talks—they should be just long enough to get the point across. Talks should almost never exceed thirty minutes.

9. Use interesting examples from personal experiences to illustrate your main points.

Most people dislike the idea of standing on their feet before a group of people and making an address. But it is a job every naval officer must do, and the only way to overcome the hesitancy of speaking publicly is actually to do it. This point cannot be overemphasized. The naval officer should welcome every opportunity to get up on his feet and talk before a group. He should take advantage of, and join, certain speaking clubs that are organized specifically for the purpose of developing the speaking ability of the individual. A good example of such an organization and one that is growing daily is the "Toastmasters" Organization. Practically every naval shore station has a speech club, and even certain combatant ships have organized speaking groups.

A typical example of the speaking job facing the officer is the case where his unit has been criticized for its appearance aboard ship and on liberty. Will the officer more effectively correct the situation by addressing the entire division or by telling his enlisted leaders to correct it? In this and similar situations, the officer who can effectively express his thoughts in a talk has a distinct advantage. The "all hands" contact is more effective in that everyone receives the same information at the same time. Naturally, a talk to all hands should be used only in situations pertinent to all hands. But such "all hands" talks should not be overdone—never too often and never too long.

Conversation

Correct speech, coupled with the capacity for interesting and intelligent conversation, constitutes one of the greatest assets of a man or woman.

Correct speech begins with individual words. And, with words, perhaps the foremost requirement is pronunciation. There is rarely any good excuse for the incorrect pronunciation of a word. Limitations in an individual's vocabulary or the lack of a ready facility to express his thoughts may be overlooked, but a mispronounced word stands out as a reproach in the conversation of intelligent people. If an individual is uncertain of the pronunciation of a word, he should avoid using it until he can pronounce it correctly.

Next in importance is enunciation. Every word should be enunciated clearly and distinctly, as well as correctly. Poor enunciation is usually caused by lack of training, by carelessness, and by thoughtlessness on the part of the individual. It is excellent practice from time to time to listen consciously to your own speech, and to endeavor to discover and to correct any careless habits. On most ships and stations a tape recorder is available where an officer can record a prepared speech and then play it back. The results may please—or they may be very disconcerting to—the individual concerned, but they are bound to be enlightening.

Choosing appropriate words is part of correct speech. Excessive use of slang is considered poor taste among educated people. Slang that is unusually expressive or exceptionally clever is permitted in a talk where it is appropriate, but to continue to use slang and colloquial expressions which have long since lost their originality is to indicate that you have a narrow and deficient vocabulary.

Profane or obscene language is always out of place in an officer's speech. The use of such language will invariably lower the leader's prestige in the eyes of his followers. The officer who resorts to swearing or who indulges in blasphemy usually does so because he is unable to express himself forcefully in proper language. Such language never impresses the people who hear it. In ordinary conversation, even where only men are present, foul language is seldom received with favor, and its use usually demonstrates a lack of tact and consideration on the part of the speaker. Use of profanity in anger, or with the intent to insult or degrade another person, betrays a lack of decency and self-control. The offense is a violation of all the principles of justice and of good discipline—and can even be grounds for disciplinary action under naval regulations.

Engaging and intelligent conversation, on the other hand, requires among other things a broad contact with literature and a familiarity with current events. It will pay any officer to devote a certain amount of time each day to reading and study. An officer should cultivate an interest in national and world affairs as well as in happenings of merely local import. While specialization appears to be the order of the day, the naval officer, now as never before, must strive to maintain a broad point of view and a lively sympathy and interest in human affairs and activities the world over.

Part of every officer's recreation time should be spent in reading good books. Reading is a habit—and, like all good habits, it must be practiced to be acquired and kept.

The Written versus the Spoken Word

The written word endures long after the spoken word has died, and for that reason its use requires considerably more care. The locale, the circumstances, the other people present, the tone of voice used, the facial expressions, and the gestures (to name but a few), all give a special emphasis and modification to the spoken word that seldom can be imparted to the written word, at least in official correspondence. Harsh words spoken may be overlooked or forgotten, but the same words in writing will rise to confront the writer again and again, and they may cause rancor to smoulder in someone's heart. Written words must be chosen with care to ensure that they are words the writer is willing to live with. Similarly, when the officer wishes to commend or thank someone, the written word carries more weight. Furthermore, written commendations can be shown, rather proudly, to others elsewhere, and later. Whenever an officer deems a junior's actions worthy of thanks, he should have the acumen and decency to send a copy of the commendation to the official who makes out that junior's fitness report (if he is an officer) or who has custody of his service record (if he is enlisted). In the naval service a person's mistakes usually are entered in his record; it is only fair, therefore, that his praiseworthy acts be accorded similar treatment.

Effective Writing

As with effective oral communications, the degree to which an officer develops techniques and abilities to express himself in concise and lucid composition will greatly affect his success. But developing the art of writing your ideas in a manner that will be acceptable to seniors is decidedly most important.

For instance, would you consider the following an example of concise and lucid composition?

> The specific techniques for interviewing the complainant must be regarded as ancillary to the additional components which form the underlying matrix of the type of interview under consideration. Clearly, these elements, cannot be disarticulated. We mention them separatively only in the interests of ease of presentation, but with the clear recognition that they are inextricably interrelated.

The deficiences here are obvious.

How do you develop the art of composition? First, you must develop, through practice and study, a sound basis in the fundamentals of English composition, and, in addition, you must acquire a well-rounded vocabulary.

Second, you must try to increase through constant study your knowledge of naval, military, and associated service matters that will aid in the generation of new ideas and the development of logical reasoning and thinking.

Third, you must know your senior's personality to the extent that you will know how far you can go in presenting new ideas, especially if your ideas are of a new and radical concept that may tend to "rock the boat." When writing up new ideas or a letter for a senior, the junior should always identify himself with the person who is going to sign the letter, and he should never project his own personality into the letter. Junior officers sometimes complain of their difficulty in getting their seniors to sign correspondence; it may be, however, that another junior officer has little difficulty in getting correspondence signed by that same senior because he is writing ideas the senior will accept. This distinction is very important; it does not mean that the latter officer is a "yes man," but it does emphasize the necessity for the junior officer to know the personality of seniors and to try to see things through their eyes.

It is vital that an officer allow sufficient time for proofreading, revision, and retyping before handing a letter, a memo, or any correspondence to anyone for processing.

Summary

The success of a naval officer can be affected by his mastery of the so-called "niceties" of life. The officer who remembers people's names, who practices tolerance and temperance, and who speaks and writes effectively is benefiting his own career and improving the lives of those who serve under him.

12

Personal Relations

Every day the junior officer is involved in personal relations with juniors, peers, seniors, and—equally important—the civilian public. To say that one relationship is more important than another is to make a relative judgment; generally, an officer's success in his relations with people in all of these groups will determine his effectiveness as an officer. The young officer may consider some relationships more important than others at a given moment, and there are some officers who consider only one relationship—that with their seniors. It goes without saying that the officer who practices this one-way relationship soon earns a reputation among his juniors, peers, and seniors.

Relations with Juniors

Interest in Others

Being able to talk to a large group and make each person in your audience feel that he is being talked to alone is an invaluable attribute. Yet acquiring this attribute may be no more difficult than understanding this simple fact: *Each man is to himself the most important person in the world*. "Watch me" is a phrase that children repeat again and again until they learn that it is not socially acceptable to demand attention so directly. Then they—and we, as adults—resort to various actions to satisfy this desire for attention. Some individuals become "smart-aleck" showoffs. Others devote themselves to serious, hard work to produce results that merit praise. In both cases, the efforts are put forth to satisfy an innate human desire for recognition. This most basic psychological need must be remembered by anyone who aspires to lead.

Nearly all the great leaders of the past—Lincoln, the Roosevelts, Nelson, Martin Luther King—had what has been called the "common touch." They were truly giants who were completely human in their dealings with everyone. People felt comfortable and welcome in their presence.

The magnetism that draws people is nothing more than the unselfish demonstration of a friendly interest in each person as an individual. Perhaps it is nothing more than a warm, cordial "good morning" when the officer greets his personnel each day, or an inquiry as to how the work is progressing. The essential point is that sincere interest from a senior makes the junior feel important as an individual. It shows that the senior recognizes each individual as an individual, and that he considers each one significant enough to deserve his attention.

This interest in others as individuals leads to a common ground of understanding. The leader is able to find out why individuals react as they do and therefore is more capable of handling personal relations with them. Leaders can develop the confidence of their personnel by getting to know them, and by making a point to discern their needs and take steps to fulfill them. Correspondingly, confidence in a leader is born from the knowledge others have of that leader as an individual. The leader must allow his subordinates to get to know him well enough to see that he has their best interests as one of his priorities and to trust that he will do everything he can for them.

Friendliness versus Familiarity

In his capacity as a leader, an officer is basically concerned with the difficult task of dealing with people. Whether they are seniors, peers, or juniors, people and his personal relations with them constantly confront the officer. To gain the complete cooperation of those with whom he works, an officer must get along with them. The leader who has a warm, friendly personality instills pride of organization into everyone he comes in contact with, making them feel that he is glad they are members of the same organization. This feeling, this being proud of the other people in the same group, is the essential element of esprit de corps.

People are unconsciously drawn to the person who has a warm, pleasant smile, a hearty greeting, and a firm handshake because that person is displaying an interest in others through these actions. The person seems glad to see them and also makes them feel as though they belong—whether it is to a social group or a military group.

As a result, the other fellow begins to repay respect and interest with similar respect and interest. If the individual has previously been difficult, he may begin to see things in an entirely different light: your light. For the very fact that interest has been shown in him as an individual makes him feel that his ideas are of importance too.

The question that arises immediately in the mind of the inexperienced officer is: How can I be friendly with those under me and still have them respect me and obey my orders? This question stems from a lack of appreciation of the difference between *friendliness* and *familiarity*. Talking to subordinates in a friendly manner, and showing concern for their problems, never cost an officer one iota of their confidence and respect. They expect that of the leader. They do not expect the leader to be their "buddy," but they do expect counseling, guidance, and recognition as individuals.

Subordinates' respect and confidence, however, is something that can never be commanded; it must be earned. The only way to earn it is for the officer to know his subordinates and their problems, their capabilities and their limitations. He cannot do this by joining in their card games or by going ashore with them; these are not the sort of personal relations that they expect. But if they find their officer friendly and easy to approach, subordinates will begin seeking counsel and advice. This leads to the payoff: better effort and performance.

Being friendly and interested does not mean that the officer has to sacrifice discipline in any way. You can be just as strict as the occasion demands, as long as you are fair and understanding. Neither is there any reason for the enlisted personnel or their officers to feel that the door is being left open for bypassing the chain of command. They will instinctively know how to react to a warm personality.

As always, there will be those few individuals who will misinterpret and try to take advantage of friendly interest shown in them by their officer. But these will be few, indeed, compared to those who will not—and a courteous but firm check here will soon straighten out those who presume.

If one key element to the successful exercise of leadership had to be singled out, it would probably be fairness. This is the one principle that every officer, regardless of rank, must scrupulously observe. Subordinates always want to get everything to which they are fairly entitled—they not only want it, but they expect it. Whether it is good food, liberty, not being compelled to do more than their share of work, or even being brought to mast when they deserve it, the enlisted personnel expect their officer to have a personal interest and concern in their affairs. There is nothing the officer can do that will bring greater returns.

Relations with Peers

A peer, in the military service, is a person of the same or approximate rank, duty assignment, or experience. Peers are the people with whom the officer will have the greatest number of personal contacts, and with whom he will be naturally most at ease. Since his relationship with peers is such a large part of an officer's life and will take up much more time than any of his other relationships, it would be well to explore the subject a little further. Some officers may forget the importance of this relationship and feel that their worth is measured entirely by their efficiency as leaders and their loyalty as followers. But it is the officer's peers and co-workers who know him best and whose opinions will possibly be the greatest factor in the establishment of a "service reputation."

Helping a Peer

An eminent naval officer once made a statement to the effect that if he had to choose one road to success in the navy, the desire and effort to help shipmates and peers would be the one path from which he would never deviate. Gratitude is usually undying, and the help you can give to contemporaries will never be forgotten. This approach to success can be started at the beginning of your career. The officer who enjoys helping others may, naturally, experience encroachment on his time. But it is time well spent.

Cooperation versus Competition

The military life has always stressed the value of the competitive spirit in developing group morale, discipline, and esprit de corps. Competition has been considered the lifeblood of the "free enterprise" or capitalist economic system, and the individual has been considered the point from which the competitive spirit originates.

Recently, selection boards have dropped several hundred numbers below the promotion zone to select certain officers who apparently stand far above their peers and immediate seniors and accelerate them in promotion over their peers by two or three years. This practice has been justified by its proponents with the reasoning that the junior officer, in proceeding up the promotion ladder, must be imbued with that "spirit of competition"; he must not "grow old together with his contemporaries of the moment."

The individual officer, if he is not extremely wary, may find his efforts oriented toward personal achievement and individual goals, rather than toward the unit or institution's goal. He may forget that few leaders in history have accomplished their mission and achieved enduring results without the aid and cooperation of peers, juniors, and seniors.

As an officer, you may work as a subordinate to an officer of the same rank and approximate length of service. Complete loyalty and cooperation will be owed this officer, because of the billet the senior fills in the structure of the naval service. It will be the junior's duty to give his peer his wholehearted cooperation, even though the junior may not agree with the senior's methods; the senior has the responsibility, the junior does not. The naval officer must have faith in the navy as an institution: faith that it will provide rewards with increased command and responsibility as he develops in experience and judgment. At times he may suspect that he is getting the worst billet assignments in the navy. But not every billet in the navy can be of the individual's own choosing, and the needs of the naval service are paramount to the needs of the individual. Any officer can, because of his particular experience or availability, be selected for such a billet.

Usually the officer in command, although he is not obligated to do so, will invite suggestions from his peers with regard to how and what should be done. However, there should be no ill feelings if an officer does not choose to ask a peer's advice. Any officer, placed in a like situation, may find it impractical to ask peers for advice or assistance. It should always be remembered that the officer holding a billet, even though he is senior to a subordinate by only one number, has the full responsibility; he should receive the same degree of loyalty and respect that a far more senior officer filling the same billet would.

Relations with Seniors

Although this book is intended primarily to help junior officers improve their leadership capacity, every officer, whether junior or senior, is always a follower as well as a leader. There will always be a senior to whom the officer will be responsible and accountable. The official record of each officer will doubtless be a very accurate measure of his worth as a follower, whereas, if the marking senior is not in very close association with the officer, the junior's true worth as a leader may not be realized.

The saving factor in this situation is that the best juniors are usually better leaders. Possibly this stems from the interest that the junior has in the matter of human relations and his closeness to the subject, regardless of whether he is dealing with an admiral or a seaman. Though there may be exceptions to this statement, as there are to all generalities, the man who learns to get along with an admiral usually takes the same pains to get along with a seaman.

Every officer in the armed services must be inherently and unfailingly a faithful follower before he can ever be trusted with the authority to lead others. Throughout an officer's career, seniors will assign tasks with the assumption—without any question—that they will be correctly accomplished.

The Leader-Follower Relationship

When considering leadership instruction, the tendency is to consider only the role of the leader. However, it should be kept ever in mind that in any concept of institutional leadership, the role of the follower is important. Some of the attributes that make a good leader have been considered, but what are the characteristics of a good follower?

The characteristics listed below, adapted from *Selected Readings in Leadership*, pinpoint the follower's responsibilities to the leader. The student may pursue the discussion further by referring to the article "Leadership Is Not Enough" in that publication.

The good follower

- knows his job and how it contributes to mission accomplishment
- knows the characteristics of the leader
- has the capacity for inspiration
- exercises loyalty up as well as down
- exercises initiative commensurate with knowledge
- readily accepts and is prepared to accept delegated authority
- accepts the decisions of the leader and wholeheartedly tries to implement these decisions

is aware that the leader has limitations in his ability to provide for personal welfare of subordinates and does not add to the leadership burden by ureasonable expectations

All officers should make sure that they carry out their own responsibilities as followers before they look for weaknesses in their leader. They might be contributing more to the failure of leadership in their unit than are those they are criticizing.

Those who today would be leaders must first learn to follow. This does not mean that the longer you are a follower the better leader you will be. It is necessary to "learn by doing" in the field of leadership just as in other fields. But every service officer must serve an apprenticeship in which he is "low man on the totem pole." As he progresses up the chain of command he will have a dual role: leader to those below, and follower to those above.

Getting Off on the Right Foot

The importance of the first impression the young officer makes on seniors cannot be overemphasized. When you report to a new assignment you should make it a point to arrive in the best possible physical and mental condition, and *on time.* The general rule is to report to a new duty station a few days early to provide time to take care of family or business and to provide a cushion against transportation delays. No young officer can afford to take a chance of being late in reporting, for doing so can cause at a minimum an official reprimand that can ruin service reputation and career at the very outset.

Of course there sometimes are extenuating circumstances, such as serious sickness or injury. Under such circumstances the officer concerned should request emergency leave from the command issuing orders and keep the unit to which he has been ordered fully advised of the circumstances.

In reporting aboard for a new assignment, it should be stressed, the officer should always report in uniform, and squared away (haircut, shave, shined shoes, etc.).

Study Your Seniors

The senior officer under whom a junior officer is serving may be the captain of a carrier or a lieutenant colonel of a marine battalion. Whatever his position, he is the officer immediately senior to other officers in that chain of command. One of his duties is to prepare fitness reports on subordinate officers. Since the fitness report is the permanent record of an officer's career as well as the basis for selection to each rank, and has some weight in certain duty assignments, it is highly sensible for every officer to do his best at all times.

The senior may be an excellent naval officer in every sense of the word. On the other hand—though this is rare—the senior may be disinterested in subordinates as individuals, caring only how well they do their jobs. For instance, the senior may issue orders without consideration for his subordinates' personal reactions. He may have forgotten that these subordinates would do more and better work if he used better command and leadership techniques.

However, there are compensations for the junior officer even in this case, for the junior can see here an example of what not to do when he becomes a senior officer. He can improve his own leadership technique by learning how to be a good follower—even under adverse conditions—and by doing his best to please the senior.

Studying the senior can help the junior be a better follower in other ways. Officers are required to prepare all correspondence, messages, and notes in correct English and grammatical format, and a good way to satisfy a senior in the matter of preparing his correspondence is to study his previous correspondence. Another example is of a junior officer who is serving as mess treasurer; if he found that the commanding officer had an aversion to beans, then only the tactless mess treasurer would serve them very frequently.

The application of the principles of tact and adaptability is vital in relationships with seniors, as the case of the mess treasurer points out.

Starting Slowly

The best way, perhaps, to emphasize how important it is for a new officer to exercise modesty on first reporting aboard is to cite the example of a young officer who reported to a destroyer that happened to be commanded by a very fine officer. The ship's reputation was excellent, and the ship stood high in the various fleet competitions. The captain had several years' experience in destroyers behind him and enjoyed a superb service reputation.

One day, a lieutenant (junior grade) reported on board after six months' duty on one of the other destroyers of the same force. During his first meal in the wardroom, with the captain and all other officers present, this new officer completely monopolized the conversation by expounding his theories of efficient destroyer operations and relating how he had improved the ship he had just left. He proceeded to advise the captain and to impress all with their good fortune in having him on board.

Later years proved this same young officer to be a very effective leader. He may have been as good then as he assured his shipmates that he was, but his complete lack of tact and modesty on that and other occasions seriously hampered his junior officer career. This is an extreme case, but it should indicate the necessity of being "seen and not heard" until you have carefully integrated yourself into the organization. Once the new officer has become an effective cog in the machinery, and the organization is convinced of his loyalty and sincerity, then his ideas may well get the attention that they deserve.

Friendliness

Determining how friendly he should be with his seniors can cause the inexperienced officer considerable worry. Certainly, displaying a defensive and distant attitude toward seniors is not the proper approach. The junior officer is going to have to advance halfway in establishing very necessary amicable relations.

Some inexperienced young officers who have had the misfortune to receive a rebuke from their senior feel a hesitancy thereafter about venturing on normal, friendly relations with him. The ones who have been rebuked should remember that there was nothing personal in the senior's action, and that he was merely carrying out the duties of his position. If he has the impression that because of the rebuke the senior holds a grudge against him, he is mistaken. If the junior, on next encountering the senior who has rebuked him, gives him a cheerful smile and a smart salute, he not only will erase the unpleasant occurrence from the minds of both, but in addition will have learned the lesson that every officer of the armed services has to learn sooner or later. For it is doubtful that there exists any officer, no matter how exalted his rank, who has not earned—and been given—some measure of correction during his service career.

However, there are pitfalls, too, in this matter of "friendly relations." There is a limit to certain aspects of them. On the forbidden side of that limit is the practice commonly called "greasing," that is, ostentatiously and obnoxiously lubricating the wheels of personal progress. This is not condoned by any naval officer. However, very few officers are guilty of thus pushing themselves on their seniors in an attempt to get in the latter's good graces. "Climbing" of this sort is usually so obvious that the senior senses it immediately.

The genuine, friendly attitude toward seniors, though, is anything but "greasing"; it is a "must."

Unofficial Calls

There are good reasons for an unofficial social call, a propriety and an amenity expected in the naval service. It gives the senior an opportunity to know the junior officer better, and it also gives the junior an opportunity to learn more of the senior's background. Much can be learned by both in the informal conversation that will undoubtedly take place during the visit. The junior officer should not be afraid to accept invitations from senior officers and their spouses. Seniors will be pleased to have juniors make calls and will be happy to have young officers and their spouses in their company. Young officers should relax and enjoy themselves, for, as long as they act appropriately, they will find that their visit not only will give them a better insight into what makes their seniors what they are, but will prove enjoyable, as well.

Also, juniors should never be embarrassed to have seniors and their spouses call on them. It is proper for a young officer to ask senior officers and their spouses to his home for an afternoon or evening. The junior should not be reluctant, because his home is limited; undoubtedly, the senior officer had the same difficulty when he was a junior officer and remembers it well. The home will reflect the true character of the junior officer in many respects, no matter how inexpensive it may be. Its size and grandeur are of no consequence. A true representation of the junior's own individual character and resourcefulness is far more valuable than a more colorful picture that does not present the facts. If an officer lives and entertains above his means, the only person he is harming is himself. The services respect individuals for what they are.

Keeping the Senior Informed and Seeking Advice

If a junior officer has been assigned a specific task to perform in a certain period of time and knows that the senior is basing future plans on the outcome of this task, then it is imperative that the senior be kept informed on the progress of the work. For example, one of the main engines may be out of commission due to a breakdown. The ship has a definite schedule to meet. Say the junior, as the maintenance officer, has predicted that the engine will be repaired in four hours; the captain should be notified as soon as it is determined that the job will require more—or less—time. In this connection, some officers tend to be overly optimistic in predicting how soon a casualty can be repaired. Until experience has taught the responsible officer how long it takes to do a repair job, it is best to add a margin of safety to the estimate, for contingencies' sake. However, an officer should also avoid the opposite error, of being overly cautious.

Most senior officers will be glad to have a subordinate come to them for advice, and they can be very helpful. What may seem an indecipherable problem to one person may be a very simple problem to someone with more experience. The young officer with a difficult problem should never spend sleepless nights worrying about it. After having put the very best efforts into it, without finding the solution, he should feel free to ask for the senior's advice and suggestions. The senior will not resent the request, he will welcome it.

When junior officers feel that they are not getting along with seniors as they should, generally they will find that the impression is mostly in their own minds. This is when they should go to their seniors and ask for a frank conference. Almost invariably the senior will "let his hair down" and explain the junior's deficiencies, if there are any. It is then up to the junior to accept the information, not as a rebuke, but in the helpful spirit in which it was given, and to proceed to do his utmost to remedy the deficiencies. He may be assured that his senior will be prompt to observe and react favorably to such honest effort.

Solving Problems for Yourself

The correct handling of situations that require advice, permission, or authority from a senior is a valuable means for any officer to show his mettle. The first step, when the junior is faced with a tough problem, is, of course, to gather detailed and complete information concerning the situation for which the advice or permission is needed. The second step is to determine just what course of action the junior would take if the senior was not available and the junior's judgment was required. The third step is to present the situation and recommended course of action to the senior, who then may add the benefit of greater experience and knowledge of higher policy. It will then be necessary for the senior to correct, confirm, or reject the junior's solution. In the meantime the senior officer has been given a demonstration of the junior's ability to solve problems on his own initiative. If the junior's decisions were sound, the confidence of the senior in his ability will be considerably increased.

The ability to make proper decisions is a distinctive characteristic of someone who is qualified for command. The more training the junior can get in this regard, the better prepared he will be to render logical and sound decisions when he is in a position of greater responsibility.

In the foregoing the senior officer has also had an opportunity to further his command techniques, by delegating authority. Senior officers forever comb personnel under their command for exceptional people. For this reason, capable officers tend to attract work, and their workload is often so heavy in comparison with that of their peers that they feel they are being imposed on. They should realize that the exact opposite is the truth, that in actuality they are making good in the finest way. The officer with the light load is definitely slipping.

Relations with Civilians

Too many naval officers delegate the responsibility of maintaining good personal relations with the civilian populace to the public affairs officer. Relations with the civilian world are very important, and each officer—each person in the service—from seaman apprentice to the admiral has a joint responsibility to maintain a relationship with the civilian populace which will reflect the greatest credit on, and inspire the utmost respect for, the naval service.

At times the service makes its own problems in its relations with civilians. Hard, fast, and legalistic rules formulated elsewhere can discourage attempts by local commanding officers to head off legal actions against the service through friendly personal relations with the local populace.

Take the case of the old gentleman who lived near a naval air station and became increasingly irritated by aircraft flying over his house during field carrier landing practice. Each year he wrote personal letters to the admiral in Washington, threatening law suits against the

U.S. Navy. And of course the commanding officer of the air station received letters from the admiral with the directive to "cease and desist" flying over civilian houses. Along with this came advice from the staff legal officer to get something in writing from the old gentleman on how much damage had been caused, as well as to inspect the premises of civilians for damage—in general, to give the civilians an open invitation to start a lawsuit against the navy.

The commanding officer on the spot decided to take the personal rather than the legal approach. He visited the complaining civilian, who turned out to be a very pleasant individual rather than otherwise. The commanding officer explained that the flights were part of the navy's training program for operating planes aboard carriers, and he assured the old gentleman that the navy was most interested in his complaints and would do its utmost to eliminate any cause for friction.

He left the old gentleman in a pleasant mood—not just mollified, but very gratified that the navy had been interested enough to send a personal representative to visit him. The commanding officer forwarded the legal forms, duly signed, back to the legal officer, informed the admiral of his action, and during the remainder of his tour had no further complaints from either the admiral or the civilian about low-flying aircraft.

This story is narrated to emphasize the importance of the personal approach in civilian affairs. In cases that have obvious legal aspects, every effort must be made to protect the navy's interests, but you should never forget that a few minutes of personal contact can sometimes accomplish what hours and pages of written correspondence cannot.

Today more and more, officers live in civilian communities. The alert officer will take opportunities to broaden civilian contacts. True, the average civilian cannot quite comprehend the group feeling that naval life generates in the average service family and is more concerned with local and community problems than is his military counterpart. However, the officer should not be reluctant to make overtures; he will usually find that people are pretty much the same everywhere, and that they readily respond to the friendly and sincere neighborly approach.

In essence, in relationships with the civilian populace, the officer, whether in or out of uniform, must always bear in mind that he does not shed responsibilities to the service as soon as he is away from a duty station. He always represents the naval service and needs to bring credit to it. If he keeps this thought in mind, an officer's civilian relationships will be highly rewarding and will form a valuable asset to his service life.

Summary

For a fresh start in the study of getting along with people, the young officer could do no better than to read what was published years ago in the *United States Coast Guard Magazine*. Under the title "Thirteen Mistakes," the Coast Guardsmen raised their warning flares about the pitfalls in personal relations.

1. To attempt to set up your own standard of right and wrong.
2. To try to measure the enjoyment of others by your own.
3. To expect uniformity of opinions in the world.
4. To fail to make allowance for inexperience.
5. To endeavor to mold all dispositions alike.
6. Not to yield on unimportant trifles.
7. To look for perfection in your own actions.
8. To worry yourself and others about what cannot be remedied.
9. Not to help everyone wherever, however, whenever you can.
10. To consider impossible what you cannot yourself perform.
11. To believe only what your finite mind can grasp.
12. Not to make allowances for the weakness of others.
13. To estimate by some outside quality what it is within that makes the person.

The unobserving officer will no doubt dismiss this list as just so many cliches. The reflective officer, though, will accept it as a negative guide to positive conduct, for it engages practically every principle that is vital to the growth of a strong spiritual life in relation to his fellow humans.

13

Counseling and Interviewing

One of the most time-consuming duties of the junior officer is counseling and interviewing his subordinates, but there is no more effective leadership technique for maintaining personal contact with them, and giving them recognition, than this. Some naval officers tend to avoid this procedure if there appears to be another way of solving the subordinate's problem, such as referring him to a specialist: the public relations officer or the chaplain or the legal officer. However, junior officers must bear in mind that shunting too many problems to the shoulders of the specialists will soon cause loss of personal touch with subordinates—and when this happens, the leadership position is imperilled. The officer maintains his title, but someone else has usurped his position.

Guidelines for Successful Counseling and Interviewing

Know Your Personnel

The officer-counselor must know the record, the character, and the measure of goodwill of the individual he is counseling. It should be his first order of business when he assumes command of his unit to learn the characteristics of his personnel. This duty precedes the counseling interview. It is by no means an excessive task for an officer to learn the names and a great part of the history of the personnel he sees daily, since not knowing them means that he is at a great disadvantage when he is called on to give personal counseling and guidance. It is often too late to check these details after a subordinate seeks advice from the officer. If he does not know enough about the individual to be effective in giving guidance, the officer, whenever possible, should delay the interview until he can gather information.

An officer's study of each individual in his unit should be a never-ending process. Much can be learned by studying service records;

through these the leader can get a comprehensive picture of the make-up of the unit. But service records are not enough. Each individual must be studied. The officer should know each person's temperament, weaknesses and strengths, hopes and apprehensions. The leader should know something of his subordinates' lives before they entered the service; something about their families, their educational and vocational backgrounds. The officer should constantly endeavor to know their states of mind, their attitudes toward the service, and all the minor things that tend to raise or lower their morale.

Be Accessible

Personal information often can be obtained only from the personnel themselves. But on formal questioning, an individual will often have only a minimum to say. If they lack confidence in the officer, most persons will react in this way. But if an officer is able to talk to personnel in a way that allows them to understand him, he will surely gain their confidence. When it seems appropriate, the official military relationship can be set aside temporarily, and the subordinate can be put at ease by being allowed to sit down and to talk things over informally.

The too-formal manner, the over-rigid attitude, the disposition to deal with any human problem by the numbers, as if it was only one more act in organizational routine—all these can destroy the counseling process before it has begun. Though no one can wholly change his or her personality, the officer with a cheerful manner is always ahead when it comes to human relationships.

As a further safeguard against making himself inaccessible, the officer needs to know the procedures that have been established by immediate subordinates. At all levels of command those near the top are inclined to think up new ways to keep all hands from "bothering the old man." Regardless of how positive an order to the contrary the officer issues, these "do-gooders" will not infrequently contrive to circumvent it, mistakenly believing that by this act they save the officer from himself. No alert officer will permit those in the chain of command below him to cut him off in this manner from close contact with the personnel he commands.

Receive Subordinates' Problems with Respect

It is never a waste of time for the officer to talk to his personnel about their personal problems. Even though the problem may seem small to him, it may seem highly important to the individuals concerned, and therefore it must not be dismissed lightly.

For instance, a woman's husband may be sued for damage inflicted in an automobile collision, or a man's wife may have unwisely contracted for furniture beyond the family's means, or one of the youngsters may be having trouble at school. These are typical problems that will lead subordinates to consult their officers if they are—as they should be—trusted by them as friends and counselors.

Regardless of what the home problem of an individual may be, it must be given the same consideration as performance of duty aboard ship. Although the officer may feel far removed from the home lives of his subordinates, today more than half of naval personnel maintain homes outside their navy environment, and the officer cannot afford to ignore problems arising from these outside sources.

Even worse than ignoring personal problems like these would be for the officer to ridicule, treat with sarcasm, or "give the brushoff" to anyone who takes him into his confidence on matters of any sort—unless the petitioner is using trickery for devious purposes. Even in such cases, if the subordinate provides information that shows that his own conduct has been improper, or that he is trying to get his officer to support some illegal act, it is better to hear him through than to treat what he says in an offhand manner. An officer will grow in the esteem of his subordinates only if he treats their affairs with respect. The policy of patience toward and sincere interest in the affairs of subordinates pays off tenfold, because what happens to one individual soon becomes known to the others.

It is not necessary for an officer to wet-nurse his subordinates in order to function in the role of counselor. His door should be open, but that does not mean he should create an atmosphere that promotes bypassing the petty officers or noncommissioned officers in the chain of command. Rather, he should build up the prestige of his enlisted leaders to the extent that those under them will seek out their counseling and guidance rather than bringing all their problems to the officer level.

Help the Person Help Himself

In the role of counselor, an officer should give serious attention to the problem and then follow with straightforward advice or a decision, according to the nature of the case—provided that from his own knowledge and experience he feels qualified to do so. If the officer does not feel qualified, it would be wiser for him to defer a decision or to consult with someone who has the correct information before offering a half-baked opinion. To consider for a time, and to seek counsel from others, whether in higher authority or associates, is the sound alternative when there is a great deal at stake for the person below and when the problem is too complex for its solution to be readily apparent. The spirit in which this work should be undertaken is nowhere more clearly indicated than in the words of Schuyler D. Hoslett, who, in his book *Human Factors in Management*, said this: "Counseling is advising an individual to the extent that an attempt is made to help him understand his problem so that he may carry out a plan for its solution. It is a process which stimulates the individual's ability for self-direction."

Weigh the Needs of the Organization and the Needs of the Individual

Family affairs, frictions within the organization, personal entanglements, frustrations and anxieties of varying kinds, a sense of failure, and other nameless fears that are rooted deep in the consciousness of nearly every individual—all these are the more general subjects in counseling. Whatever problem the subordinate wishes to discuss with his officer becomes the officer's rightful business. In addition, when a person's only desire is to present a recommendation, believing that it would serve the interests of the organization, the recommendation should be heard with the most careful attention.

Whether it centers on a problem or a recommendation, the counseling interview develops around two concerns. The first, and most important, is the best interests of the unit. The second concern is the good of the individual. When counseling, the officer is rarely in the role of a disinterested party. Unlike the minister, the lawyer, the teacher, or the "best friend," the officer has to look beyond what is beneficial simply to the spiritual, mental, and moral needs of one individual. All officers have a responsibility to equate the personal problem to the philosophy within which a command operates. Foremost in their minds must be the fact that, while every individual has a breaking point, the unit also is made of individuals who may have similar problems and who may be equally affected by the decision.

When undue personal favors are granted, when precedents are set without weighing the possible effects on all concerned, or when individuals are urged or sympathetically humored by their seniors into taking a weak personal course, the discipline of the organization is weakened, tension within it mounts, and personnel lose respect for the leadership capacity of their officers.

So, while personal problems are to be considered with sincere interest and compassion, the officer must not lose sight of his responsibilities to the organization as a whole. For example, within a given command, at a particular time, leaves have been restricted, for command reasons, to those with emergencies. A sailor comes forward and says that he is so homesick he can no longer do his work. If his senior granted this sailor's request because he feared that the sailor would break, he would be harassed by other requests with no better bases, and if these were not granted, there would be general dissatisfaction among the personnel. On the other hand, an individual may request emergency leave because he or she has been informed that his or her mother is dying. If the senior fails to act on this request, he will win the deserved contempt of the same personnel who were ready to take advantage of a weak decision in the first case, but who, in the second case, will seek nothing for themselves.

Consider the Problem in Light of the Individual

What the individual says of himself in relation to the problem deserves always to be judged according to the individual's record. If it is a good record, action should be taken on the basis of the problem and the record. If it is a poor record, the counselor should listen to the case with interest and sympathy, but with considerable mental reservations, pending further investigation.

Vietnam era officers had to abide by this standard in dealing with the general discontent that arose out of redeployment. When a man said that he "couldn't take it anymore," and his commander knew that he had always been a highly motivated individual and had faithfully performed his duties, it became the commander's job to attempt to get that man home. But when a second man gave the same story, and his record showed that he had little motivation and had shirked his work, the question was whether he should be given the final chance to shirk it again. To favor the first man meant furthering discipline; his comrades recognized it as a fair deal. To turn back the second man was equally constructive to the same end. In a general situation of unique pressure, commanders found that these principles worked.

Channel Problems to Appropriate Sources

Many of the problems for which men seek the advice of their officers are of a legal nature. Unless an officer is well versed in the Uniform Code of Military Justice or in civil law, the inquiry must be channeled to a qualified source. Other problems require use of the home services of such civilian organizations as the Red Cross. A knowledge of his limits, beyond which the help of a specialist or agency must be sought, is therefore as important to the officer-counselor as the ability to give an individual full information concerning the whereabouts and use of these facilities.

The official views of the naval service on the primary civilian agencies available for emergency relief for naval personnel are as follows.

The Navy Relief Society. The society, although closely affiliated with the naval service and working exclusively among naval personnel and their families, is a private organization. The objectives of the society are to collect and hold funds and to use the funds for aid in times of need of the officers and enlisted personnel of the naval service, their dependents, and the dependents of deceased personnel, with full regard for the dignity and self-respect of those who find themselves in need of its help. The chief of naval personnel is a member of the board of managers of the society and thus maintains a close liaison with the society.

The American Red Cross. The American Red Cross is authorized by navy regulations to conduct a program of social welfare which includes financial assistance for naval personnel, medical and psychiatric case work, and recreation services for the hospitalized. The Red Cross is an authorized medium of communication between families of naval personnel and the service. In furnishing information, the primary interest of the Red Cross is to develop the facts concerning matters referred to it.

The Family Service Centers. The Navy Family Service Centers form a network of navy-wide facilities that help implement the Family Support Program within the naval service. They provide a wide range of reliable and useful information, resources, and services to all active-duty and retired naval service personnel and their dependents. Their purpose is to support and enrich the lives of naval service members and their dependents. The services and programs are tailored to local needs and unique requirements. Family Service Centers assist single and married personnel and their families in solving problems, dealing with roadblocks, and finding assistance and resources when necessary.

Recognize the Importance of Immediacy

The Red Cross is usually an effective agent in checking the facts of a home situation and returning the data to the proper naval authorities. But at the command level, where officer and subordinate sit together, its resources for helping the individual—when what is needed mainly is advice and a sympathetic ear—are not likely to be any better than those his military seniors can provide for him. In any time of crisis, the average human being can draw strength and guidance far more surely from a person he knows well, and has trust and confidence in, than from a stranger.

During the Vietnam War, for example, some men overseas received word that their homes had been broken up. The counselor could talk with the man concerned, could learn whether a reconciliation was the most important thing or whether the man was groping his way, looking for a friend who could help him see the matter in proportion and let him weigh, among other things, his duty to himself. In this case, the Red Cross could check the facts of the home situation, but the man's readjustment depended primarily on the actions of those who were closest to him.

Offer Support

Sooner or later every leader has to deal with some aspect of this kind of problem. In a problem of this nature, moralizing and generalizing about the weakness of human nature serves no purpose. Calling the subordinate a fool is as useless as wasting indignation on the cause of the misfortune. Likewise, any frontal approach to the problem, such as telling the person, "Here is what you should do," should be shunned, or at the least used most sparingly. The most effective attitude can be expressed in these words: "If it had happened to me instead of to you, and I were in your same situation, here are the things I would consider, and here are the points to which I would give greatest weight."

To tell any individual to "brace up" or "be a man" is to make plain inference that he is being weak. Reflecting, rather, on the traits of a person of strong character is the gentle way to stir self-respect. Also worth remembering is that in any person's dark hour, a pat on the back and an earnest handclasp may work a small miracle.

Consider Transfer Requests with Care

Transfers are the subject of many interviews. When considering a transfer request from a subordinate, an officer should use as a criterion the overall good of the service rather than the short-range effect on his own unit. Of course no officer wants to transfer the good personnel out of his unit, but if the transfer appears to be in the best interests of the service, the request should be granted.

Unfortunately, some officers, thinking only of their own unit's success—which, naturally, affects their own record for efficiency—hold on to every able subordinate like grim death. This is a sign of weakness, not of strength, and its inevitable fruit is discontent within the organization. The sign of superior ability in any officer, at any level, is the confidence that another good person can be developed to fill any vacancy that occurs within the unit. When it is self-evident that a person can be bettered and can profit the service through transfer, it is contrary to all sound leadership principles to deny the transfer.

Allowing deserved transfers does not mean that the unit's exit door should be kept wide open, but only that it should be ready to yield on a showing of competent proof. It is not unusual, when the pressure mounts and war danger rises, for many individuals to develop a sudden conviction that they would be more useful in duty billet ashore. However, unless the great majority of the personnel remain in that line of duty which they had accepted in less dangerous circumstances, the navy would soon lose its combat efficiency.

It makes little sense, however, to keep personnel in combat who obviously are morally and physically unequipped for its rigor. Some of the ablest officers in our service have abided by this rule: never deny the person who had a legitimate reason for transfer, and never shuffle off the lemons and goldbricks under a false label. Though seemingly idealistic, the rule is also practical.

Approach Organizational Friction Objectively

Nonrated men tend to seek officer counsel when they feel discriminated against by their enlisted leaders. When this occurs, it is the duty of the officer to get at the facts, and to act fairly and impartially.

Complaints against a junior are always unpleasant to hear because they usually indicate a state of low morale in the unit. Tactless handling of complaints, without weighing the facts from both sides, can further aggravate the problem of low morale. For instance, the officer's responsibility extends further than automatically supporting a junior when the facts say that the latter is wrong. It is the duty of the leader to reduce friction wherever it is caused by a misuse of power. This implies private counseling of the offender instead of reprimanding him in public.

Take the Time to Counsel

For the officer already burdened with other duties, counseling may seem like a waste of time, an activity that more properly belongs to the chaplain or some other specialist. True, the wise and understanding chaplain may sometimes counsel personnel on their material problems and thereby assist the line officer, but in so doing, he is trespassing on the command responsibilities of the line officer unless he acts with the latter's knowledge and consent. The line officer must always be the foster father or mother of the personnel in his or her organization. When this role is renounced, a subordinate is neglected. That neglect reduces the combat efficiency of the unit through the lowering of general morale and discipline.

Accept Counsel from Below

In the military society, far more than in civil life, confidence is a two-way street. Wise advice can be obtained from below as well as handed down. Many junior officers in the past have learned to rely on the friendly counsel of a veteran senior enlisted; they have usually received it straight from the shoulder, but with respect. The breaking-in of most young officers, and their acclimation to their role in a command system, is due, in large measure, to support from this source. Even senior commanders are not reluctant to receive moral comfort from this same source in periods of crisis.

Principles of Counseling and Interviewing

The officer who determines to conduct helpful counseling interviews should follow the eleven principles outlined here.

1. Good counseling is personalized and individualized. The officer

must indicate that the individual's problem is important to him as a person, that it is not considered as a "type" problem to be handled in a routine way.

2. A need for counseling arises when a person faces a difficulty that cannot be resolved without help. The person may or may not be able to identify or to define the problem alone. The problem must be explored.

3. The function of counseling is to help people to help themselves. True counseling does not consist of telling people what to do. It is a process of assisting a person to analyze his own problems, of supplying him with or directing him to needed information so that he can think intelligently about his situation, and of considering together possible solutions. After this is done, the person is in a position to work out a solution or constructive program of action that can be accepted as his own.

4. The counselor should be a good listener. Some personnel who seek advice will already be on the right track. They are quite certain of what they need to do, and merely want support and confirmation of their thinking. In some cases, "talking it through" may provide emotional release as well as assist the person to become more objective. If the person's own plans appear to give a reasonably happy solution to the problem, the counselor should encourage him to carry them out.

5. Effective counseling is dependent on adequate data rather than on just a desire to help people. The counselor should be quick to ascertain what additional information will be needed and from what sources it may be obtained.

6. The counselor should recognize his own limitations, particularly if he suspects that difficulties of personality adjustment are involved, and he should make a referral to a navy psychologist when he is in doubt.

7. The counselor should treat as confidential the information he is given in an interview. Adherence to this ethical principle is very important, because it will help establish the counselor's reputation as a "square shooter" and will promote this relationship and relationships with his other personnel.

8. In the course of an interview it is good practice to stop periodically and review the facts and conditions covered up to that point. This not only helps in the action-planning phase, but also enables the counselor to maintain control of the interview.

9. During the counseling process, the interviewer establishes himself not only as someone who is willing and anxious to help, but also as someone who is interested in the results of the plan of action. He should keep in touch with the individual afterwards in order to assist with the "follow through."

10. Skill in counseling and interviewing develops with experience, as do most other abilities. The naval officer can build on his experience, and he can improve his technique through reading and through discussion with those who have made clinical counseling their profession.

11. Sympathy for the problems of your subordinates may get you so involved that you will be no more capable of solving them than they are. What the officer needs is empathy for the subordinates' problems; he needs to understand the problem as if it were his own, without losing sight of the "as if" part of the equation. The leader is then able to take action to ease "the pain," as it were, and still remain effective in his own job.

Summary

Described in cold type, the counseling process probably appears a little "sticky." Actually, it is not. The techniques of counseling have been used by leaders through the ages. Counseling is a force in all organized human relationships, beginning in infancy and lasting through old age. No group has good morale or discipline unless each member identifies with the group and feels that the group is interested in his welfare. For this reason, there is a need to imbue each member of the unit with the philosophy that he, as well as the unit, will benefit when he assists personnel who are in need of help.

33

14

Discipline, Morale, and Esprit de Corps

Discipline, morale, and esprit de corps are inseparable, and trying to decide which comes first is similar to the pointless argument about the chicken and the egg—it doesn't matter. A unit without morale cannot have true discipline; and, conversely, without discipline, no organization will have good morale. The point is that discipline and morale are mutually reinforcing. They are also both primary responsibilities of the leader.

Discipline

To the average person, the word *discipline* carries with it the connotations of severity, an unreasonable curtailment of freedom, unnecessary restraints on personal conduct, endless restrictions, and required adherence to arbitrary or unreasonable demands of authority. Actually, discipline is the basis of true democracy, for it means the adherence of the individual to the set of rules that people through the experience of ages have found best suited to govern relations between individual members of society so as to protect the interests of the whole. Some of these rules are made by duly constituted authority and are set down in writing. These are called *laws*. Others have been sanctioned by custom and usage, and they are called *conventions*. Every person is subject to some sort of discipline. The decent citizen, and the happy one, is the one who accepts this discipline cheerfully.

Discipline implies subjection to a control exerted for the good of the whole, the adherence to rules or policies intended for the orderly coordination of effort. Obviously, orderliness and discipline are indispensable to a military organization. In fact, without the requisite degree of orderliness, a military organization ceases to be a military organization and becomes merely a mob. One of the primary responsibilities of a leader is the inculcation of discipline in his organization.

There are various ways of securing discipline. For instance, there is the discipline based on the fear of consequences for violation of rules: the discipline of fear, or the negative aspect of discipline. Then there is what we like to consider as the American ideal of discipline: a cheerful and spontaneous discipline to which personnel willingly and gladly subject themselves out of faith in the cause for which they are striving and out of respect for, and confidence in, their leaders. This is the positive aspect of discipline.

An organization may be said to have been brought to an ideal state of discipline when there exists in it a maximum of efficiency and contentment generated through positive discipline techniques, with a minimum use of negative discipline (punishment).

In the naval service, discipline means "a prompt, willing responsiveness to commands." The best discipline is self-discipline, the individual doing the right thing because he wants to do the right thing. It is gained through building willingness, enthusiasm, and cooperation; it exists not only while personnel are under the eyes of their superiors, but while they are off duty, as well.

Admiral Arleigh A. Burke wrote: "A well-disciplined organization is one whose members work with enthusiasm, willingness, and zest as individuals and as a group to fulfill the mission of the organization with expectation of success. Lack of discipline results in loss of smooth, determined operating action and combat efficiency."

In striving for a high level of discipline, leaders must remember that personnel admire an individual who lives in accordance with the code that is enforced. Nothing but resentment can result when a leader demands behavior from followers which he does not exhibit himself. The officer who expects unflinching obedience and cooperation from subordinates will do well to give the same obedience and cooperation to his seniors. If the officer combines this trait with ability and a genuine interest in the well-being of personnel, then many disciplinary problems will be avoided.

Positive Discipline

Positive discipline is the development of a state of mind in individuals in which they endeavor to do the right thing, with or without specific instructions. In order for positive discipline to operate effectively, it is necessary that personnel know their jobs thoroughly. Training, therefore, is one of the basic factors involved in this type of discipline. The individual officer must strive constantly to train personnel to perform their duties in such a way as not to break regulations. In this way discipline is being exercised just as surely as by punishing personnel after an infraction, but it is being exercised in a much more productive manner.

The person in authority can assist in the achievement of positive discipline through his own actions. The leader must:

1. Maintain a general attitude of approval of the organization. A feeling of distrust on the part of the leader is soon transmitted to subordinates and causes a general sense of insecurity.
2. Let subordinates know what is expected of them. This can be done by formal directives and by clear verbal instructions.
3. Keep subordinates informed of their mission in any specific job. An individual works better when he fully understands the relationship of what is done and how it is done to the whole task of operation.
4. Let subordinates know that their officers are behind them as long as they perform their duties to the best of their abilities.
5. Keep subordinates informed on the progress they are making. This is equally important whether their work is good or bad.
6. Keep subordinates informed, within security restrictions, of any changes that will affect their future.
7. Assure subordinates by his actions that each of them will receive fair and impartial treatment.
8. Improve his own professional ability. Enlisted personnel have been asked what they think makes a good leader. They say they like and respect professional competence in a leader more than any other single attribute.
9. Delegate authority, with corresponding responsibility, as far down in the organization as competence exists.

Negative Discipline

From the point of view of the leader, discipline and punishment should never become synonymous. The training and educational phase of discipline should be kept constantly in mind, even when it becomes necessary to resort to awarding punishment, the ultimate method of attaining discipline. Some individuals are so constituted that they do not respond to ordinary methods of training. In dealing with these individuals, the leader should first attempt to influence them by the positive methods of discipline. However, when the individual fails to respond to these methods, the leader should not hesitate to utilize punishment, or negative discipline, as a leadership technique. Punishment is an element of discipline, albeit the final one.

Except in its relation to discipline, punishment is not a pleasant thing, either to talk about or to use as an instrument in the control of subordinates. It would be better if punishment was a force that needed never to be invoked, but, human nature being what it is, the leader can scarcely get along without it. Punishment is like dynamite: strong and dangerous, valuable and destructive, effective to a degree when used correctly, alarmingly destructive when used incorrectly.

People are very largely controlled by two motives, the hope of reward and the fear of punishment. The following words express the sentiments of one of our early naval leaders, John Paul Jones, on the subject of reward and punishment:

> No meritorious act of a subordinate should escape his [naval officer's] attention or be left to pass without its reward, if even the reward be only one word of approval. Conversely, he should not be blind to a single fault in any subordinate, though at the same time he should be quick and unfailing to distinguish error from malice, thoughtlessness from incompetency, and well-meant shortcoming from heedless and stupid blunder. As he should be universal and impartial in his rewards and approval of merit, so should he be judicial and unbending in his punishment or reproof of misconduct.

Some of the factors to be considered in the administration of negative discipline are discussed below.

Punishment must be prompt. To be effective, punishment must be prompt. This principle is so well recognized that, with few exceptions (such as murder, desertion, and fraud against the United States), statutes of limitation operate to bar trial of an accused person after a certain lapse of time if the suspected offender has not placed himself out of reach of justice during that time. If the officer were to reprove a subordinate for some minor breach of discipline committed several months before, the offender might well have forgotten the incident entirely, might wonder why he was being taken to task, and might rightfully entertain some doubts as to the quality of leadership exhibited by the officer. If reprimand or punishment is not given reasonably soon after the offense has been committed, the whole thing had best be forgotten.

Punishment must be impersonal and just. Punishment should

never be personal, and it should never be vindictive; that is, it should never be inflicted in revenge for misconduct. It cannot make right the wrong that has resulted from an act of dereliction. Its only value lies in the object lesson it furnishes the wrongdoer and others: that the offense must not be repeated. It appeals to the fear of punishment in people.

Not only must punishment be just, but, if it is to accomplish its purpose, the recipient and his peers must recognize it as just. Just punishment is punishment that is administered as soon after the offense as possible, that is not of such a nature as to lower a person's self-respect, and that is not so severe as to be out of all proportion to the gravity of the offense.

People range from extreme sensitivity to great callousness in their reactions to punishment; therefore, any set scale of punishments for specific offenses has its limitations. Punishment not only should "fit the crime," but should fit the individual, also—after all, he is the person being punished. Some subordinates are so constituted that a glance or expression of disapproval, a word of reproof, or even a conveyance that the officer believes that they have failed to measure up to what he expected of them, will be all that is needed to correct their breach of discipline. Others are so accustomed or hardened to the knocks of life that it takes more severe forms of punishment to make any impression. The foregoing bears out rather emphatically Dr. Douglas Southall Freeman's injunction "Know your men." Because the junior officer is the one who presumably knows the character of his personnel, he is the one who is required to represent any offenders from his unit when nonjudicial punishment is applied.

The Uniform Code of Military Justice provides maximum, and, in some cases, minimum sentences. Sometimes these sentences are of an "either . . . or" variety, or else several alternatives are permitted. Reference to the *Manual for Court-Martial* will disclose the sentences that both commanding officers and court-martial are permitted to give. In sentencing an individual, an officer should make certain that the sentence is no more severe than adjudged necessary, and that care is taken to avoid punishing a person's family through—or instead of—him. Loss of pay may work hardship on the family of an individual who is married and has children. Extra duty or deprivation of leave might be more keenly felt by him and far less harmful to his family. On the other hand, a severe fine usually will be effective punishment for the single individual who loves his night life. This case points up the importance of the admonition "Know your men."

Reprimand privately; praise publicly. It is a cardinal rule to reprimand only in private, but to praise publicly. At one time Benedict Arnold was one of the ablest and bravest officers in the Continental Army. George Washington was ordered by the Continental Congress to give him a public reprimand, and it was given in the setting that is normally associated with the conferring of a high decoration. Washington personally delivered the reprimand, but he did as much as possible to leaven the censure with praise. Nevertheless, it was galling to Arnold's high-spirited nature. The reprimand rankled, and it can only be surmised how much part this played in his later treason.

The officer must not push an individual beyond allowable limits:

> A reasonable leader can, however, avert many, many arraignments before courts-martial. He will sense that there are limits beyond which the human being cannot be pushed. At times, during the pursuit of exasperating tasks, nothing goes well. Sufficient harassing by an unperceptive leader can make the mildest man explode or harbor enough suppressed irritation to push him blindly into infractions of regulations.

Punishment is a command function. Punishment, like positive discipline, which it is intended to uphold, is a command function. It cannot be delegated, and it can legally be awarded only by the accused's commanding officer or by a legally convened court-martial acting in accordance with the Uniform Code of Military Justice. No officer except the one who is in command status has any authority to inflict any punishment over the personnel he is assigned to control. Officers must be careful not to assume this authority under the assumption that they will save time for the commanding officer or that the accused will get a fairer deal from them than from the commanding officer, or for any other reason. They can only report offending personnel to their commanding officer and exercise positive discipline techniques in guiding the offender's future actions. Each officer should find out for himself how these matters are handled.

The indiscriminate use of nonjudicial punishment against personnel on charges that subsequently are found to be largely unfounded is a direct reflection on the officer concerned. An officer should carefully investigate all angles of the case before he places an individual on report, and then he should only do so when he is convinced of the guilt of the person or when such grave doubt of the person's innocence exists that he feels further investigation and more mature judgment by the commanding officer is necessary to exercise justice.

Morale and Esprit de Corps

Another essential purpose of good leadership is developing good morale. High morale is the index of effective leadership. No control of human behavior is possible without it, and no failure is final unless the failure destroys morale. Morale is based on the belief of each person in himself and in the cause.

Before high morale can be instilled in an individual, there must first exist personal convictions and standards which provide a positive goal and make day-by-day life meaningful and worth living. Second, the person must be made aware of specific tasks and problems that must be completed and solved in order to reach his goal or the unit's goal. However, before any individual will identify closely with any group, that group usually must offer tangible and satisfying rewards. In other words, there must be immediate tasks to complete which are part of the overall plan of operation for the unit. Third, in order for the individual to sustain personal morale during periods of stress, his basic convictions and aims must be in harmony with those of the other members of the unit; otherwise, group action will be uncoordinated and the possibility of failure of the unit will be greatly increased.

How does a junior officer proceed in building morale in his unit, and how does he know when he has a good outfit with high morale? Actually there will be little doubt in his mind as to whether or not his unit has a high state of morale—the result achieved by the division will provide the answer.

The following principles for building and maintaining morale in both the individual and the unit should be studied by the junior officer. However, the leader will not find morale building an easy task. It is a task that must be worked at constantly, always remembering that each decision or each action will have an effect on the morale of the entire unit.

Building Morale

Much has been said about the morale of the members of service units. Napoleon pointed out that morale is to material as three is to one. He is also credited with saying that an army moves on its stomach. All of this emphasizes the point that the state of mind of service personnel has a tremendous bearing on what they are capable of doing. Morale is given many definitions, but the one that will concern the leader most as an officer is as follows: morale is the state of mind of an individual that has been produced by all the circumstances that make his membership in a group rewarding and satisfying. It is what an individual is getting out of being a member of that group that determines his mental state. Living conditions, food, quarters, discipline, pay, and duties all have a bearing. How important individual members of the group are made to feel will determine how good or how bad group morale is at any given time.

It has been said that "morale is a lot of little things." Probably nothing comes closer to describing accurately this important factor, because everything that makes a person feel well and satisfied builds up his morale, and everything that bothers him as an individual can lower his morale. If the officer aspiring to leadership will work out the difficult and seemingly thankless task of knowing everything he can about each of his personnel, the knowledge thus gained will give him a trusty weapon with which to attack the problems that are keeping his personnel from being alert and on their toes, and from doing the job of which they are capable.

There are certain points that the leader must constantly analyze and correct. He must realize

1. that subordinates' attitudes are a dependable measure of morale;
2. that high morale is present only in those groups that have discipline and efficiency; and
3. that subordinates' attitudes toward their officers are important as a morale factor.

Measuring morale. Morale can be measured in two ways:

1. By inspections. If the appearance of an organization is smart and the equipment is in efficient operating condition, the morale is high.
2. By interviews with subordinates. If they are happy and contented, the morale is high. Conversely, if they are restrained, unhappy, and desirous of a transfer, the morale is low.

Components of morale. If there is to be high morale, each person must believe the following statements.

1. It is desirable to be in the naval service.

2. Naval service policies and practices are reasonable and sound, particularly as they apply in his own unit.

3. Training is thorough and good. If an individual is asked to do a job and he can do it well, his feeling of accomplishment will improve morale.

4. The job is appropriate to his abilities and interests.

5. All work receives proper recognition and reward.

6. He is receiving consistent and impartial treatment.

7. Living conditions are as good as other conditions permit.

8. His health and personal problems are being cared for.

9. He is receiving as much free time and opportunity for recreation as service requirements permit.

10. He is an accepted member of a first-class unit.

Guidelines for the officer. The following general rules are laid down for the officer who desires to build or maintain high morale. He should

1. make his subordinates confident of his professional ability

2. keep in touch with their problems and wishes and look after their welfare carefully and continually

3. keep his personnel informed regarding policies and practices which affect them

4. be strictly consistent and impartial in assigning duties and in giving rewards and punishment

5. show his subordinates that he respects them as individuals with dignity and that he is proud to be associated with them

6. keep well informed of the attitudes of his personnel

7. be accessible to his subordinates to the maximum extent possible

8. participate actively in planning and executing unit functions

9. actively supervise affairs in order to ensure that the senior enlisted do their jobs with the welfare of the personnel in mind

10. see that his subordinates have ample opportunity for educational development

11. always be friendly, courteous, and tactful

12. know each individual by name

The following specific points are recommended for the officer who is building morale. He should

1. see that his outfit has the best mess possible, both as to quality

and preparation of the food (a sparkling mess hall produced by an efficient mess force can contribute to the morale of the unit just as good leadership on the commanding officer's part does)

2. check sanitation and health conditions in his unit constantly

3. see that the supply of clothing and equipment for his unit is adequate, and that the laundry is efficient

4. make sure that his subordinates get their proper amount of liberty and leave

5. ensure that his subordinates receive just treatment, with respect to promotions, awards, and privileges

Youth is generally impatient. This, coupled with the fact that new personnel and new officers are assigned the less important jobs, may produce a feeling of discouragement. The junior officer should make his men realize two things about their jobs. First, that oiling the bearings of a machine is important to its proper operation, just as is the ship-handling of the captain, and, second, that every job well done leads to a better job later on. The junior officer must never let himself or his personnel lose sight of the fact that there is no unimportant job.

Probably the greatest single destroyer of morale anywhere is prolonged inactivity and the boredom that results from it. On the other hand, no individual likes to have every minute of his time obligated. Everyone enjoys moments of relaxation and freedom to go his own way. Too much activity over too long a time can be as unfortunate in its results as too little activity; for instance, the athlete who is overtrained can go "stale." All work and no play does indeed make Jack a dull boy. The problem of what to do with spare time is unlikely to occur these days, but it has existed in the past and conceivably could again. In times of forced inactivity much can be done by holding "smokers," contests, tournaments, projects, and even competitive drills. Anything is preferable to idleness and boredom.

The problem in the naval service is far more likely to be too heavy an operating schedule, too much work and too little time in which to do it, and too much time away from home. If this proves to be the case and morale is adversely affected, it is the duty of the effective leader to report the fact to his seniors and see what can be done to alleviate conditions. Information must flow upward as well as downward.

A wise and thoughtful leader will keep careful watch on the morale of his men and do all that he can to maintain it at a high level.

Building Esprit de Corps

Esprit de corps is the common spirit pervading the members of a unit. It implies enthusiasm, devotion, and zealous regard for the honor of the unit. While morale may be used in referring to one person or many, esprit de corps is a unit spirit embodying a definite bond between the individual members, between members and their leaders, and between all hands in regard to the organization they serve.

Esprit de corps does not necessarily appear in units that are efficient and well disciplined, nor does it depend entirely on the unit being successful in competition with other units. The production of esprit de corps is not as difficult as the production of efficiency or discipline, but, in the final analysis, it is the driving force of a unit's endeavor. If an outfit is efficient and well disciplined and, in addition, has esprit de corps, it will be hard to beat.

Measuring esprit de corps. Esprit de corps can be indicated or measured by the following.

1. The expression of enthusiasm and pride in their unit by its members.
2. The reputation of the unit among other units.
3. The competitive spirit in the unit.
4. The unit's staying power under conditions of stress.
5. The attitude of the members toward one another and toward their leaders.
6. The members' readiness to help one another.

The most accurate measure of esprit de corps is the readiness of members of a unit to help one another. The officer who would build up esprit de corps in his outfit should point out to his personnel the value of this spirit of brotherhood and sisterhood. In small, closely knit units, it is a simple matter to persuade members that helping one another is an investment that always pays dividends.

For example, on one ship no one ever sat on deck if anyone else was loading stores; the educated machinist's mates first class spent their spare time teaching the strikers; and, when there was a tough job to do, all hands immediately volunteered. Every new man who reported on board was made to feel immediately that he was wanted, that all hands wanted to help him, and that he was a part of an organization whose members enjoyed living and working together.

Finally, there came a time when five of the leading petty officers were to be transferred to the United States, having completed more than three years on the Asiatic station. These men had talked for weeks of the joy they felt in going home. But the international situation was tense. On the day before they were to be detached they went to the commanding officer as a group and said that they wanted to stay; that they just could not leave the ship, because there might be war; and that if they had to fight, they wanted to do it with the officers and men with whom they had lived during the past three years. The date was 15 November 1941.

Guidelines for the officer. The achievement and maintenance of esprit de corps will be difficult unless the following problems that may arise are overcome.

1. Lack of confidence in leadership.
2. Presence in the unit of conflicting groups of personnel.
3. Presence of noncooperators who hamper unit performance.
4. Rapid turnover of unit personnel, especially of the leaders.
5. Lack of proper recognition for unit achievement.

Although the naval officer can do little to prevent rapid turnover of personnel, or to choose the location and assignment to duty of his unit, he would do well to realize the importance of these factors and to try to offset them by giving great attention to those problems over which he has control.

True spirit and pride in the outfit can be developed if each member recognizes the group's common interest and will cooperate toward the common goal. This spirit is dependent on the satisfactions that each man gets from being a member of the group, and is aided by the following.

1. The approval each participating member gets from other members.
2. The disapproval or punishment received by noncooperators.
3. Competition with standards in other groups.
4. The successes of the group and the recognition given to it.
5. Ceremonies and the use of symbols of membership.

The U.S. Marine Corps has, throughout the years, maintained an esprit de corps that is the envy of other military services. The marines have achieved this by a close attention to the principles outlined here. Coupled with morale and discipline, this group spirit makes the marines unbeatable—as proved by the fact that the corps has not once failed in reaching its military objective: "The marines have landed and have the situation well in hand."

Summary

Discipline, morale, and esprit de corps, although seemingly quite different and unrelated, are all necessary for the efficient and effective functioning of an organization. Discipline, by encouraging people to do the right thing, leads to high morale and esprit de corps, which are attained when members of an organization are relating to one another in a positive, rather than a negative, way. Conversely, when morale is high, members are more inclined to do what is right and necessary—to display self-discipline, which is the most effective form of discipline.

15

Training

In the final analysis, all services exist for one purpose. That purpose is to fight and to win battles. This does not mean that every service person will actually be a trigger puller, but every service person will have a function that will bring destruction on the enemy or that will support those who are destroying the enemy. To be successful, all military personnel must know their job and be proficient at it. This requires training.

Training must be carried on continually, both in peacetime and in wartime. In peacetime, training is the primary occupation of the services. This statement is not as sensational as it may seem, for training is nothing more than teaching personnel to do their present jobs as well as the jobs that they will do after they are promoted. This part of the book will discuss some of the basic principles of training, the methods of instruction available, and the tools the instructor uses.

Principles of Training

The first thing to be studied is the training responsibilities that the junior officer must face. Navy Regulation 1948 states that a division officer is responsible for training his personnel in their present duties and also the duties to which they may succeed, and that he shall encourage them to qualify for advancement and to improve their education. This directive divides training into three areas, all of which overlap.

Training for Immediate Duties

It is absolutely necessary to train personnel for their immediate duties, so this is the field that must be studied first. The officer knows all the jobs for which his organization is responsible, and he can find out whether or not they are being properly performed. If they are, he has a person who is trained for the job; if they are not, he does not.

Assuming that he does have a properly trained person doing each job, he should not feel complacent. The trained person will not stay aboard forever, so the officer should begin at once to train his successor.

Usually it will be found that all jobs are being performed adequately, but that they are not being performed as well as they might be. This situation can be remedied by additional training. Equipment is constantly changing, and the personnel must be trained on the new equipment. Furthermore, new personnel are constantly coming into the unit. They must be instructed, not only in their duties, but also in their rights and benefits, and in the provisions of the Uniform Code of Military Justice.

A training plan should be developed in advance of the start of training. The officer should also investigate formal schools to see if these will help meet the needs of the unit. After these sources have been checked and the training available there has been utilized, the remaining training must be accomplished at the unit level.

Once it is known what training is necessary, and which personnel need this training, it is necessary to determine when it should be accomplished and who should do it. Finding the time to hold training instruction is not difficult if you use a little ingenuity. Good advice is to use odd moments of time that are generally wasted. There are times when personnel must stand around doing nothing productive, such as standing by for an inspection or waiting at quarters. By planning to use these scraps of time, the junior officer can accomplish a great deal.

Training personnel while they are on watch is also productive. Even when an individual is doing a job fairly well, he can be taught to do it better. Of course, it will also be possible to schedule regular drills and instruction periods when the plan of the day allows time for this.

So far the officer has provided for everything—except instructors. A unit always contains a built-in group of expert petty officers and noncommissioned officers. They should be used to the maximum extent possible. The junior officer should not remove himself from the instructor list, either. There are many subjects in which he will be the most appropriate person to do the instructing. For instance, it might be necessary for him to instruct petty officers or noncommissioned officers in the techniques of instructing before they will actually be qualified to act as instructors. If he does not feel capable of teaching his subordinates how to become teachers, then it is his responsibility to learn how—and with no delay.

Training for Advancement and Improving Education

Training for advancement and maintaining professional competence overlaps the training personnel receive in their duties. Technical and military promotion requirements for higher ratings demand more knowledge by personnel on their special ratings and an increased knowledge of their military and leadership responsibilities. Therefore, any professional training that they receive helps them toward advancement and retaining competence. There is also the requirement that they take correspondence courses peculiar to their rating prior to being promoted. These courses are furnished by the Naval Education Training Program Development Center in the form of correspondence courses.

The Bibliography for Advancement Examination is available on all ships and stations. It lists the qualifications necessary for advancement in ratings. The officer must refer to this manual in order to determine what training personnel will acquire, in addition to the correspondence courses, before they are qualified for promotion.

General education correspondence courses are available from the Defense Activity Non-Traditional Education Support officer (DANTES). Interested personnel should be referred to the local Education Services Office, where arrangements can be made to enroll in high school completion programs as well as in courses for college credit given by correspondence by selected colleges around the country. DANTES can also arrange for personnel to take examinations to receive credit for college-level courses. The officer should inform personnel as to the availability of these courses and encourage their use.

While the advantages for the naval service of the use of DANTES courses may not be immediately apparent, they are many. First of all, there is some transfer or carry-over of knowledge from these courses that is useful to military training. Courses tend to raise the general educational level in the naval service, which in turn permits the military to raise its performance standards. The fact that the courses are available also raises morale and has a certain recruiting value. Last but not least, there is an advantage that may seem totally unrelated: it has been statistically demonstrated that the unauthorized absence rate among the personnel who take these courses is significantly lower than the general rate. There are many more advantages for the naval service of having personnel make use of the educational opportunities available to them.

Encouraging Learning through Enthusiasm

Thus far only the mechanics of training personnel have been discussed. There is still one thing missing that will put life into a training program: ENTHUSIASM!

Nothing is quite as dull as a drill or training session that is expected to be dull. Subordinates will attend because they are ordered to, but they will not learn anything. They will go through the motions, but their minds will be occupied with their next liberty and other thoughts.

The division officer can change this with a little imagination and a lot of enthusiasm of his own. He must enjoy the drills, and he must force himself to be enthusiastic. He must constantly think of ways to make the training more interesting to the men. He can profitably use smoke, noise, fire (where it is safe), live ammunition, drone planes and good targets to fire at, real water in compartments that will not be damaged by it, phony blood on simulated casualties, and imaginary enemy planes and torpedoes—anything his imagination can produce to make the training more interesting and realistic. He should never let a feeling of sophistication prevent his enjoyment of training drills. Training is deadly serious business, but that does not mean that it cannot also be fun and exciting too. An experienced officer has a favorite saying that applies here: "If it isn't fun, we are doing it wrong." There is much truth to this statement, and it contains the answer to the problem of selling the training program to your men. The officer must enjoy it himself and be enthusiastic. The attitude is contagious.

Being a Good Instructor

The most important link in the training chain is the instructor, who translates the plans into action and whose effectiveness determines whether the plans succeed or fail. The instructor's objective is to help the students learn. Chapter 4 discussed the idea that learning is the process of acquiring more effective behavior patterns; that people will learn only if they have a need to learn; and that there are various ways in which people learn. These principles help give direction to the efforts of the instructor.

Provide motivation. The instructor must assume initially that his students are not motivated; that they do not feel a need to learn what he wants them to learn. The first thing that he must do for them, then, is to point out the advantages they will gain from learning the material to be studied. He must show them that they have a "need to know."

In the naval service there are many reasons why service personnel should learn. They are more likely to be promoted when they learn. Some types of information will save their lives or make them more comfortable. Some subjects will assist the student to gain respect and prestige. There is a valid need for the student to learn everything that is taught to him in the naval service. It takes very little perception on the instructor's part to find these motivational forces so that they can be emphasized to the student.

Use every method of learning. Chapter 3 emphasized that people learn by transfer, observation, trial and error, and mechanical guidance. Transfer is the most effective method of learning, so the instructor should relate everything he is trying to teach to something with which the students are already familiar.

Observation is also an effective method of learning, and it is the one most instructors use to make their appeal. Observation means both seeing and hearing. For it to be effective, students must be able to see what the instructor is demonstrating and hear what he is saying. In addition, they must *comprehend* what they see and hear. The instructor must speak loudly enough to be heard by all the students, and he must use words that they understand. This is something that the young officer must be particularly careful of. He will probably be a college graduate, while the average enlisted man may have a high school education, or even less. The officer's vocabulary is quite likely to contain words that the students will not readily understand, so extra care in his choice of words is needed. After students have observed the instructor do something, they should have an opportunity to be guided by him in doing it themselves.

Trial and error is nothing more than trying responses at random and selecting the useful one if it appears. A refined version of this is employed in the navy when the students practice what they are learning. However, this practice comes only after all the other learning methods have been employed. The student has had the subject related to other behavior patterns that are familiar, has observed the proper way to perform the act to be learned, and has been guided through the act itself by the instructor. However, it often happens that the student still can not perform it successfully. In that case, incorrect responses must be eliminated by trial and error. This becomes something more than a completely random choosing of responses, however, because the field from which to make choices has been limited by the instruction that has preceded the practice session. This form of practice should always be conducted under close supervision until the correct sequence of responses has been learned.

Once the student has learned the correct response, it can be stamped in by repetition. Repetition is the most effective way of preventing the student from forgetting, but its use must be tempered. Prolonged repetition will produce boredom and apathy. It is better to practice one hour a day for eight days than to practice eight hours in one day. This principle should always be borne in mind when any type of training is being conducted.

Encourage participation. As was noted previously, the student must be given a reason for learning. But while this reason will put the student in the proper state of mind, it will not keep him there. The instructor must provide a psychological reward for learning, he must give the learning a meaning, if the student is to maintain interest. The psychological reward we mentioned is the satisfaction that comes from success. When the student recites correctly or performs well, the instructor should acknowledge the success by a simple compliment or by some other show of appreciation, such as a smile.

Students should be allowed and encouraged to participate as much as possible in the class. Participation is its own reward, especially if it is successful. From it the student gains recognition from the instructor and from classmates, as well as a better self-opinion.

Student participation also provides advantages for the instructor, who has the opportunity to evaluate the individual students, is relieved of part of the responsibility of making the class a success, and is aided in the accomplishment of his objective. He is helping the students to learn, because the students are helping themselves.

Participation combines many principles, such as practicing, interest production, and satisfaction of needs. It merits a great deal of emphasis.

Present information in manageable form. To repeat once again, the learning must have meaning to the student. The instructor implements this principle by breaking the complete task into logical sections that can be learned in a reasonable length of time, and by relating all the sections to the whole. Simple tasks should not be broken into sections, because usually there is no logical breaking point, and they can normally be taught in a reasonable length of time. Complicated tasks, however, such as firing a rifle, can normally be broken at natural division points. Furthermore, it is generally necessary to divide them into units because of physical limitations. Except in emergencies, material on complicated tasks should not be presented at one session or completed in one day because of the time necessary to present the material, and because students can absorb only a limited amount of material at one time.

When presenting these separate parts, the instructor must remember to show how they fit into the whole. Also important is to allow the students to practice the task as an entity as soon as possible, with all the parts combined. Practicing a skill by parts results in inefficiency and difficulty in remembering the order in which the parts should be accomplished.

Follow sound teaching principles. Up to this point the discussion of the instructor has been rather general, but there are several specific requirements concerning the personal actions of the instructor in the classroom that must be adhered to.

The instructor must provide a classroom atmosphere that places the students at ease while at the same time it permits order to be maintained. To do this, the instructor should be firm and friendly, should insist on the maintenance of order, but should not be overbearing in his attitude toward the students. This atmosphere is not difficult to create in the naval service because the trainees are accustomed to the same kind of discipline in their daily lives from their officers and senior enlisted personnel.

The instructor is in the same position as any other leader in the naval service. He has a responsibility to set the proper example in bearing, dress, and attitude. This responsibility is accentuated by the fact that students are more impressionable than other groups. There are strong influences working on students to make them receptive to the ideas that are being presented by the instructor. They tend to open their minds to everything that the instructor represents, whether it is proper or improper.

The instructor must be particularly careful to remember that the students are sensitive individuals and must be treated as such. He has the advantage, and the students cannot defend themselves, so it is something less than sporting for the instructor to use sarcasm or to be unfair or partial with the students. For the instructor to be effective, he must have the students' trust. And to maintain this trust, he must make the students feel that he is worthy of it. He must never bluff, because either he will be found out or he will give the students incorrect answers. Both results are undesirable. When a student asks a question that the instructor cannot answer, he should frankly say that he does not know, and then either find out himself or assign the question to one of the students as a research project.

It would almost go without saying that the students will not learn what the instructor tells them if they cannot hear him. Therefore the experienced instructor will always speak loudly enough for those farthest away to hear clearly.

The instructor should always look at the students when speaking to them. This technique is known as maintaining eye contact. The instructor should look from student to student so that each one will feel that the instructor is talking to him individually. Then, by watching their expressions, the instructor can tell whether or not students are grasping what he is saying.

Most instructors feel a certain amount of nervousness when they first get up in front of the class. This frequently causes them to develop small nervous habits such as clicking their ballpoint pens, tossing chalk into the air, waving a pencil, or staring out the window. These actions occur involuntarily, and the instructor is usually not conscious of them, but they are quite apparent to the students. And extraneous actions tend to direct students' attention away from what the instructor is saying. It stands to reason, therefore, that the instructor should make every effort to eliminate these habits the moment he becomes aware that he is developing them.

The last point to cover is preparation. The instructor must know a subject thoroughly before he attempts to teach it. He should not be satisfied with knowing just what he intends to teach to the students, but should make a study of the past history of his subject, recent developments in the field, and even advanced work. This preparation will enable him to answer the inevitable questions that occur when the students' minds are stimulated, and it will give him the broad insight and understanding that is necessary if he is to teach properly.

While it is very important that the instructor be prepared, just knowing the subject does not completely prepare him to teach it. He must plan the training session and prepare himself for every eventuality. He must arrange the time and place of the session and notify the students accordingly. He must choose a method of presentation, select the training aids to be used, and make a lesson plan. In fact, he will find that he usually spends several times the length of the presentation period in preparing the lesson that he is going to present.

Methods of Instruction

The basic methods of instruction, or presentation methods, are meant to be combined in any way the instructor feels will be effective. He should choose those that will allow him to present most effectively his particular subject or the portion of that subject that he is teaching at the time.

The Recitation

The recitation is the type of class presentation with which everyone is most familiar. Instructors have been using it for years in grade school and in college. It is useful in a course where the students have been assigned a lesson and are required to know its contents.

In a recitation, the instructor holds a question-and-answer period with the students—with the students furnishing the answers. The instructor must be thoroughly prepared for this type of instruction. He must have prepared questions that develop the lesson and bring out the knowledge of the students. It goes without saying that he must be prepared to answer these questions to the students' satisfaction.

Asking a good question is an art in itself. Questions should not be of the type that can be answered with a yes or a no. Answers to such questions impart no knowledge to the remainder of the class; furthermore, even a student who had not read the lesson would have a 50 percent chance of guessing the right answer.

Questions should be phrased in such a way that the student can confine his answer to that question and must furnish the facts himself. They should not be asked in rotation, alphabetical order, or any other system. Systems are easily figured out by the students, and they then have a tendency to daydream or to lose interest before and after their turn to recite. *It is best to put the question to the whole class, and then to pick a volunteer or name a student to answer the question.* This forces all the students to participate mentally and to think of the answer.

When an answer is given, the instructor should acknowledge it if it is correct, and then go on to the next question unless another student has something additional to contribute. A small compliment such as "Good!" helps to give the student a sense of accomplishment, and should be given for correct answers.

If the student's answer is incorrect, the instructor should allow another student to give the correct answer if there is a volunteer, or he should call on another student if there is no volunteer. Later in the recitation the instructor should permit the students who gave wrong answers a chance to redeem themselves by answering another question, preferably one for which they volunteer.

One thing the instructor must guard against is the tendency to answer the questions himself. He should give the students time to think of the answers, and he should compel their participation if none is forthcoming.

This procedure for instruction will become more relaxed as the students and teacher become accustomed to each other. It can be varied at will by the instructor, who can give brief explanations of points that are not clear to the students, or hold discussions of certain points as they occur, or even allow students to ask questions of the instructor.

The Lecture

Lectures are useful in presenting large amounts of material in the shortest period of time. However, when students are expected to learn the material thoroughly, the instructor should never use this method. Unless the instructor is an outstanding lecturer, and a showman in addition, a lecture tends to be dull for the students, and they have a tendency to let their minds wander.

If this form of instruction must be used, the lecturer should keep the following points in mind.

1. Do not lecture right after a meal, because people with full stomachs have a tendency to go to sleep.
2. Ventilate the area where the audience is assembled in order to prevent sleep, or at least to discourage it.
3. Remove all interesting pictures and devices from the front and sides of the lecture area; this makes the audience look at the lecturer for lack of anything better to look at.
4. In some instances it may be appropriate to stand on an elevation above the audience so that you can be seen. Stand on a box if necessary.

After all the physical barriers that hamper the presentation have been removed, the lecturer must consider what he should do to get the material across most effectively and so keep the attention of the audience. Some suggestions follow.

1. Speak loudly enough for everyone to hear clearly. If the audience has to strain to hear the speaker, it will sooner or later decide that straining is not worth the effort, and it will sound mental "liberty call."

2. Know the material thoroughly, and, above all, practice the lecture beforehand until you are convinced that you can give it well.

3. Use jokes that are appropriate to the subject matter. Laughing is a form of audience participation, and audience participation makes the audience more receptive to the lecture.

4. Ask questions and then answer them. This has a tendency to make the audience participate mentally by thinking of answers.

5. Be relaxed and friendly, and look at individuals in the audience while talking. Being relaxed has a desirable effect that is difficult to describe but nonetheless valuable, and looking at people has a tendency to make them listen.

6. During a lecture it is often appropriate to make motions, such as arm gestures, that will attract attention. Make the action appropriate to the talk.

The main objective in good lecture technique is to keep the audience looking at, and listening to, the lecturer. The material presented may not be very interesting by nature, but much can be done to motivate the audience to listen and learn. The instructor should treat the audience as a group of individuals, not as a mob. And they should be told the purpose of the lecture and how it should benefit them as individuals.

These are the keys to a successful lecture. Each member of the audience is interested primarily in himself, so talk to each one of them!

The Discussion

The discussion is a very useful type of presentation when the students have prior knowledge of the subject. This knowledge may have been gained either from past experience or from a study assignment. A discussion allows maximum participation from the students, and therefore it is enjoyable and conducive to learning. The most effective discussion group contains about fifteen people, but a discussion group can include up to twenty-five students. However, such a large group does not normally allow all students to participate, and unless the instructor is very careful, some of the students will never take part in the discussions.

The instructor usually acts as the discussion leader. He starts the discussion by making a short statement concerning the individual problems to be discussed. At the conclusion of the discussion he summarizes the points and states the solution to the problems that have been arrived at by the group. However, he must be very careful not to impose his own solution on the class without their consent. He may influence the discussion tactfully, but he should never give the appearance of stating his solution as the only one.

Neither should he allow a faulty solution to stand as the accepted one. He should point out the errors as they appear in the discussion if one of the students does not do this. It is most desirable that the students themselves arrive at a correct solution so they will feel that it is theirs and that they are responsible for, and important to, the discussion.

There are several techniques that the instructor should be familiar with in order to keep the discussion going smoothly and spontaneously. First of all, he must motivate the students if they are not already interested in the discussion topic; he must show them why they, as individuals, should want to discuss the topic. After stating the problem and motivating the students, the instructor should call for someone in the group to give a personal opinion on the problem. If no one participates at this point, a student can be called on. This probably will not be necessary if the topic is interesting enough to be the subject of a discussion.

If the discussion should lag on a certain point, and it becomes apparent that no solution will be reached, the instructor should take control, give a solution to the point, and go on to the next point. And if the discussion starts to go astray from the matters under consideration, the instructor should steer it back to the main problem. One effective technique that the leader can use to generate discussion is deliberately to misstate the solution to the problem under discussion. This should lead one of the students to correct the instructor and thus spark further discussion.

The instructor should be studiously careful himself not to embarrass any individual in the group, and equally alert to prevent the group from embarrassing any of its own members. He should attempt to build the ego of the students by allowing them to participate in the discussion to the maximum extent, and he should compliment them for particularly good ideas and comments. One of the most successful devices that can be used is to make sure that the group receives credit where credit is due.

On-the-Job Training

On-the-job training is the type of instruction that is used to great advantage in the service to teach specific jobs. It may or may not be backed up by more formal instruction, depending on the material being taught.

On-the-job training is most useful for teaching skills. The size of the group under instruction is necessarily limited to the number who can physically see and operate the equipment that is the subject of instruction. This usually limits the size of the instruction group to not more than five students.

On-the-job training is necessarily held on the spot where the job is taking place. This limiting condition is likely to be considered disadvantageous when it is compared to the physical conditions the instructor tries to arrange for in most instruction areas. As an example, if the equipment on which the students are being instructed is located in the engine room of a ship, the physical condition there is going to be hot and noisy. Any such disadvantage is more than offset, however, by the amount of interest the students will generate through being able to participate in the actual operation of the equipment.

While it may appear that this type of instruction is strictly informal, the normal amount of preparation and planning is required of the instructor. He must decide how much material to teach in the time available, without covering so much that the students cannot absorb it. He will need a plan so as to present all major points in a logical order without slighting any. The obvious answer, of course, is a lesson plan, just such as is used in more formal instruction. However, the use of a lesson plan, except in the planning stage, may be impractical because of the location of the equipment on which the students are to be instructed.

On-the-job instruction can be used any time the instructor has students near equipment he desires to instruct them about. This can be on watch, at general quarters, or any time people are required to stay in a specific area.

There are four easily remembered methods for on-the-job training.

1. The instructor performs the operation and tells the students what he is doing, step by step.

2. The students tell the instructor the steps to take, and the instructor then performs the manual operations.

3. The students perform the operations while telling the instructor what they are doing.

4. The students perform the operations under actual conditions while the instructor supervises—in other words, they practice under supervision. This last method is very important, as it is here that the student smoothes out his technique and the instructor weeds out faulty responses as they occur.

It is well to emphasize at this time that on-the-job training is the method most often used in the naval service to teach personnel their actual and specific jobs. The officer should realize, however, that it is a type of instructional method and that it requires as much formal planning as any other method. The quality of the instruction is the responsibility of the officer, so he should closely supervise the preparation of his petty officers who will be doing the actual instruction.

Tools for Training

The lesson plan and training aids are tools the instructor uses to put together a presentation so that it runs smoothly and accomplishes the objectives.

The Lesson Plan

A lesson plan is essential to every instruction period. It is the instructor's assurance that he will carry out the plans he has made for his class. The lesson plan

1. maintains proper sequence of presentation
2. prevents omissions
3. serves as a time table
4. gives new instructors confidence
5. can be filed for reference and future use—it eliminates much of the preparation for future presentations on the same subject

The form of a lesson plan is not important. Some units may require that a standard form be used for administrative reasons, but for the instructor's own use, the form that best meets his needs is the most desirable.

The following items are found on most lesson plans used in the naval service:

1. *Heading*, indicating ship or unit.
2. *Date, time*, and *location*.
3. *Instructor's name*.
4. *Title*, which should be an exact description of the lesson.
5. *Objective*, or what the instructor desires to accomplish.
6. *References* from which material has been extracted.
7. *Training aids*, listed by number if standard, or described if nonstandard.
8. *Student assignment*, if any.
9. *Introduction*, including a brief description of the present lesson, its relationship to past and future lessons, and motivation for the trainees.
10. *Presentation*, which is an outline of the material to be presented. This should indicate the length of time to be spent on each main point, the questions to be asked, the demonstrations to be given, the training aids to be used at appropriate places in the lesson, tests to be given, etc.
11. *Summary*, which should include a reemphasis of the main points of the lesson.
12. *Next assignment*, if applicable.

Table 15.1 follows one of many types of lesson plans that can make up a one-hour presentation. The exact format may be specified by the particular command.

Table 15.1. Sample lesson plan, U.S. Navy

	F DIVISION	
2 September 1983	USS *Nimitz*	
	0830–0930	Crew's Lounge
Instructor:	Ens. Marsup, E. L.	
Title:	Instructor training, the lesson plan.	
Objective:	To familiarize petty officers with preparation and use of lesson plans.	
References:	*Shipboard Training Manual*, NAVPERS 90110; *Manual for Navy Instructors*, NAVPERS 16103-B; *Naval Leadership*, U.S. Naval Institute, 1984	

Table 15.1. Sample lesson plan, U.S. Navy (*continued*)

F DIVISION	
Training Aids:	Film MN 7016 (10 minutes), "Preparation and Use of the Lesson Plan"; Blackboard
Student Assignment:	Chap. 6, *Manual for Navy Instructors*; Appendix I, *Shipboard Training Manual*
Introduction: (3 minutes)	"Good morning. As you know, today we are going to study the lesson plan. We saw in our last meeting how to select our presentation method and plan the instruction. The lesson plan is used to record all our planning and assure that we follow it when we give the instruction. A good lesson plan will save you many headaches."
Presentation: (5 minutes)	A. Uses and advantages: 1. Maintains presentation sequence 2. Prevents omissions 3. Controls time 4. Gives confidence 5. Provides future reference
(20 minutes)	B. Form and content: 1. Standard form required by this command a. Illustrated on blackboard 2. Content a. Heading as illustrated b. Location and instructor c. Title and objective d. References, training aids, and assignment e. Introduction: (1) Tie-in (2) Motivation (3) Preview of instruction f. Presentation: (1) Outline of material (2) Time schedule (3) Use of training aids (4) Demonstrations (5) Questions to be asked

Table 15.1. Sample lesson plan, U.S. Navy (*continued*)

	F DIVISION
	g. Summary
	h. Next assignment
(10 minutes)	C. Discussion period:
	1. "Are there any questions?"
	2. Questions to ask students:
	a. "What are the advantages of a lesson plan?"
	b. "What should be contained in the introduction?"
	c. Etc.
(15 minutes)	D. Film:
	1. "Watch for these points in the film:"
	a. "Etc."
	2. Show film.
	3. "Are there any questions?"
Summary: (5 minutes)	A. Uses and advantages:
	1. Etc.
	B. Form and content:
	1. Heading
	2. Etc.
Next Assignment: (2 minutes)	Prepare a 15-minute instruction on use of a piece of equipment in the department.

Training Aids

Training aids are devices used to facilitate learning. The principle behind their use is that the more senses the students use in learning, the more learning that can take place. A training aid permits the instructor to do more than just tell his students what characteristics his subject has. He can let them hear the characteristic, smell it, feel it, and see it, if the object has the capabilities of exciting these senses. But the question arises, "Why not expose the students to the real thing instead of using a training aid?"

If it is practical to use the actual object being studied, the instructor will use the real thing instead of the training aid. But suppose the instructor wants to show the students the characteristics of the F-18 or how corrosion on a ship develops between dissimilar metals. Under most circumstances showing these things would be impractical or impossible because of extreme size, either large or small, or because of danger, invisibility, or extreme speed, either fast or slow. Therefore, when it is not practical to use the real object, a training aid should be used if its use will facilitate learning.

The naval service has many standard training aids, ranging from cardboard signal flashers to training planes. These instructional aids are produced for the Navy by the Naval Training Center and for the Marine Corps by the Training Aids Visual Support Center. Local commands often are able to manufacture needed devices when they are not readily available in the naval service. These training aids are all catalogued and have standard numbers for identification and ease of procurement. Even though all these devices are available, however, the instructor will frequently still prefer to construct his own training aid. The only limitation here is the extent of the instructor's imagination and ingenuity. If he feels that he needs a certain type of training aid to help students learn, and no such aid is available, it should be built.

The training aids most frequently used and most generally available in the naval service are the blackboard, movie projector, closed-circuit TV, overhead projector, and computer.

The blackboard is so simple and obvious that most people never consider it a training aid, but it is. And some instructors use it incorrectly. When he writes on it, the instructor should make his letters large enough for the student farthest away to read clearly. He should write legibly. If he is right-handed, he should face to the left and back up as he writes. This prevents him from blocking the students' view and allows him to see both the students and the blackboard. If the lessons call for complicated drawings, these should be completed on the blackboard before class; or, if it is important for the student to see the drawings developed, these should be outlined on the board in pencil prior to class and then traced in chalk as the lesson develops (pencil writing can be seen up close, but it cannot be seen from a distance). The main points can be accentuated by using colored chalk to draw or describe them.

The movie projector and video tape for closed-circuit TV are training aids that can be found in most units. They are very popular, and rightly so, but they do not solve all training and instructing problems.

The armed forces have vast stores of training films to cover almost any subject that would be approprite to teach a serviceman or servicewoman. These films are listed in the *Navy Film Catalogue* issued by the Naval Photographic Center. The instructor's problem is to find a film or tape that is applicable to the scope of instruction. In making the choice, the instructor must bear in mind, however, that the movie or tape is inflexible and cannot be changed to suit the instruction; it must be presented in exactly the same way every time it is used. For this reason it is not a substitute for good instruction, though it is an addition to it. Thus, a word of caution is necessary because it is so easy to fall into the trap of just showing a training film or tape and assuming that the students have absorbed everything in it.

The proper way to utilize a film or tape is to find one that illustrates the special points the instructor wants to cover. The instructor should preview the film and make notes for its presentation and the main points to be covered.

Before showing the film or tape, the instructor should tell the students just what they are expected to learn and in general what the presentation is about. After the showing, he should hold a discussion and answer any questions that the students have. It is sometimes profitable to re-show a film or tape to the students when it is probable that they will absorb additional knowledge from it. This would apply especially to demonstrations of skills, etc.

The classroom will need some special preparation before the film showing. It must have facilities for making the room reasonably dark. It should be well-ventilated, and the temperature should be comfortable—on the cool side. Additionally, a film or tape should never be shown within an hour after a meal, if it is possible to avoid this, because full stomachs induce sleep—and a sleeping student learns little. When closed-circuit TV is used, an adequate number of sets for easy viewing must be obtained.

The overhead projector is a device for projecting figures from a transparent plate, sheet, or roll onto a screen. Its primary advantage is flexibility, because it can be fitted into the instructor's presentation in so many ways. It is usually available on the larger naval ships and in marine units of battalion size or larger.

The overhead projector has most of the advantages of a blackboard and some additional ones that make it desirable in special situations. Complicated drawings can be produced on sheets of acetate prior to class, and can be projected as needed, thus saving the class time required to produce the drawings on the blackboard. The instructor can sit beside the projector facing the class, and he can write on the roll of acetate built into the machine as he talks, thereby maintaining better eye contact with his students than he can if he has to turn away to write on a blackboard.

The overhead projector can also be used in cases where a blackboard would be too small for all of the trainees to read or see. Normal handwriting can be projected to a size that can be read at distances up to seventy feet. The same darkness that is required by the movie projector is required by the overhead projector. The instructor should remember, however, that he cannot expect to work an overhead projector smoothly into his presentation without practice beforehand.

As there are infinite computer approaches to instructional development, instructors would do well to consult knowledgeable individuals for guidance in making use of a computer in their instructional programs.

The number of other training aids that are available to the instructor is so great that it would require a large book to describe them and their uses. However, the instructor should not use a training aid just because another instructor uses it or because it is available. On the other hand, he should not fail to use training aids for the opposite reasons. He should consider each of the presentation problems in the light of the principles expressed in this book and use such training aids as are necessary to make his instruction more effective.

Summary

Training is one of the most important facets of the junior officer's responsibility to the naval service and its people. It is the officer's duty to ensure that all personnel in the unit are properly trained and that all training within the division is effective. The officer must use all of the available resources to make the training meaningful to the trainees, and he must teach petty officers and noncommissioned officers to be competent instructors.

For, after all, it is the instructor who translates all training plans into action. If one fails, the program fails. To get results, the instructor must motivate students by giving them a reason for learning and must present the material in such a way that the students will understand it, absorb it, and maintain interest in it.

There are a number of proven presentation methods, teaching practices, and instructor techniques that may be used to fulfill a mission.

The basic presentation methods are: the recitation, the lecture, the discussion, and on-the-job instruction. There is some overlap in these methods, and they are usually used in combinations to produce the desired results. The case-study method is described in chapter 19.

Any good instruction period can only be a result of much prior planning and rehearsal. These plans are recorded in the lesson plan so that the instructor will be sure to carry them out in the way intended.

The instructor frequently uses a training aid to help students to learn. The training aid makes learning easier and more effective by employing additional senses. Many standard training aids are issued; others can be constructed by the instructor. The only limitation or qualification of what is to be used is that it helps the student to learn and is economically feasible.

In conclusion, it need only be said that the state of training determines the state of effectiveness of our naval service. Therefore, it behooves all officers and senior enlisted to emphasize training and to ensure that their personnel are as well trained as possible.

16

Organization and Administration

Organization is the tool with which the commander performs command functions, while administration is the operation and manipulation of the organization. Naval organization establishes the channels and levels of command through which the various units, commands, and large shore-based activities are administered. Organization, administration, and command leadership are inseparably interwoven. Not one of these can exist long without the other two. An organization without adequate leadership is only a hollow shell, and administration can be inefficient if it is based on an unsound organizational structure or on poor leadership.

Organization

Leadership and organization are inseparable because a leader accomplishes his job through an organization. An early instance of the need for an organization is to be found in Exodus 18:20–23, wherein Jethro, father-in-law of Moses, counsels Moses, leader of the Tribes of Israel:

> And thou shalt teach them ordinances and laws, and shalt show them the way wherein they must walk, and the work they must do. Moreover thou shalt provide out of all the people able men, such as fear God, men of truth, hating covetousness; and place such over them to be rulers of thousands, and rulers of hundreds, rulers of fifties, and rulers of tens: And let them judge the people at all seasons: and it shall be, that every great matter they shall bring unto thee, but every small matter they shall judge: so shall it be easier for thyself, and they shall bear the burden with thee. If thou shalt do this thing, and God command thee so, then thou shalt be able to endure, and all this people shall also go to their place in peace.

This was singularly good advice, covering as it did rules and regulations, laws, work, official channels ("the way wherein they must walk"), qualifications for subordinate leaders, the span of control, the levels at which decisions should be made, and sharing the burden of leadership so that the leader might endure and all might dwell in peace.

In considering the development of an organizational structure, it should be remembered that an organization must be flexible, and that flexibility often results from a series of compromises made primarily because of the particular mission of the organization. An organizational structure represents the activities of people who react and respond to stimuli from both within and outside the organizations.

Principles of Organization

The new officer will find that the naval organizational structure has been well established and has been tested with time, but an understanding of the basic principles of organization which go into establishing an organizational structure should be well understood. The twelve principles of organization discussed below have been accepted in the armed forces as being highly valid in any organization.

Every task necessary to accomplish the assigned mission or objective of a command must be assigned to a unit or element of that command for accomplishment. This requires the use of imagination and an analysis of responsibilities to ensure that all tasks will be accomplished without overlapping functions.

Responsibilities and tasks assigned to units and members of the organization must be specific, clear-cut, and well understood. Adherence to this principle prevents confusion in lines of authority and ensures that everyone clearly understands the nature of his job and the steps necessary and authorized to perform that job. Organizational directives, orders, and manuals should be checked periodically to assure that they adhere to this principle.

No task is assigned to more than one unit or individual for accomplishment. This principle prevents overlapping responsibilities, which causes confusion and delays in carrying out assigned tasks. This principle is most frequently violated by individuals who assign the same task to different people with the idea that one of them will be certain to accomplish it. This practice is basically unsound, as it lowers the morale and prestige of the individuals involved and leads to half-hearted performance of tasks assigned.

The same organizational structure should be used throughout the command. Standard organization within each division of a unit, exemplified by a standard ship organization, is highly desirable. Broken down to the division level, it means that each division aboard ship should use the same organizational structure except where obvious deviations are necessary to carry out the assigned task of the division.

Each member of an organization must know to whom he reports and who reports to him. Adherence to this principle eliminates confusion resulting from conflicting orders and dual responsibilities.

No member of an organization reports to more than one supervisor unless there is careful coordination between supervisors. The results of violations of this principle are obvious.

The responsibility to perform a task must be matched with the authority necessary to ensure its accomplishment. Nothing is more frustrating to an individual with an assigned task than to have to check continually with the supervisor for authority to carry out procedures to accomplish the task.

No commander or individual has more units or persons reporting directly to him than he can effectively coordinate and direct. Violation of this principle (the span of control) results in lowering of the morale and efficiency of a unit because of the slowing down of necessary work. Also, ideas will stagnate on the desk of a supervisor or commander who feels the duty personally to review and comment on every detail of his organization.

The normal chain of line command is not violated by staff members. This principle sets forth the basic idea that the staff of a commander must work directly through the units in the chain of command in the name of the commander, and that the staff should never bypass the unit commander and work directly with corresponding members of unit organizations. This does not imply, however, that division head or staff members may not confer directly with one another in an advisory capacity or on an informal basis.

Authority and responsibility for action must be delegated to the lowest possible level commensurate with the personnel available and qualified to assume such authority and responsibility. This calls for maximum decentralization, as long as the necessary policy control and standardization of procedures are not lost in the process.

Senior officers should exercise control through policy rather than through detailed procedures. Again, violation of this principle implies attention to too much detail on the part of the commander. Authority to act on all matters not involving policy must be delegated to subordinates.

Organizations should be as simply constructed as the tasks assigned the unit will permit. Organization and procedures should never become so cumbersome as to obstruct the effective accomplishment of the assigned tasks of the missions.

Checklist for Evaluating an Organizational Plan

The following checklist can be used to evaluate any organizational plan before or after its implementation.

1. Are all the functions that are necessary to accomplish the objectives of the command provided?
2. Are any unnecessary functions that should be eliminated provided?
3. Are the functions, responsibilities, relationships, and authority of each unit of organization clearly defined?
4. Are the functions assigned to the proper unit, and are they grouped properly within that unit?
5. Is there duplication or overlapping of functions, responsibilities, or authority between units of the organization?
6. Is authority commensurate with responsibility?
7. Is the organizational structure in the simplest form capable of fulfilling the requirements of the command?
8. Is the organization properly balanced? Are too many units responsible to one individual?
9. Are the functions, duties, responsibilities, and authority delegated in such a manner that definite accountability for operating results can be established?
10. Does the organization lend itself to internal checks and controls?
11. Are titles and other organizational nomenclature clearly descriptive, and are they used consistently?
12. Have individuals been selected to fit the organizational plan, or has the plan been made to fit the individuals?

Organizational Charts

It is necessary to prepare organizational charts that show the command relationships—who is directly under whom. As it is manifestly impossible to indicate the entire organization on one chart, sometimes whole booklets of charts are necessary to cover the entire organization, just as in the case of blueprints for a ship or a house. Each chart should be captioned and numbered for ready reference.

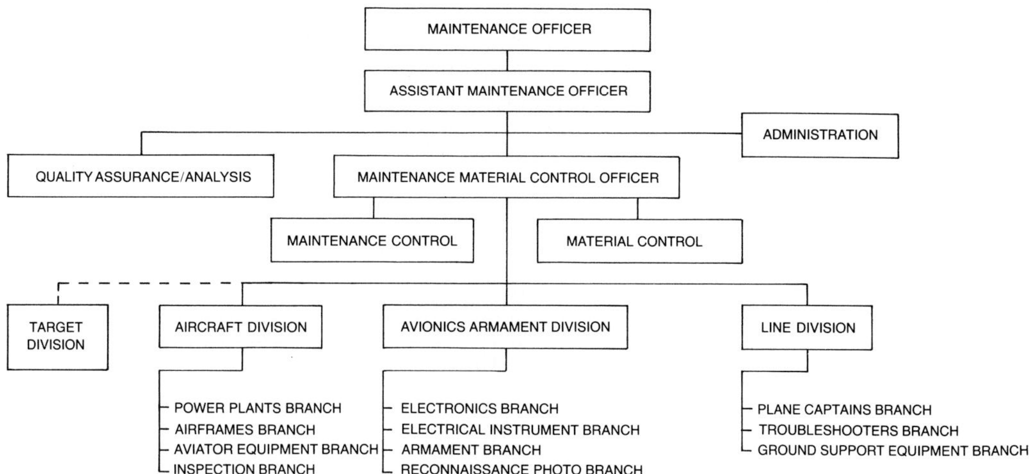

Figure 16.1. Organizational chart: Squadron Maintenance Department

In organizational charts, the title of the office, not the name of the person occupying it, is used (for example, "Executive Officer," not "Major Jones"), and each office is usually represented by a rectangle, properly labeled. Slightly below the head officer's rectangle, and abreast of each other, are the boxes representing the offices directly under the head office, and a little farther down are the boxes representing the third echelon. Subsequent echelons are similarly drawn and stepped down from the one above it, space permitting. Usually all the offices shown on the same echelon are considered to be of equal, or approximately equal, rank. These rectangles then are connected by lines to indicate their relationships; solid lines are used to indicate full control, dotted, dashed, broken, or thin lines to indicate partial or special control.

Chain of Command

The captain of a ship, or commanding officer, is at the head of the ship's organization. Directly under him is his "aide and executive officer," who is generally referred to as the XO. All persons in the ship who are subject to the orders of the commanding officer are subject to the orders of the executive officer just as if these orders emanated directly from the commanding officer, and access to the commanding officer is normally obtained through the executive officer. Exceptions are the operations officer, navigator, and officer-of-the-deck, all of whom have direct and immediate access to the commanding officer in navigational and tactical matters. The commanding officer may, of course, confer directly with his department heads on matters directly affecting operations, but the executive officer should be kept informed of the matters discussed.

One echelon below the executive officer are the heads of departments: operations, navigation, gunnery or deck, engineering, medical, supply, air (in carriers), and repair (in tenders). Each of these has one or more divisions, which in turn may be divided into sections or other units, and these may be even further subdivided.

From the lowest office in the organization, no matter who occupies it, there is a sequence of direct contact extending up to the commanding officer. This is often referred to as the official channel, or the "chain of command." Requests and information flow up and orders and information flow down.

Using the chain of command. Except under extraordinary circumstances all business is accomplished via this chain of command. As in the Biblical example, "every great matter" is sent up to the commanding officer for decision, but "every small matter" is judged at a lower level—the lower, the better. In this way the commanding officer is kept from being overwhelmed by a multitude of minor details, perhaps to the extent that he cannot deal with a "great matter" when he is faced with one.

Administration

Administration means "management," "control," "direction"—the exercise of the executive functions. It is important to differentiate clearly between organization and administration; the first is an instrument, the second is the method of using this instrument. The first is a form; the second is a mode of action—it is work itself.

One of the most important lessons learned through war is that modern military operations require excellent administrative support for their success. Otherwise the necessarily complex and widespread activities cannot be performed—or at least not in time. And if they are late, they are usually of little value. That is why it is necessary to have large fleet and force staffs on shore. The administration of a vast and far-flung operation could not be carried on efficiently in the confined space and facilities of a ship at sea.

Almost every duty, from piping sweepers to holding target practice and maneuvers, to a large degree is administrative. The work of officers at our great shore establishments, whether shipyards or command or other stations, is at least 90 percent administration.

The defects in organization may be covered by good administration, but no organization, however good, can escape the penalties of bad administration. Commanders may issue regulations and orders forever, but unless administration sees to their proper execution, they are futile. Administration, then, is one of the most important elements of leadership. No officer who fails to comprehend and apply its principles is a sufficiently capable leader, or officer.

The dominating principle of administration is cooperation to obtain the objective under a sole directing plan and impulse. The central object of administration is coordination. This is obtained by ensuring a common knowledge of the objective by all concerned; a common knowledge of the plan for attaining the objective on the part of the coordinating parts of the organization; the maintenance of discipline; the enforcement of efficient work; and a general spirit of loyalty.

Successful administration depends on certain underlying conditions that emanate from the spirit of the administrator. Successful administration is indicated by not only the leader's general bearing toward subordinates and his manner of approaching the functions of discipline and inspections, but also the consistency in personal conduct and the administrative control of others. At all times everyone should know what can and what cannot be done, what is expected and what someone else will do. Then each individual can adapt accordingly.

The Naval and Marine Corps Officer as an Administrator

Once the organization has been established and the personnel have been selected for the different echelons of responsibility, the organization begins to function. The officer, as the head of an organization, acts as an administrator and will spend the greatest amount of his time in the naval service in this role. As an administrator, the officer will be concerned with the clothing, feeding, pay, training, education, family problems, mail, recreation, liberty, leave, reward and punishment of the subordinates. While the officer may have no direct responsibility for many of these items, the conditions surrounding some of them may be improved by his constantly observing these things closely to ensure that the personnel are getting the best possible care in every instance.

All the points mentioned have a great bearing on the mental and spiritual well-being of every person of the command. If, through close attention to these and other details concerning them, the officer shows his subordinates that he has their best interests at heart, they will have confidence in and respect for their leader. Through sincere interest in the welfare of the subordinates the leader will come to know them intimately and to learn which of them are the more dependable. From this will develop the mutual respect and understanding that is so essential to successful handling of personnel in the service of their country.

Unfortunately, some officers feel that their job is done when they have trained their subordinates in their technical duties, and that the administrative details should be supervised by a senior subordinate. But, in order to be aware of those administrative details which affect the daily performance of his personnel, the officer must actively supervise the administration of such details, although their actual accomplishment should be delegated to the petty officers, noncommissioned officers, or other juniors. In his role of administrator, the junior officer will be required to supervise the work of his personnel.

The naval officer supervises primarily through policy, procedure, and personal supervision. This last—personal supervision—will fall principally within the province of the junior officer.

Policy

Policy is a statement of the broad objectives established by a senior which permit subordinates to exercise good judgment, ability, and initiative in making the decisions necessary to achieve the assigned missions of their units. Policy statements from a commander should form the basis for governing future actions of subordinates, and they should be of a continuing nature, changing only by gradual evolution dictated primarily by changes in the assigned mission of the commander. Their primary purpose is to sanction in advance the action to be taken in repetitive situations.

Policy, therefore, ensures uniformity of action with a minimum of supervision. Control through policy permits a much greater degree of delegation and provides the basis for evaluating the performance of subordinates. If the personnel have been indoctrinated with an intelligent singleness of purpose, the need for review of actions taken within an established policy is minimized.

Procedure

Procedure determines who will engage in a given task, what the responsibilities will be, and in what order action will be taken. By establishing a procedure, the proper control is simplified and reduced to routine.

Procedures should be reviewed periodically to ensure that those in effect are still necessary and have not become obsolete with changing events.

Personal Supervision

This involves proper delegation of authority, planning of routine work and drills, and control through adequate inspections. It is not enough that proper instructions for work be given; the officer must be sure that the completed work has been done to his own satisfaction and that of his seniors.

Keep hands off. The senior should never do a job that has been assigned to an officer or enlisted person in the organization, as long as the subordinate is doing it to the senior's satisfaction. If the individual assigned the task cannot do it, someone who can do it should be assigned the task, and the former worker should be told why he has been replaced.

The junior officer may observe a few direct violations of this axiom after his arrival, but he must realize the importance of keeping hands off the work that has already been delegated to a competent petty officer and he must resist the temptation to don dungarees and climb into the crankcase to help a chief machinist's mate remove a wiped bearing. By such actions on the part of the junior officer, the petty officer is relieved of his responsibilities and the petty officer's prestige is lowered in the eyes of his men. In addition, the officer leaves the petty officer with the feeling that the officer does not have confidence in his ability, and the efficiency of his work thereafter will almost surely drop. Worse still, by concentrating on one detail of the job, the junior officer decreases the supervision over the rest of the organization. The junior officer should always remember that the job of a leader is one of assuming responsibilities and exercising supervision; it is not a job that requires him to assume the role of a "busybody."

Define jobs and responsibilities. When a young officer assumes control of his first organization, he will doubtless believe that the duties and responsibilities of each of the personnel have already been clearly defined. True, general duties and responsibilities have been defined, but real leadership requires that the organization be constantly adapted to changing needs. It may be that the gunner's mate will come up and complain that he is unable to load ordnance because the chief boatswain's mate has all hands chipping paint on the forecastle and won't let them go. Or it may be any one of a thousand similar situations. The officer will do well to eliminate the cause before the trouble starts by seeing that his men, particularly the subordinates, know their duties and the limits of their responsibilities.

In doing this, he must make sure that no man serves two masters if this can possibly be avoided. Dual duties and responsibilities inevitably lead to trouble. In other words, the chain of command must be kept clear of extraneous cross links to another chain in another part of the organization.

Elicit ideas. An officer can easily get suggestions from the subordinates, but he must let them know the suggestions are wanted. And he must be prepared to screen ideas without dampening the enthusiasm of the personnel. This requires considerable diplomacy and time, for the leader must make clear to each person why his idea cannot be used. In this connection, it must be remembered that many ideas, when they are first presented, may not appear to be very good. Therefore, the officer must be careful not to reject a new thought until there has been ample time to consider it and discuss it with others. It is a good plan never to accept or reject an idea when it is first presented. The officer should question the suggestor until he has a complete picture of the suggestion on the subject, and then he should reserve judgment until he has had time for further consideration of the project.

The young officer may wonder just how he should go about persuading personnel to come to him with their ideas. First, he should tell them at quarters what his policy in the matter is, and then he should show a keen interest in their ideas and in their work. This is all there is to it. There is no reason why every good idea for improvement should not be utilized if every officer would follow these simple rules.

Be available. Since leadership is primarily the art of influencing human behavior, a leader cannot afford to be cut off from contact with his followers. If that occurs, they will follow someone else. During the French Revolution one of its leaders was sitting at a table in a sidewalk cafe, having a drink with a friend, when he saw a mob come running down the street. Excusing himself to his friend, he said, "There goes my following. I must run and get in front of them!"

Leadership is not something to be practiced from an ivory tower. The leader should be available for consultation by his subordinates at certain established times each day for routine business, and seldom should he be where he cannot be reached in an emergency. There are few things more annoying to most personnel than being unable to see the boss when they need to. When the boss has to be chased in order to be seen, routine matters assume the air of emergencies—and emergencies become crises. It is not necessary for an officer to announce that he has an open-door policy. Rather, by visiting subordinates in their working areas and listening to their comments, he will make it clear he is interested in the comments of others.

Delegating Authority

Empowering a subordinate to act for a senior, and normally without making reference to the senior, is known as "delegating" authority. Since a leader cannot personally do everything that is required, maximum use should be made of this principle. It gives the leader some freedom and, in addition, is excellent training for the subordinates. What, when, and to whom to delegate requires sound judgment born of knowledge and experience.

Delegating to others the authority to perform certain tasks for a senior does not relieve that senior of the responsibility to superiors for their successful accomplishment. "I delegated that to so-and-so!" is not a satisfactory explanation of a bungled job. The delegating officer can rightfully hold the person to whom he entrusted the task responsible, but he himself will similarly be held responsible and accountable by the superior who gave it to him.

Certain tasks, however, can never be delegated. A commanding officer, for instance, is prohibited from delegating to a subordinate the authority to inflict punishments authorized by the Uniform Code of Military Justice.

Bypassing

Shortcutting by skipping one or more persons in the chain of command is known as "bypassing." Any person in the naval service has the right to communicate directly with any subordinate, bypassing whoever he wishes in doing so, but this right should never be exercised *except in emergencies*. First, the bypassed persons will feel that they do not have the confidence of their senior, and they may harbor resentment, up and down. Second, it may make them hesitant to act in a similar situation in the future. ("Didn't the boss handle that without reference to me last time?" they may remind themselves.) Third, the senior officer is not helping the subordinates by doing their work for them. They can be instructed and guided as necessary, but they should never be cut. Fourth, the senior should be training himself for higher, not lower, command.

In an emergency the officer having the responsibility should by all means act, but when time permits, circumstances should be explained to anyone who has been bypassed in the process. But if it is necessary to bypass a junior in order to accomplish a purely routine task, then the leader has an obligation to himself, to the junior, and to the naval service to relieve the junior of his duties. But in any other circumstance, nothing will so effectively destroy the command organization as the practice of bypassing.

Reversing the process and bypassing a senior or two is likely to have unpleasant consequences—except, of course, in emergencies. First, there are few more damning things that can be said of a person than that he does not know what is going on in his outfit—and that is the position the bypassed senior will be put in. Second, the bypassed person might himself have been able to act favorably on the matter, or the commanding officer might wish to know his opinion or recommendation before taking action. In an emergency, a junior officer should unhesitatingly act—but he should be equally prompt to inform his bypassed seniors immediately afterward.

Cooperation

It is essential to efficiency and harmony in the organization that there be hearty cooperation among all units. Settling disputes is generally a time-consuming and fruitless task, pleasing to no one.

Human beings are not small rectangles on a chart, just labeled and connected by lines. Some persons never quite fill a job, and others habitually overflow theirs and assume additional functions; very few fit the requirements of a position exactly. A certain amount of give and take is usually necessary.

Planning

The efficient administration of the organization requires that the leader make the most of time. Time is always passing and never returns, and it can be wasted just as energy and materials are wasted. It is lost through poor planning, poor instruction, and procrastination.

Victor Hugo put it well by observing that whoever plans the transactions of the day, and follows out that plan, carries a thread that will guide him through the maze of the most busy life. But where no plan is made, where the disposal of time is surrendered merely to the chance of incidence, chaos will soon reign.

In planning any work, the officer should use the time and ability of subordinates as much as possible. A written plan should be made wherever it can help in the performance of assigned duties. The senior should never do the work that others in the same organization should be doing, but he should attempt to eliminate all unnecessary details from the supervisor's load.

Much time can be lost if subordinates are not given proper instructions. Men have reported to wrong ships, ships have gone to wrong piers, truckloads of equipment have gone to wrong cities, just because some senior took it for granted that the subordinate knew what to do. The only way to prevent this is for the senior to give his instructions clearly and simply. An excellent practice is to have subordinates repeat the orders they have been given. In this manner the leader not only determines whether the subordinate understands orders, but also learns his own capabilities in giving orders. It should never be taken for granted that a subordinate knows his instructions. Repetition is a minor annoyance when compared to the error of misdirection.

Procrastination is the thief of time. It is based on the theory that you can "put off until tomorrow what you should do today." For the officer who follows this practice, paper work soon becomes a mountainous obstacle never to be overcome. The papers on the desk pile higher and higher, and the worry and mental strain of the situation become tremendous. The officer must determine to do today's work today. It is a satisfying feeling for an officer to know, when he leaves the ship at night, that everything is cleared up and ready to go in the morning. The officer who practices this procedure will be more efficient and better thought of by seniors as well as by juniors.

Inspections

One of the important duties of an officer, from senior to junior, is housekeeping. This is accomplished primarily through routine personal inspections. "A place for everything and everything in its place" is the motto that housekeepers have followed for centuries. In time of peace, housekeeping may take on the appearance of "spit and polish" routine to inspecting officers, so the officer should explain to personnel and impress on them the value of cleanliness to battle efficiency. Ships have been lost because damage control equipment was missing from its place at a critical time. Men have been trapped below decks in sinking ships because of clothing left carelessly adrift to tangle their legs, or because emergency battle lamps were not tested or replaced. Fires have spread from compartment to compartment because of dust in ventilation lines or paint on threads of critical cut-out valves. Through years of war experience the navy has learned that the ship that stays afloat and fights is the one that pays complete attention to details of cleanliness and stowage. This same attention to cleanliness is important to the Marine Corps, where weapons, vehicles, and other equipment are adversely affected by dirt.

Personal cleanliness and neatness of appearance also have a bearing on military efficiency. The neat, clean individual is the one who insists on neatness and cleanliness in living quarters. He is also the person who, if wounded in action, stands the least chance of infection from dirty skin or clothing. That person will have a lifejacket, first-aid kit, knife, and flashlight always available in emergency situations. Moreover, the clean ship with a clean crew is a happy ship, for few people enjoy living in dirt or disorder.

Maintaining a high standard of cleanliness and orderliness requires a great deal of effort on the part of the officer in charge. Routine inspections of personnel at quarters should be carefully carried out with words of praise and encouragement given to those who look well or have shown improvement in their personal appearance. When formal inspections are held, the officer should make certain that every person and every piece of equipment is carefully scrutinized. There is nothing that will destroy the value of inspections as quickly as announcing an inspection and then carrying it out halfheartedly, or not at all. When a man has gone to great pains to clean up himself and his equipment, he wants to be inspected, and he will soon become indifferent and disinterested if he is not.

In addition, the officer should make frequent and unannounced inspections of the living spaces and equipment assigned to the unit so that orderliness and preparedness will become habitual rather than performances that are staged especially for the inspector.

Many officers think that to inspect means to find fault with what has not been done. This is only a small part of the value of inspections. A simple rule to follow which will do much to increase the pride people take in themselves and their work is to commend them for the things they have done well before pointing out the things that they have not done as well as they should have.

Typical of this is the case of a seaman apprentice who was assigned duty as a compartment cleaner. At every inspection the division officer did nothing but find fault with the individual's work. At first the compartment cleaner worked very hard to correct the faults, and then he waited for the officer to notice and say something about the improvement. However, this never happened, and the officer continued to find fault, no matter how hard the person worked. So the seaman finally said, "It doesn't make any difference whether I clean the compartment or not. I always get bawled out, so I won't bother to clean it up anymore." The officer, petty officer, or noncommissioned officer must learn to reward subordinates' efforts with words of praise and encouragement if he is expecting a better job.

Public praise should be given to personnel who have exceptionally clean compartments or outstanding personal appearances, and appropriate commendation entries should also be made in their service records. Subpar performances should be carefully investigated, the reasons determined, and necessary steps taken to correct the deficiency. However, the officer should avoid, if possible, any form of public censure or disciplinary measure, and should rely primarily on explanation and precept to remedy the situation.

Summary

Organization must be as flexible and as simple as the mission to be accomplished will permit. The major part of an officer's noncombatant duties are concerned with administration. In the naval service, an established organization is administered by capable leaders who, to ensure performance of routine administrative details, must actively control the organization by the assignment of responsibilities and the delegation of authority to juniors in the chain of command.

17

Leadership and the Code of the U.S. Fighting Force

The backwash of the Korean War left the average American a little stunned over what had happened to our prisoners of war in Korea. What sinister thing was it that had brought about the most extensive collaboration with the enemy since the Civil War? What force was strong enough to make our servicepeople fail to live up to the Code of Conduct of the U.S. Fighting Force? Misconceptions of the conduct of American prisoners of war (POWs) in Korea are abundant. For the most part these are based on erroneous generalities and deductions. For a fuller understanding of today's prisoner of war problem, background knowledge of the past is essential. History has established precedents that provide the knowledge necessary to shed light on preparation for the future.

Historical Background

Ancient man and his barbarian descendent usually annihilated or enslaved captured foemen. In time it occurred to the conqueror to hold a captured headman or leader as hostage. (Such a victim was Lot, who, according to Scripture, in perhaps the earliest recorded prisoner rescue, was freed by the forces of Abraham.) But the vanquished of the ancient world usually faced extermination, as this passage in the book of Samuel testifies: "Thus saith the Lord of Hosts . . . go and smite Amalek and utterly destroy all they have, and spare them not." Saul was considered disobedient because he took a few Amalekite prisoners. Six centuries later, Hemocritus of Syracuse was exiled for refusing to slaughter all Athenian captives.

The conscience of mankind found voice in India in the Code of Manu (about 200 B.C.). The Hindu warrior was enjoined to do no injury to the defenseless or to the subdued enemy.

Less humane, the Romans sported with their war prisoners, often using them for target practice or gladiatorial shows. Captives were tortured for public amusement. Enslaved warriors rowed Caesar's naval galleys to North Africa and Britain; those who could no longer pull an oar were killed. "Slay, and slay on!" Germanicus ordered his Rhineland invaders. "Do not take prisoners! We will have no peace until all are destroyed." Thumbs sometimes went up for the valiant foreign gladiator or the stalwart warrior who begged no quarter, and mercy to the conquered foe was usually granted on a whim.

Chivalry, the concept of "Do unto others as you would have them do unto you" developed in the Western World with the rise of Christian civilization. In the Middle Ages, warfare among the common soldiers remained savage, but the codes of chivalry served to temper the warrior knight's steel. The true knight refused to slay for slaughter's sake. Conquering, he could be merciful to a gallant opponent. His prisoner was not a plaything for sadistic entertainment.

If the chivalric code was sometimes more honored in the breach than in the observance, the ideal, the Golden Rule, was there. It often was threatened by intolerant ideologies and the fanaticism that fosters atrocities. Cruel pogroms and religious wars bloodied medieval Europe. The Islamic conquests were savage. Woe to the unbeliever captured by the stepsons of Abu Bekr! But even as it clashed with the sword, the scimitar acquired tempering. Possessed of his own code, the Moslem warrior could appreciate gallantry.

The Christian knight was called on to assume the obligations of noblesse oblige. Warrior or liegeman, facing battle, was pledged to remain true to his king or cause, even if he was captured. Under any circumstance, treason would merit retributive punishment. Treachery, the disclosure of a trust, or the deliverance of a friend to the enemy, was perfidious—the mark of Judas the Betrayer. Thus, rules for the fighting man in combat or in captivity were linked to knightly concepts of duty, honor, loyalty to friend, and gallantry to foe.

At some time during the Crusades a rule evolved regarding what a prisoner could divulge under interrogation. The captive knight was permitted to divulge his name and rank, admissions made necessary by the game of ransom. In Europe during the seventeenth century, the concept emerged that prisoners of war were in the custody of the capturing sovereign or state. No rules for their treatment had yet been formulated, but they were protected from servitude and personal revenge. During the eighteenth century, captivity was considered a means of preventing the prisoners from returning to their own or allied forces to fight again. This was a step forward. Military prisoners were no longer to be considered guilty of crimes against the captor's state.

During the Revolutionary War, in order to discourage desertion, the United States established the death penalty for prisoners who took up arms in the service of the enemy after their capture. No amnesty was granted to those who deserted to the enemy. This was the first American definition of required prisoner conduct.

During the U.S. Civil War, there was some regression in the treatment afforded prisoners. This was induced by the fact that about 3,200 Federals, prisoners of the Confederate forces, joined the Confederate armies; and about 5,400 Confederates, prisoners of the Federal forces, joined the Federal armies. Prisoner conduct was mentioned in War Department General Order no. 207 on 3 July 1863. This order provided that it was the duty of a prisoner of war to escape. Apparently this order was intended to curb the widespread practice of surrender and subsequent parole in order to escape further combatant service. Prosecution for misconduct was based on three criteria: misconduct where there was no duress or coercion, active participation in combat against Federal forces, and failure to return voluntarily.

Nine years after the Civil War ended, a declaration establishing the rights of prisoners was drafted by the Congress of Brussels of 1874. It was signed by fifteen nations, none of which, however, ratified the agreement. The Hague Convention of 1907 established further rules concerning captivity in war, and was complemented by the Geneva Conventions of 1929 and 1949. The United States signed and ratified all three of these conventions without reservation. The conventions set forth in detail the rights and protections that should be afforded prisoners taken from the enemy forces, but they do not specifically prescribe the conduct that a power may require of its own personnel who become prisoners. This is rightly left for prescription by sovereign powers.

There are several provisions of the conventions which do require specific conduct. Prisoners of war are subject to the laws, regulations, and orders in force within the armed forces of the detaining power. Although all of the U.S. services had regulations, the U.S. Armed Forces have never had a clearly defined code of conduct applicable to American prisoners after capture. While there were piecemeal legal restrictions and regulations, there was no comprehensive codification. Despite this lack of a definitive system of rules, American troops have demonstrated throughout all wars that they do not surrender easily—they have never surrendered in large numbers—and that they conduct themselves generally well when they are made prisoners of war.

The Korean Conflict

In the undeclared war in Korea, the motives of the United States were simple and just. The causes of the war, the objectives of the United Nations, the need for United States intervention, and the objectives of the United States were not clearly understood by the public. The Communists attempted to exploit this condition to the fullest in international propaganda and in dealing with prisoners of war.

The Korean War had three aspects. There was the Soviet-contrived civil war aspect—supposedly, North Koreans fighting South Koreans for control of a divided country. There was the collective aspect—the first United Nations endeavor to stop a treaty-breaking aggressor. And there was the cold war aspect—the Western powers blocking expansion of Communist imperialism.

During the Korean War 7,190 Americans were captured by the enemy: 6,656 were army troops; 263 were air force men; 231 were marines; 40 were navy men. The army bore the heaviest burden of prisoner losses.

The captives were marched to twenty prison camps in the North Korean interior. The first, and often the worst, ordeal the prisoner had to suffer was the march to one of these camps. The North Koreans frequently tied a prisoner's hands behind his back or bound his arms with wire. Wounded prisoners were jammed into trucks that jolted, dripping blood, along broken roads. Many of the wounded received no medical attention until they reached the camp. Some were not attended to until days thereafter.

The marching prisoners were liable to be beaten or kicked to their feet if they fell. A number of the North Korean officers were bullwhip barbarians, products of a semiprimitive environment. Probably they had never heard of the Geneva Conventions or any other code of war. The worst of this breed were responsible for the murder of men who staggered out of line or collapsed at the roadside. They were particularly brutal to South Korean captives. Evidence indicates that many ROK prisoners were forced to dig their own graves before they were shot (an old oriental custom in the execution of criminals). Some Americans, with hands tied behind their backs, were shot by the enemy.

So the journeys to the prison camps were "death marches," especially in the winter of 1950–51, when the trails were knee-deep in snow and polar winds flogged the toiling column. On one of these marches, 700 men were headed north. Before the camp was reached, 500 men had perished.

Prisoner of War Camps

The prisoner of war camps in Korea were generally no better or no worse than might be expected of camps located in a remote corner of Asia. Unlike the Chinese and Koreans, who were inured to a rice diet, the average American did badly on such fare. He was plagued with long sieges of sickness and dysentery. The weather was abnormally cold or hot. Water was often scarce, bathing became difficult, and barracks were foul and unsanitary. In the worst of the camps, the prisoners existed by the skin of their teeth and raw courage alone. Men in the "bad" camps were known to lose fifty pounds in a matter of weeks.

The "bad" camps included the so-called "Bean Camp" near Suan, a camp known as "Death Valley" near Pukchong, and another camp called "The Valley," apparently in the vicinity of Kanggye. Among the worst camps were the "Interrogation Center" near Pukchong and a neighboring disciplinary center called "The Caves."

"The Caves" was literally composed of caverns in which the men were confined. Here they were forced to sleep without blankets. Their food was thrown at them. They had no latrine facilities. In "The Caves" the prisoners were reduced to a degree of misery and degradation almost unimaginable. Those sent to "The Caves" were prisoners accused of insubordination, breaking camp rules, attempting to escape, or committing other so-called crimes. The testimony of survivors suggests that the "crime" was seldom fitted by the punishment. Some men who refused to talk to military interrogators were threatened with, or sent to, "The Caves."

Possibly the worst camp endured by American prisoners of war in Korea was the one known as "Pak's Palace." This was a highly specialized interrogation center located near the city of Pyongyang. The place was a brickyard flanked by Korean houses. It was a North

Korean establishment dominated by a chief interrogator, Colonel Pak. Pak was ably assisted by a henchman who came to be called "Dirty Pictures" Wong by the prisoners.

Prisoner of War Interrogation

The "Palace" wanted military information. Coercion was used to obtain it. To the surprise of some U.S. prisoners at the "Palace," the interrogation team would sometimes open up with a wild political harangue. Then came the word that the enemy had established a system of indoctrination courses. The prisoner might react to the indoctrination by a hostile attitude—and be punished by restricted rations and other privations. If he began to show the "proper spirit"—that is, to cooperate with his captors—he was lectured and handed Communist literature. A docile prisoner who read the literature, and listened politely to the lectures, was graduated to a better class. Finally he might be sent to "Peaceful Valley." In this lenient camp the food was relatively good. Prisoners might even have tobacco. And here they were given all sorts of Marxian propaganda. The graduates from "Peaceful Valley" and others who accepted Communist schooling were called "Progressives." Prisoners who refused to go along with the program often remained in tougher circumstances. They were considered "Reactionaries."

To obtain military information, the Communists also would question the prisoner on his home life and educational background. The interrogator would make him put this information in writing, produce a biographical sketch. Seldom did this brief autobiography prove sufficient. The prisoner was usually compelled to write more, and in greater detail. If his literary efforts were painful, the discomfort was only a beginning. His autobiography was used against him. The slightest discrepancy was used to accuse him of lying. He might discover eventually that, in his efforts to explain the discrepancy, he had written a confession of some kind.

The enemy followed no rigid system for dealing with those who refused to cooperate. Rather, his treatment of prisoners was capricious. Sometimes he showed contempt for the man who readily submitted to bullying. The prisoner who stood up to the bluster, threats, and blows of an interrogator might be dismissed with a shrug and sent to relatively mild quarters—if any prison barracks in North Korea could be described as mild.

All in all, the docile prisoner did not gain much by his docility—and sometimes he gained nothing. The prisoner who defied Pak and his breed might take a beating, but again, he might not. The ordeal was never easy. But things were not easy, either, for the combat troops battling out there in the trenches.

Failure of Leadership

The POW "political" schools in North Korea were, of course, patterned after the Soviet Russian design. They were part of a mass program to spread Marxian ideology and gain converts for international communism. The "Progressives" among the prisoners were called on to deliver lectures to, write pamphlets for, and make propaganda broadcasts to other prisoners. Progressive leaders were sent among reactionary groups to harangue the men. They wrote speeches condemning capitalism and "American aggression in Korea." They organized a group known as "Peace Fighters."

Fortunately, only a few officers were Progressives, but their influence was, unfortunately, strong on the enlisted men: If the captain can do it, why can't I? If the colonel signs a peace petition and orders the rest of us to do it, we have to follow orders, don't we? That most of them refused to join the Progressives—and rejected promises, sometimes unfulfilled, of better food, minor luxuries, and mail call—says something for the spirit of privates and noncommissioned officers. The men who gave the Progressives an argument—the active Reactionaries—were a rugged group.

Sundry group techniques, designed to undermine the spirit of all the prisoners, were employed. Those prisoners who were leaders by virtue of rank were segregated early in captivity. When natural leaders emerged from among the rest of the prisoners, they were quietly transferred elsewhere and supplanted by spies and informers of the Reds' choosing, with care taken to avoid raising group antagonism. The Chinese always were meticulous in avoiding, or immediately abandoning, any action that tended to engender or solidify group feeling. In furtherance of the design to destroy organizational spirit, the Communists directed that military titles be dropped and prisoners be known only by their last names.

For lack of leadership—due principally to the method of segregating leaders, but also in some degree to officers' failure to assume leadership when possible—the situation in the camps degenerated into one of "every man for himself." There was no discipline. Prisoners refused to take care of the sick. As may be expected in such a state of affairs, bullies took over and oppressed those they could. Some men lost the will to live. Organizational spirit was nonexistent. The Communists had seen to that by destroying the identity of the individual as a member of any unit except a prisoner of war camp, and even his identity by military grade. With informers in every group, a general feeling of distrust and isolation prevailed. There was no sanitation. Prisoners struggled with each other for food. The total effect was deplorable. Lives were lost as a result of the misery that prisoners collectively brought on themselves.

Nevertheless, many U.S. servicemen exhibited pride in themselves and their units. This was particularly pronounced where they had belonged to the same unit for years. They stood by one another like the "band of brothers" inspired by Nelson. If a prisoner was sick, his fellow prisoners took care of him. They washed his clothes, bathed him, and pulled him through. They exhibited true fraternal spirit, comradeship, and military pride. These prisoners did not let each other down. Nor could the Reds win much cooperation from them.

Why Some Prisoners Broke

When he was plunged into a Communist indoctrination mill, the average American POW was under a serious handicap. Lectures, study groups, and discussion groups, with blizzards of propaganda and hurricanes of violent oratory, were all a part of the enemy technique. The POW was lured into reading Marxist literature. Often he was conned along by devices no more subtle than rewards for yielding and punishments for resisting. He was threatened by enemy political officers into participating in debates and inveigled into telling what he knew about American politics and American history. And many times the Chinese or Korean instructors knew more of these subjects than he did. This brainstorming caught many American prisoners off guard. To most of them it came as a complete surprise. They were unprepared.

A large number of American prisoners did not know what the Communist program was all about. Some were confused by it. Self-seekers accepted it as any easy out. A few actually may have believed the business. They signed peace petitions and peddled Communist literature. Although they were confronted with a difficult choice, those

POWs alone were responsible for their decision to collaborate. It was not an inspiring spectacle. It set loyal groups against cooperative groups; it broke down camp organization and discipline. It made fools of some men and tools of others; it provided stooges for enemy propaganda shows.

Few of the POWs became sincere converts to communism; indeed, the percentage seems infinitesimal. Yet for every weak prisoner who became an active collaborator there were many others who passively "went along." These people lacked sufficient patriotism because of their limited knowledge of American democracy. These had lost their battle before they had ever entered the service.

Much of the trouble can be laid to ignorance. A great many servicemen were teenagers who at home had thought of politics as dry editorials or uninteresting speeches, dull as ditchwater. Many POWs, and some who became defectors, had heard of communism only as a name. Many had never heard of Karl Marx. And here was communism held up as the world's salvation and Marx as mankind's benefactor.

The loyal prisoners were up against it. To themselves they were unable to refute the commissar's argument in favor of communism with arguments in favor of Americanism. They were frustrated in their inability to stand up for democracy because they knew very little of their own America. Yet, when they were provoked by the commissars they seldom had sense enough to "shut up." For his own reassurance—not for dialectical discussion with his captors—the American prisoner's knowledge was a defense weapon, and almost his only one.

Perhaps the Red enemy worked harder on the Americans than he did on the other prisoners. An American who signed a propaganda leaflet, a peace petition, or a germ warfare confession was a big feather in the enemy's hat. The mistake of the prisoners who wrote autobiographies was in ever taking pen in hand in the first place: the information supplied the interrogators with a useful leverage for more pressure. Many Americans in Communist POW camps signed something or wrote something that benefited the enemy. For instance, of seventy-eight men under various forms of duress, thirty-eight signed germ warfare confessions. The other forty did not. Both groups were under coercion. Why did some men break, and some refuse to bend? The answer is to be found in the moral development of these men before they were captured.

Under tough military interrogation only a handful of the POWs in Korea were able to remain resolute in adhering to the limits prescribed by the Geneva Convention. Nearly all went beyond giving name, rank, date of birth, number, and appropriate information of individual health, welfare, and matters of camp administration. In the atmosphere of a captor's prison few people have the precise judgment essential for determining what provides aid and comfort to the enemy. The avoidance or evasion of interrogations that seek further disclosures is mandatory.

Training for the Future

The responsibility for building good citizens and loyal Americans lies within the home, the school, the church, and the community. When civilians enter the armed forces it is up to the armed forces to see that they develop in their knowledge of the American way of life. In a war for the minds of people, the enemy's methods can be successfully combatted by this civil education and proper military training. In battle or in captivity the fighting American is no better than the inherent human capabilities as they are tempered by this training, education, and moral development.

Military schooling can teach combat skills. Such "know-how" is a must. The first phase of military schooling is general training, which must be conducted throughout the careers of all servicemen and servicewomen during both active and reserve duty. Second is the specific training, which is designed for and applied to combat-ready troops. A code of conduct must apply uniformly to all services, and training must be uniform among the services to the greatest degree practicable.

In all service, training should be adapted to cover the needs of every rank, from lower enlisted to unit commander. It must be realistic as well as idealistic training. Above all, it must be presented with understanding, skill, and devotion sufficient to implant a conviction in the heart, conscience, and mind of the serviceman and servicewoman that full and loyal support of the code is in the best interests of his country, his comrades, and himself.

But skill must be reinforced by will, by moral character and by basic beliefs that have been instilled in home and classroom long before a person enters the military service. Pride in country and respect for its principles, a sense of honor, a sense of responsibility—such basics should be established long before conventional "basic training," and they should be further developed after an individual enters the armed forces.

War has been defined as "a contest of wills." A trained hand holds the weapon, but the will, the character, the spirit of the individual—these control the hand. In the war for the minds of men, moral character, will, and spirit are supremely important.

Code of the U.S. Fighting Force

The Code of Conduct for members of the armed forces of the United States was first promulgated by President Dwight Eisenhower on 17 August 1955. The code, including its basic philosophy, was reaffirmed on 8 July 1964, in Department of Defense (DoD) Directive no. 1300.7. On 3 November 1977, President Jimmy Carter amended article 5 of the code. Although it was first expressed in its written form in 1955, the code is based on time-honored concepts and traditions that date back to the days of the American Revolution.

As a member of the armed forces of the United States, you are protecting your nation. It is your duty to oppose all enemies of the United States in combat or, if a captive, in a prisoner of war compound. Your behavior is guided by the Code of Conduct, which has evolved from the heroic lives, experiences, and deeds of Americans from the Revolutionary War to the Southeast Asian Conflict.

Your obligations as a U.S. citizen and a member of the armed forces result from the traditional values that underlie the American experience as a nation. These values are best expressed in the U.S. Constitution and Bill of Rights, which you have sworn to uphold and defend. You would have these obligations to your country, your service and unit, and your fellow Americans even if the Code of Conduct had never been formulated as a high standard of general behavior.

Just as you have responsibility to your country under the Code of Conduct, the U.S. government has an equal responsibility always to keep faith with you and stand by you as you fight for your country. If you are unfortunate enough to become a prisoner of war, you may rest assured that your government will care for your dependents and will never forget you. Furthermore, the government will use every practical means to contact, support, and gain release for you and for all other prisoners of war.

To live up to the code, you must know not only its words but also the ideas and principles behind those words. The Code of Conduct is an ethical guide. Its six articles deal with your chief concerns as an American in combat; these concerns become critical when you must evade capture, resist while a prisoner, or escape from the enemy.

Experiences of captured Americans reveal that to survive captivity honorably would demand from you great courage, deep dedication, and high motivation. To sustain these personal values throughout captivity requires that you understand and believe strongly in the free and democratic institutions of the United States, love your country, trust in the justness of its cause, keep faithful and loyal to your fellow prisoners, and hold firmly to your religious and moral beliefs in time of trial.

Your courage, dedication, and motivation, supported by understanding, trust, and fidelity, will help you endure the terrors of captivity, prevail over your captors, and return to your family, home, and nation with honor and pride.

The following pages present the six articles of the Code of Conduct, an explanation of its principles, and a statement of the standards expected of you.

Code of Conduct 1. I AM AN AMERICAN FIGHTING MAN. I SERVE IN THE FORCES WHICH GUARD MY COUNTRY AND OUR WAY OF LIFE. I AM PREPARED TO GIVE MY LIFE IN THEIR DEFENSE.

All men and women in the armed forces have the duty at all times and under all circumstances to oppose the enemies of the United States and support this country's national interests. In training or in combat, alone or with others, while evading capture or enduring captivity, this duty belongs to each American defending our nation regardless of circumstances.

Code of Conduct 2. I WILL NEVER SURRENDER OF MY OWN FREE WILL. IF IN COMMAND, I WILL NEVER SURRENDER MY MEN WHILE THEY STILL HAVE THE MEANS TO RESIST.

As an individual, a member of the armed forces may never voluntarily surrender. When isolated and no longer able to inflict casualties on the enemy, the American soldier has an obligation to evade capture and rejoin friendly forces.

Only when evasion by an individual is impossible and further fighting would lead only to death with no significant loss to the enemy should an individual consider surrender. When all reasonable means of resistance are exhausted and when certain death is the only alternative, capture does not imply dishonor.

The responsibility and authority of a commander never extends to the surrender of a command to the enemy while the command has the power to fight and evade. When isolated, cut off, or surrounded, a unit must continue to fight until relieved or able to rejoin friendly forces through continued efforts to break out or evade the enemy.

Code of Conduct 3. IF I AM CAPTURED I WILL CONTINUE TO RESIST BY ALL MEANS AVAILABLE. I WILL MAKE EVERY EFFORT TO ESCAPE AND AID OTHERS TO ESCAPE. I WILL ACCEPT NEITHER PAROLE NOR SPECIAL FAVORS FROM THE ENEMY.

The duty of a member of the armed forces to use all means available to resist the enemy is not lessened by the misfortune of captivity. A POW is still legally bound by the Uniform Code of Military Justice and ethically guided by the Code of Conduct. Under provisions of the Geneva Convention, a prisoner of war is also subject to certain rules imposed by the captor nation. When repatriated, a prisoner of war will not be condemned for having obeyed reasonable captor rules, such as sanitation regulations. The duty of a member of the Armed Forces to continue to resist does not mean a prisoner should engage in unreasonable harassment as a form of resistance. Retaliation by captors to the detriment of that prisoner and other prisoners is frequently the primary result of such harassment.

The Geneva Convention recognized that a POW may have the duty to attempt escape. In fact, the Geneva Convention prohibits a captor nation from executing a POW simply for attempting escape. Under the authority of the senior official (often called the senior ranking officer, or "SRO"), a POW must be prepared to escape whenever the opportunity presents itself. In a POW compound, the senior POW must consider the welfare of those remaining behind after an escape. However, as a matter of conscious determination, a POW must plan to escape, try to escape, and assist others to escape.

Contrary to the spirit of the Geneva Convention, enemies engaged by U.S. forces since 1950 have regarded the POW compound as an extension of the battlefield. In doing so, they have used a variety of tactics and pressures, including physical and mental mistreatment, torture, and medical neglect to exploit POWs for propaganda purposes, to obtain military information, or to undermine POW organization, communication, and resistance.

These enemies have attempted to lure American POWs into accepting special favors or privileges in exchange for statements, acts, or information. Unless it is essential to the life or welfare of that person or another prisoner of war or to the success of efforts to resist or escape, a POW must neither seek nor accept special favors or privileges.

One such privilege is called parole. Parole is a promise by a prisoner of war to a captor to fulfill certain conditions—such as agreeing not to escape or to fight again once released—in return for such favors as relief from physical bondage, improved food and living conditions, or repatriation ahead of the sick, injured, or longer-held prisoners. Unless specifically directed by the senior American prisoner of war at the same place of captivity, an American POW will never sign or otherwise accept parole.

Code of Conduct 4. IF I BECOME A PRISONER OF WAR, I WILL KEEP FAITH WITH MY FELLOW PRISONERS. I WILL GIVE NO INFORMATION OR TAKE PART IN ANY ACTION WHICH MIGHT BE HARMFUL TO COMRADES. IF I AM SENIOR, I WILL TAKE COMMAND. IF NOT, I WILL OBEY THE LAWFUL ORDERS OF THOSE APPOINTED OVER ME AND WILL BACK THEM UP IN EVERY WAY.

Informing, or any other action taken to the detriment of a fellow prisoner, is despicable and is expressly forbidden. Prisoners of war must avoid helping the enemy identify fellow prisoners who may have knowledge of particular value to the enemy and who may, therefore, be made to suffer coercive interrogation.

Strong leadership and communication are essential to discipline. Discipline is the key to camp organization, resistance, and even survival. Personal hygiene, camp sanitation, and care of the sick and wounded are imperative. Officers and noncommissioned officers of the United States must continue to carry out their responsibilities and exercise their authority in captivity. The senior, regardless of his service, must accept command. This responsibility, and accountability, may not be evaded.

If the senior is incapacitated or is otherwise unable to act, the next senior person will assume command. Camp leaders should make every effort to inform all POWs of the chain of command and try to represent them in dealing with enemy authorities. The responsibility of subordinates to obey the lawful orders of ranking American military personnel remains unchanged in captivity.

The Geneva Convention Relative to Treatment of Prisoners of War provides for election of a "prisoners' representative" in a POW camp containing enlisted personnel but no commissioned officers. American POWs should understand that such a representative is only a spokesman for the actual senior ranking person. Should the enemy appoint a POW chain of command for its own purposes, American POWs should make all efforts to adhere to the principles of article 4.

As with other provisions of the code, common sense and the conditions of captivity will affect the way in which the senior person and the other POWs organize to carry out their responsibilities. What is important is that everyone support and work within the POW organization.

Code of Conduct 5. WHEN QUESTIONED, SHOULD I BECOME A PRISONER OF WAR, I AM REQUIRED TO GIVE NAME, RANK, SERVICE NUMBER, AND DATE OF BIRTH. I WILL EVADE ANSWERING FURTHER QUESTIONS TO THE UTMOST OF MY ABILITY. I WILL MAKE NO ORAL OR WRITTEN STATEMENTS DISLOYAL TO MY COUNTRY AND ITS ALLIES OR HARMFUL TO THEIR CAUSE.

When questioned, a prisoner of war is required by the Geneva Convention and this code to give name, rank, service number (social security number), and date of birth. The prisoner should make every effort to avoid giving the captor any additional information. The prisoner may communicate with captors on matters of health and welfare, and he may write letters home and fill out a Geneva Convention "capture card."

It is a violation of the Geneva Convention to place a prisoner under physical or mental duress or torture or to use any other form of coercion in an effort to secure information. If under such intense coercion, a POW discloses unauthorized information, makes an unauthorized statement, or performs an unauthorized act, that prisoner's peace of mind and survival require a quick recovery of courage, dedication, and motivation to resist anew each subsequent coercion.

Actions every POW should resist include making oral or written confessions and apologies, answering questionnaires, providing personal histories, creating propaganda recordings, broadcasting appeals to other prisoners of war, providing any other material readily usable for propaganda purposes, appealing for surrender or parole, furnishing self-criticisms, and communicating on behalf of the enemy to the detriment of the United States, its allies, its armed forces, or other POWs.

Every POW should also recognize that any confession signed or any statement made may be used by the enemy as a false evidence that the person is a "war criminal" rather than a POW. Several countries have made reservations to the Geneva Convention in which they assert that a "war criminal" conviction deprives the convicted individual of prisoner of war status, removes that person from protection under the Geneva Convention, and revokes all rights to repatriation until a prison sentence is served.

Recent experiences of American prisoners of war have proved that, although enemy interrogation sessions may be harsh and cruel, it is possible to resist brutal mistreatment when the will to resist remains intact. The best way for a prisoner to keep faith with country, fellow prisoners, and self is to provide the enemy with as little information as possible.

Code of Conduct 6. I WILL NEVER FORGET THAT I AM AN AMERICAN FIGHTING MAN, RESPONSIBLE FOR MY ACTIONS, AND DEDICATED TO THE PRINCIPLES WHICH MADE MY COUNTRY FREE. I WILL TRUST IN MY GOD AND IN THE UNITED STATES OF AMERICA.

A member of the armed forces remains responsible for personal actions at all times. A member of the armed forces who is captured has a continuing obligation to resist and to remain loyal to country, service, unit, and fellow prisoners.

Upon repatriation, POWs can expect their actions to be reviewed as to both circumstances of capture and conduct during detention. The purpose of such review is to recognize meritorious performance as well as to investigate possible misconduct. Each review will be conducted with due regard for the rights of the individual and consideration for the conditions of captivity; for captivity of itself is not a condition of culpability.

Members of the armed forces should remember that they and their dependents will be taken care of by the appropriate service and that pay and allowances, eligibility and procedures for promotion, and benefits for dependents continue while the service member is detained. Service members should assure that their personal affairs and family matters (such as pay, powers of attorney, current will, and provisions for family maintenance and education) are properly and currently arranged. Failure to so arrange matters can create a serious sense of guilt for a POW and place unnecessary hardship on family members.

Summary

The life of a prisoner of war is hard. Each person in this stressful situation must always sustain hope, must resist enemy indoctrination. Prisoners of war standing firm and united against the enemy will support and inspire one another in surviving their ordeal and in prevailing over misfortune with honor.

18

Conclusion: Positive Leadership Techniques

There are a great number of leadership techniques, all based on well-established principles, that can be employed in motivating personnel. These have been thoroughly tried out through generations of Navy and Marine Corps leadership and have proven to be highly effective. The leader's problem frequently is not so much knowing what leadership techniques are available as it is knowing which of them to employ in a specific situation. Only a careful analysis of the techniques and their underlying principles will eliminate this uncertainty.

Leadership Techniques for Leadership Responsibilities

Every act of leadership should make the follower feel that, as long as he is doing his best to follow, he will be secure and his efforts will receive recognition. There are a great many techniques that the leader can use to encourage these feelings, and an attempt will be made here to list these techniques according to the nature of the leadership act. For instance, a leader who allows himself to form the habit of giving indefinite commands will soon discover that the resulting confusion in the minds of his men will make them lose confidence in him. Thus a technique in the giving of commands is that a command must be definite.

Though no all-inclusive list can be made, the techniques of leadership can be grouped into the following categories:

1. Giving commands
2. Giving orders
3. Getting cooperation
4. Establishing discipline
5. Improving morale that is low because of feelings of insecurity
6. Improving morale that is low because of feelings of lack of recognition
7. Properly using organization and administration

The lists that follow should never be considered by the student to be complete or established, and the student may have occasion to add techniques that he finds through experience to be workable and to fit to individual personalities. Additional techniques may become evident when various leadership situations arise, and they will be learned by repeated use.

Leadership Techniques Involved in Giving Commands

1. A command must be definite.
2. A command must be positive. It must be given in a tone of voice that leaves no doubt that it is to be executed.
3. The leader must look at subordinates when he gives them a command.
4. A command must be concise. It must not be so long or involved that the men cannot remember it.

Unquestioning obedience to a command is the basic concept of military life. A command given by a proper authority demands the follower's immediate response to do the will of the leader. The objective of the disciplined way of life of any military school, such as the Naval Academy, is to indoctrinate the student with this concept. When a command is issued, there can be no question on the part of the follower as to whether the command is correct or whether there is any option other than carrying it out. The subordinate must be so trained that he immediately carries out the instructions contained in the command to the very best of his ability.

A command does not permit any question or discussion. Some of the familiar commands used in the naval service are: "Forward, March!" "Right Full Rudder!" "All Engines Ahead Full!" and "Commence Firing!" Immediate and instinctive obedience is the only reaction possible to a properly worded and properly delivered command.

Commands become familiar as the result of constant usage. However, a command is not necessarily stereotyped. Situations that require commands often develop quickly and perhaps without precedent. For example, a junior officer might be inspecting the paint locker when he discovers a fire. In this situation he would immediately issue commands to personnel in the vicinity. One command, to the nearest enlisted person, might be, "Report to the officer of the deck that there is a fire in the paint locker. On the double!" Another command, to a second enlisted person, might be, "Get the fire extinguisher from the next compartment." In a situation such as this, command may be expected to follow command until the fire is extinguished. Every person receiving one of these commands has no alternative but to do exactly as he is told, immediately and without question. The combination of the leadership ability of commanders and the disciplined obedience of followers produces the team that wins competition in peacetime and victory in battle.

Leadership Techniques Involved in Giving Orders

1. Explain what is to be done. Discourage the tendency of the junior to ask how to do it, but leave an opening for questions of confused subordinates.
2. Don't talk down to the enlisted in giving instructions.
3. Give orders to the person in charge, and not to the group. The chain of command must be followed.
4. Encourage and coach the enlisted when they encounter difficulties.
5. Remember that the man is serving his country, not the officer as an individual.
6. In giving an order, try to get across the feeling of "Let's go!" instead of "Get going!"
7. Avoid an overbearing attitude.
8. Show confidence in the ability of subordinates.
9. Don't use a senior's name to lend weight to your own order.
10. Give a reason for your order if time permits, or if it appears that the orders will be clearer if subordinates understand the reason behind them.

Leadership Techniques Involved in Getting Cooperation

1. Stimulate unit or organizational pride by showing your own pride and enthusiasm for the service.
2. Don't criticize another officer or another organization before your subordinates.
3. Keep your subordinates informed so that they may have an intelligent sense of participation.
4. Use the word *we* instead of the word *I* whenever appropriate and possible.
5. Accept responsibility for corrections from higher authority, and take remedial action.

6. Give full credit to members of the organization whose work and ideas have brought progress.

7. Let your enlisted know that you think they are good, and maintain high standards through alert supervision.

8. Make sure that all subordinates know your policy.

9. Don't be sarcastic.

10. Don't threaten punishment to make an order effective.

11. Don't invent jobs just to keep subordinates busy.

Leadership Techniques Involved in Establishing Discipline

1. Praise in public; censure in private.
2. Give subordinates the benefit of the doubt.
3. Punish the individual concerned, not the group.
4. Take into account whether or not an infraction of rules or regulations was intentional.
5. Consider a person's record.
6. Be impartial, consistent, and humane in giving rewards and punishment.
7. Never use severe punishment for minor offenses.
8. As soon as possible, remove senior enlisted who have demonstrated their unfitness.
9. Teach understanding of discipline rather than fear of it: punish the guilty promptly, and defend the innocent stoutly.
10. Support the correct actions of subordinates.

Leadership Techniques Involved in Improving Feelings of Security

1. Let subordinates know what is expected of them.
2. If you are pleased with their work, tell them so.
3. If possible, keep subordinates informed of what is in store for them.
4. Don't make promises you cannot keep.
5. Grant deserved favors willingly.
6. Know the state of the morale of your personnel.
7. Never "pick on" an individual!
8. Be certain that a subordinate understands why he is being censured.
9. Evaluate your own performance in terms of the individual morale and group esprit de corps that exists in your organization.

Leadership Techniques Involved in Giving Recognition

1. Praise when praise is due. Don't flatter.
2. Be on the job whenever your enlisted are working.
3. Be interested in the promotion of your personnel. Encourage them to prepare for advancement.
4. See to it that you are the first person to whom a subordinate turns in case of trouble.
5. Express interest in ideas even though you might disagree with them.
6. Take a keen interest in the quarters and mess. Insist that these be the best available.
7. Study your personnel. Learn all about them: where they come from, their problems and interests, etc.

Leadership Techniques Involved in Improving Organization and Administration

1. Require use of the chain of command.
2. Conform to the rules of the organization.
3. Discover weaknesses of the organization by observing and questioning.
4. Never issue an order that is not going to be enforced.
5. Be fair about promotions.
6. Demote incompetents.

Summary

Chapter 19 presents several leadership situations whose solution requires the use of the leadership principles and techniques discussed in this book. When the student is involved in solving these leadership situations, the instructor should make sure that the leadership principle and technique involved is well understood. Only through constant use and conscious application of these principles and techniques will they gradually become second nature to the new officer as he progresses along the road to effective leadership.

41
MARINES

19

Case Studies in Leadership

There are many possible solutions to each leadership problem, but in most cases fundamental leadership principles establish a starting point for determining the best solutions. Once the process of handling a problem has started, many contributing factors come to light and it is difficult to set forth an established procedure. On the following pages, many situations are presented for the student's study and solution. In each case, the student should state the fundamental principles involved. Once the principles are recognized, the solution best suited to the leader, as well as to the individual or individuals who require a leadership act, should be described in detail. The student's solution will not be criticized or considered wrong unless well-established rules of human relationships are broken, in which case the instructor will explain the reasons behind the rule. After students have completed their solutions, the instructor will usually present an acceptable solution to the situation, but students should remember that there are many proper solutions to every situation.

Solving Leadership Problems

The various principles and techniques of leadership can be applied to a specific case only by the use of problem-solving methods, which embody a careful analysis of the case followed by a study of the possible results of specific techniques. The capable leader instinctively follows the problem-solving steps outlined here in his every act of leadership. They become automatic.

1. State the situation clearly: isolate and state the problem or problems to be solved.

2. Assemble all pertinent facts. Facts about the environment, the personnel, the material, the leader, must be carefully set forth.

3. Analyze the problem in the light of the facts. Knowledge of the leader and his judgment and reasoning powers will be called into operation in this step.

4. Set up a tentative solution, a plan of action and a method of carrying it out, by weighing various alternatives.

5. Check the solution to determine whether it is consistent with the facts, with the experience of the leader, and with the experience of others, and whether it is the most logical solution in light of the facts and personalities in the case.

By considering every leadership act on an individual basis, the leader will avoid the pitfall of following a typical approach to every situation. Each situation is unique and requires an approach that is based on the facts and personalities involved in it.

The Case Study Method

The case study method of teaching leadership is an excellent method of educating people to solve leadership problems. Experienced officers will have little difficulty in recalling situations that required some thought—and perhaps adroit working with the personalities involved—before they were solved. Situations used in case studies should be reduced to their basic facts; all unnecessary details should be eliminated. The problems used do not have to be clear-cut, nor do they have to allow only one solution. However, the problems must be realistic.

The problems presented here are practical problems, representing actual situations of the type a service officer can expect to encounter.

Putting the Case Study Method to Use

An effective technique in utilizing the case study method in leadership instruction is quite simple. The case is presented to the class and the students are allowed a reasonable time to think the problems of the case through and to develop a course of action. One student is then called on to present his solution to the class orally. He conducts a discussion of each salient point of the solution as he progresses. After he presents his complete solution, the student (or the instructor) summarizes the solution reached by the class in the discussion. Other students are then asked to present their solutions if they are radically different from the one reached by the class. The discussion of each solution is considered the most important feature of the presentation, because this is where good or bad leadership ideas are exposed, adopted, criticized, and rejected by the individual. The instructor should point out any fallacies or violations of basic principles as they appear, so that the entire discussion will be constructive.

It is neither required nor desirable for all students to adopt the same methods and techniques of solving a particular problem. They should be apprised of the fact that many different approaches will satisfactorily solve these problems, and that the student should adopt those methods which best fit his personality.

These case studies illustrate to the student that human-relation problems such as those encountered in leadership can best be solved in a logical and systematic manner while each problem is still treated on its own merits. To solve the problems, the student (or officer in the actual situation) must consider each separate facet of the problem and work out a solution for each which is consistent with his own experience and capabilities and with the experience and capabilities of each of the other people involved. These individual solutions must fit together to form an acceptable solution to the whole problem. In selecting a solution the problem solver must consider each possible course of action, and must then project it to its logical conclusion so that he may select the most desirable course.

The use of the case study has an additional advantage in the training of officer candidates. It motivates students to increase their professional knowledge by demonstrating their lack of information in certain areas, areas where knowledge is necessary to the execution of their duties as an officer.

Case Studies

Situation 1

You reported on board the USS *California* at the Philadelphia Naval Shipyard on 5 July, and you have been moving into your quarters and acquainting yourself with the ship. You have met all the officers. The *California* has been undergoing yard overhaul and is scheduled to leave the yard on 12 July for post-repair trials off the mouth of the Delaware River. On 19 July the *California* is scheduled to go to Guantanamo Bay, Cuba, to conduct gunnery rehearsals and firing.

At 0800, on 6 July, the executive officer informs you that you will relieve the optics officer, Lieutenant (junior grade) Dexter, who is being detached suddenly and will leave the ship during the afternoon of 7 July. You spend the 6th with Dexter, who spends most of this time telling you how well he has run the optics gang, and how much better everything is now than it was when he took the gang over from another officer one year ago. He is very proud of his part of the division and of the fourteen men assigned him. The optics gang is a part of the F Division, and the optics officer acts as a junior division officer of the division, but he has direct supervision over the optics gang. After the inspection, you are quite satisfied with the condition, efficiency, and accountability of the equipment and you write your letter of relief to the division officer.

At quarters on 7 July, Lieutenant Commander Rex, the F Division officer, introduces you to the division. After dismissal, you find that Lieutenant Dexter has kept the optics gang at quarters. He introduces you to each one of the men individually. He calls several of the petty officers by their nicknames as well as by their last names.

PROBLEMS:

1. If the first man introduced held out his hand, would you shake hands with him, or not?

2. Would you repeat the given nickname, or only the last name, of each individual in acknowledging each introduction?

3. After the introductions are over, Lieutenant Dexter tells the men that you have relieved him. He makes a farewell speech of about two minutes, and tells the men how much he hates to leave, how well they have performed their duties, and how much he appreciates their loyalty. He closes by saying that they are very fortunate in having you as their new officer-in-charge, and that he wishes you all success in the future. His closing sentences are: "Ensign ——— is a fine officer and I know you will give him the same support you gave me. I wish you every good fortune together. I am sure that Ensign ——— has a few words he would like to say to you." Write or deliver the speech you would give on this occasion.

Situation 2

Shortly after his ship entered dry dock, the executive officer of the USS *Coronado* ordered all hands, including the embarked marines, over the side to scrape the bottom. An ensign who had reported aboard only two days previously for his first duty was on watch as junior officer of the deck. The officer of the deck, who had been called to the captain's cabin, had turned the watch over to the ensign before leaving the quarterdeck.

A few minutes later, a marine private was brought to the junior officer of the deck by the marine sergeant with the report that the man had refused to turn to as ordered. The marine sergeant requested authority to put the man in the brig. The ensign asked the man if it was true that he refused this duty, and, after hearing the man persist in his refusal, he acceded to the marine sergeant's request and had the corporal of the guard lock the man up in the brig.

A few minutes later the officer of the deck returned and assumed his duties. The ensign immediately reported the circumstances of the affair to him. The officer of the deck advised the ensign not to make a formal report just yet, but to let the man cool off in the brig for a little while. In about an hour, the officer of the deck sent for the man and explained that the order he had received to go over the side was lawful, and that the penalty for refusing might extend to dismissal and imprisonment in a federal prison. He then formally ordered the marine private over the side to turn to with the rest of his division. The man obeyed with alacrity and worked very hard.

PROBLEM:

As the ensign in this case, what report, if any, would you make against the man? State the reasons for your decision. Did the ensign himself violate any regulations? If so, how? Did the officer of the deck act properly in this case?

Situation 3

Ensign Alfredo was engineer officer of the squadron and squadron duty officer, and Ensign Brand was communications officer. At about 1545, Ensign Brand received a dispatch from the commander of the wing requesting that the squadron report by 2000 the amount of gasoline used during the past thirty days. Ensign Brand personally delivered a copy of the dispatch to the engineer officer for action and reply. Ensign Brand then went ashore, having been assured by Ensign Alfredo that the wing commander's dispatch would be answered before the deadline.

The following morning the squadron commander had Ensign Brand on the carpet because the dispatch had not been answered. It developed that Ensign Alfredo had fully intended to answer the dispatch but had forgotten it in the excitement of a crash that had occurred on the field at 1630.

PROBLEM:

Which of the two ensigns is the responsible officer in this case? Why?

Situation 4

Seaman recruit Jones is a loader on a five-inch 54 gun. He has been in the navy eight months but has never been a member of a gun crew during actual firing. He is nineteen years old, immature, and very straightforward in his relations with his shipmates and officers. Throughout the period of training preceding battle practice, Jones performed his duties as loader in an exemplary manner.

Jones's gun had blown out its recoil cylinders during the last battle practice. There were no casualties to personnel, but considerable talk had ensued among the men concerning the safety of the gun.

During the actual firing of his first practice, Jones deserted the gun and took cover immediately after the first shell had been loaded. The officer in charge of the battery ordered Jones back to his station. Jones obeyed quickly, resuming his position and performing the duties of loader satisfactorily for the remainder of the practice. However, the delay in getting the second shell loaded ruined the crew's chances of getting a high score on the practice.

Later in the day, the battery officer, an ensign, questioned Jones concerning his apparently cowardly action. Jones would give no reasons for what he had done. The ensign continued his investigation without success until one of the pharmacist's mates, who had a first-aid station in the vicinity, told him that he thought it was a "frame-up." After this remark, the ensign questioned each member of the gun crew at length and found that several of the experienced men serving on the gun had said they were going to leave the gun and take cover when the "Commence firing" order was given. This talk was evidently for the benefit of Jones, who took it seriously and who thought he was merely doing what the other members of the crew intended to do.

PROBLEM:

As the battery officer, what action would you take in this case concerning Jones and the other members of the gun crew?

Situation 5

An ensign in civilian clothes arrived at the Norfolk Naval Base gate in a car with friends, a civilian couple, who knew little about the navy. The civilians were returning the officer to her ship. The car stopped near the gate, and as the ensign stood beside the car saying good night, a sailor, obviously intoxicated, reeled up and stuck his head in the opposite car window. The sailor commenced talking in a loud manner on various innocuous subjects; his speech gradually degenerated as he used profanity and obscenities. At this point, the ensign told the sailor who she was and ordered the sailor to move on. The sailor refused, saying, "How do I know if you are an officer? And even if you are, I don't give a damn for any damned officer anyway!" The ensign managed to keep her temper in check and apologized to her friends for the sailor's conduct.

Since the sailor was still hanging around near the gate after the officer's civilian friends had departed, the ensign asked the marine sentry if he could take the offender into custody. The marine replied that he had no jurisdiction outside the base. During the conversation, the sailor walked in the gate to find out what was going on, and, on demand, produced his liberty card, which indicated that he was from one of the ships in the yard. The marine sentry immediately took him into custody and returned him to his ship.

The next morning (Sunday) the ensign went over to the sailor's ship, reported the incident to the duty officer (a lieutenant), and preferred charges against the sailor. She was told that the man in question was very steady and had never been in serious trouble before.

As the ensign left the ship, she was followed and stopped by the sailor of the previous night, now very sober and very worried. He pleaded with the ensign to drop the charges, saying that he had never been drunk before and that he didn't yet know everything he had said and done the night before. The ensign, in polite official language, reprimanded the sailor for his actions. The sailor apologized profusely, offering to do anything to make up for his actions if the officer would only drop the charges against him.

PROBLEMS:

1. How should the ensign have handled the situation at the gate? Give reasons.

2. Do you think she should proceed differently after her talk with the sailor?

Situation 6

An ensign, one year after graduation, was assigned the duties of assistant engineer officer of a destroyer, with additional duties of commissary officer and stores officer. He was directed by the commanding officer to learn his duties thoroughly, and, in the process, to consult, as necessary, the officers senior to him, particularly the executive officer and the commanding officer. The officer who had previously performed these duties had been detached.

After the ensign had been aboard six months, he notified the heads of departments that existing regulations and instructions required an inventory of equipment at this time. Because of the shortage of officer personnel and his desire to get the inventory finished and books properly balanced, he proceeded to take inventory in all departments.

As he attempted to balance the books after the inventory, the ensign found the first-class storekeeper to be evasive and unreliable. He then removed the stock cards to his room and found a total discrepancy of approximately $20,000 between the amount of equipment shown to be on hand by the cards and that actually on hand. He immediately notified the commanding officer.

The commanding officer requested a Board of Investigation from the division commander. The board found that the stock cards had been improperly kept since the ship had been commissioned, in that practically no expenditures had been recorded on them; that the inventory for the previous year had apparently been made from the cards, as no discrepancies had been found; and that the storekeeper, who had been on the ship since its commissioning, as well as all of the previous stores officers, had been negligent and inefficient. It also found that there had been very little actual loss to the government. The ensign received a letter of reprimand from the commanding officer, and an unsatisfactory fitness report, and was confined to his room for a period of ten days.

PROBLEMS:

1. What mistakes, if any, were made by the ensign?
2. By the commanding officer?

Situation 7

As the engineer officer of USS *Barney* (DDG-6), you are preparing for post-repair trials after an extensive shipyard overhaul period. During the overhaul period a steam line had carried away in a fireroom, killing one workman and seriously burning several others. You are proceeding to sea and preparing for the trials when you hear a rumor, which is apparently rampant in the engineer force of the ship, that the boilers and piping have not been adequately tested. As a result of this rumor, the men are fearful of a steam explosion.

PROBLEM:

How would you proceed from here?

Situation 8

A lieutenant (junior grade) was the first division officer aboard the USS *New Jersey*. The division furnished the crew for No. 1 motor launch, which was usually secured on the boat deck with a motor whaleboat nested inside. Both boats were hoisted in and out by use of the boat crane. In addition to these boats, the ship was also equipped with two motor whaleboats slung on davits, one on each side of the ship, one of which was normally kept manned at sea for immediate use as a lifeboat.

One night at sea, during a stormy and cold midwatch in the North Atlantic, the officer of the deck received a report that the duty motor whaleboat (lifeboat) was out of commission. The other two motor whaleboats were also out of commission at this time. On receipt of this information, the officer of the deck, at 0100, ordered the boatswain's mate of the watch to break out the boat crew on No. 1 motor launch and station them in their boat as a lifeboat crew. At 0730 they were relieved by the relief boat crew from the same division. An hour later the motor whaleboat (lifeboat) was back in commission and the crew of No. 1 motor launch was secured.

At morning quarters, the division officer found that his division petty officers were upset over the treatment of the boat crew by the officer of the deck, inasmuch as their duties as boat crew normally terminated when the ship was at sea, and the crew involved had previously stood an 8-to-12 watch before being called to man No. 1 motor launch. The leading boatswain's mate in the division asked if something couldn't be done to prevent a recurrence of the incident.

The division officer investigated and found that the officer of the deck had never prepared No. 1 motor launch for lowering as a lifeboat. The motor whaleboat nested in No. 1 motor launch had not been moved; No. 1 motor launch had not been hooked on to the crane; no sea painter had been rigged; and no crane operators were standing by to operate the boat crane. All in all, it would have taken at least thirty minutes to use No. 1 motor launch as a lifeboat even with the crew stationed in it.

PROBLEM:

As the division officer in this case, six years junior to the officer of the deck, what action would you take? Why?

Situation 9

A seaman apprentice of seven months was reported to his division officer by the division boatswain's mate as being generally useless. The division officer, who had been aboard about three weeks, investigated and found that the report was true, that the seaman was the sort of man who required two good men to keep him busy. A week later the seaman was reported by the boatswain's mate in charge of the side cleaners for shirking duty.

The division officer had an interview with the man and discovered that he held grudges against the navy and was generally dissatisfied. He claimed that he was not strong enough to go over the side as a side cleaner, and that the petty officers in the division were down on him. The division officer lectured the man concerning the seriousness of disobeying orders or refusing duty, and the man went back to work with some indication that his attitude had improved.

In two weeks he was his old self and was again reported. The division officer had another interview with him, after which the seaman requested that he be given an undesirable discharge.

The case was referred to the executive officer by the department head for a decision. The executive officer refused to consider an undesirable discharge, giving as a reason that the officer had a responsibility to make a man out of the seaman, as it was one of the commanding officer's principal responsibilities to train a man so that he could pull his own oar. The man's division officer was given full responsibility of the case and was authorized to take whatever steps he deemed necessary to straighten the man out.

During his investigation, the division officer found that the previous division officer had carefully gone through the records of all of the men in the division at the time the seaman reported aboard and had noted that this seaman and one other in the division were high school graduates who had some college credits. The former division officer had decided against assigning these men to normal routine division duties of mess cooks or compartment cleaners; he decided to assign them to tasks that would utilize their apparently higher educational achievements. Naturally, the petty officers had resented this favoritism.

PROBLEM:

As the division officer in this case, how would you proceed from this point?

Situation 10

You are the division officer of the "B" Division. One of your men, a machinist's mate second class with an excellent record over a period of four years in the navy, remained absent over leave. After he had served his punishment, he repeated the offense and returned to the ship intoxicated.

PROBLEM:

What steps would you take, if any, to straighten this man out?

Situation 11

You report to the USS *Iowa*, having received your commission as ensign six weeks before, and are assigned as a junior officer of the Second (deck) Division. You are aboard after working hours and are in the gunnery office alone, studying, when one of the seamen apprentices in your division enters and requests permission to speak to you. You do not know him except to recognize him as one of your men. He is in clean uniform, appears intelligent, and is most respectful in manner. He requests that you use your influence to get him assigned as a striker in the Fire Control Division. He states that his present cleaning station is on the forecastle; that the boatswain's mate in charge of the forecastle (whom you know as a capable but tough old-timer) is down on him because he is better educated and is trying to improve himself by studying; that the division officer won't talk to him because the boatswain's mate has prejudiced the division officer against him. Your examination of the man's record indicates that he has been in the navy for two and one-half years, on one destroyer and two cruisers. His marks are average. He had received a warning at Captain's Mast for two hours absence over leave. He had attended Fire Control School following recruit training but had failed early in the course.

PROBLEM:

How would you proceed from this point?

Situation 12

Ensign New is attached to the USS *Ticonderoga* (CG-47), which is in the naval shipyard for overhaul. He is detailed by the commanding officer to proceed, with a group of twenty selected enlisted men, to a small town in Massachusetts to participate in a celebration in honor of a local hero who was wounded in action on board the *Ticonderoga* during the war. Ensign New is met at the station by the mayor of the town. He and his men are taken to a local hotel, are given very comfortable rooms, are offered the hospitality of the town, and are asked to take part in the ceremonies by acting as a guard of honor for the hero and his parents during the afternoon parade and attending a banquet in the local town hall that evening as well as a dance in the town hall following the banquet.

Everything proceeds without difficulty until the dance starts at about 2130. By this time, some local toughs have crashed the gate and are mingling with the invited guests, while more are gathering outside. At this point the mayor approaches Ensign New and requests that he detail his enlisted personnel as police; he states that the local police force is inadequate and that he is afraid that the subversive elements in the town are so rowdy that the whole affair may well turn into a riot before the evening is over. He offers to pay the enlisted men five dollars each from the profits earned from the banquet and dance that were originally intended for local charities.

PROBLEM:

As Ensign New, how would you handle the mayor's request?

Situation 13

You are officer of the deck. A seaman reports to you at 1500, saying that after he came off the forenoon watch, he was sent away from the ship on a working party without lunch by his leading petty officer.

PROBLEM:

What would you do?

Situation 14

Lieutenant (junior grade) Alvarez is First Division officer of the USS *Nashville* (LPD-13). Turret No. 1 is part of the space for which he is responsible. The ship is at sea on routine operation not involving turret gunnery. On Wednesday, Lieutenant Alvarez gave his boatswain's mate and gunner's mate instructions to clean up and paint the living spaces and inside of the turret in preparation for captain's inspection Friday afternoon and Saturday. The entire division would be involved, and the work would take until Friday noon. The ship was expected to return to port Friday morning. The top of turret No. 1 was dirty, and Lieutenant Alvarez instructed his boatswain's mate to delay scrubbing it until late Friday afternoon, after return to port and during the below-deck inspection.

On Thursday afternoon, the officer of the deck sent for the boatswain's mate and ordered him to scrub the top of turret No. 1 immediately. Since all of the men were engaged in a job that would require their full time to complete by the deadline, the boatswain's mate went to Lieutenant Alvarez for advice.

PROBLEMS:

1. What should Lieutenant Alvarez do if the officer of the deck issued the order on his own authority?
2. What, if anything, did the officer of the deck do wrong in each case?
3. Did the boatswain's mate act properly in this case?

Situation 15

The USS *Guam* (LPH-9) has been deployed in the Western Pacific for three months, during which time the morale has dropped to a low point. There has been little worthwhile liberty, and the ship has been participating in a series of fleet operations which has required practically a watch-and-watch basis ever since deployment from the West Coast. The ship is given a three-week upkeep period in Cubi Point, the Philippines.

You are in charge of a deck division, and your leading boatswain's mate is a very popular man with his shipmates. He is a good athlete and an excellent seaman but a hail fellow well met on the beach and not very dependable as far as discipline is concerned.

In order to build up ship's morale, the commanding officer has announced a competition involving athletic events on the beach, smartness at inspection, cleanliness of living quarters, and various other routine activities over the period of the three-week upkeep. The winning division is to be given extra liberty in Hong Kong, the next good liberty port. Your boatswain's mate works very hard to win, and your division wins almost entirely through his efforts. The morale of the division is high and the boatswain's mate popularity with the men is greater than ever.

At a Saturday inspection just prior to going ashore at Hong Kong, the commanding officer congratulates the division at quarters after he has inspected them and announced them the winner. As the commanding officer walks from the division, your boatswain's mate turns around to his men, and, without realizing that you are near enough to hear him, makes the following statement: "Well, we sure fooled the old Son of a B that time, didn't we?"

PROBLEM:

What action would you take, if any? Why?

Situation 16

As captain of the USS *Manitowoc* (LST 1180), you find that theft is widespread throughout the ship, involving the loss of clothing and money.

PROBLEMS:

1. What actions would you take, if any, when underway? Why?
2. What actions would you take, if any, when in port? Why?

Situation 17

As an ensign officer of the deck, you have had the smoking lamp put out and have personally ordered a pair of welders working over the side to knock off until you finish fueling boats. Fifteen minutes later, while fueling is still in progress, you note that the welders have returned to work. On questioning them, you ascertain that the assistant engineer officer, with the rank of lieutenant commander, had observed the welders sitting on the deck and had ordered them over the side to resume their work, even though the men had informed him of the officer of the deck's order. The assistant engineer officer had replied that the fueling was on the opposite side of the ship, and that there was no danger of fire and explosion.

PROBLEM:

What would you do?

Situation 18

As executive officer of the USS *Saginaw* (LST 1188), you find evidence of liquor on board in the form of empty whisky bottles in trash cans and the odor of liquor on breath at questionable times.

PROBLEM:

What would you do to combat this situation?

Situation 19

A squadron of P-3 planes was scheduled to depart at 0600 on a flight from San Diego to Panama. At the muster of the crews at 0530, the chief petty officer with the day's duty reported one man absent, a second mechanic on one of the planes. About 0550, the chief petty officer reported that this man had shown up. All the officers were, at this time, in the squadron office getting their last-minute instructions.

When the plane commander whose second mechanic had been absent went out to his plane, he was informed by the plane captain that the man in question was very much under the influence of liquor but was trying not to show it and was being very quiet. The officer talked to the man and considered it would not be dangerous to have him aboard. He therefore ordered the man to get in the plane and go to sleep. During the flight this man caused no trouble, and by the time the squadron landed that night he was sober enough to do his work properly.

This man had been in the navy for eleven years, was a first-class aviation machinist's mate, and had had a 3.9 or 4.0 in conduct every quarter since he had been in the navy. He was a hard worker and he was intelligent and an all-around good man.

PROBLEM:

As the plane commander, what action would you take in this case, and why?

Situation 20

The executive officer has issued an order that the uniform of the day would be worn during working hours by all hands, except those actually involved in dirty work. As the ship's secretary, you order the three yeomen under your charge to wear the uniform of the day at all times.

About a month later your senior yeoman complains that the yeomen in the first lieutenant, gunnery, and engineer offices are wearing dungarees, and he requests that the yeomen in the captain and executive offices also be allowed to wear dungarees during working hours.

PROBLEM:

What would you do?

Situation 21

The USS *Coontz* (DLG-9) has arrived during the forenoon at the Philadelphia Naval Shipyard, after a three months' antisubmarine sweep as a member of an Escort Carrier Task Group in the North and

Middle Atlantic. The officers and men had not been ashore on liberty during this entire period. Ensign Eaton, who had been married just before the ship left port, was particularly anxious to get ashore.

Immediately on arrival, Ensign Eaton, who was communications officer and, as such, custodian of confidential publications, collected the confidential matter that had previously been issued to the officers on board. He took a quick sight check, destroyed the individual custody cards, threw the publications in the communications safe, and went ashore.

That afternoon, workmen from the Yard Radio Material Office came aboard with a job order to remove the high frequency direction-finding equipment to make room for a new type of radar. This job was accomplished during the next twenty-four hours.

Four days later, on the last day of the quarter, Ensign Eaton made the quarterly inventory of his confidential publications as required by regulations, and located them all except CSP 000 (HF/DF Operating Instructions and Frequencies). Ensign Slack, his roommate, assisted him, and, as required, sighted all publications except CSP 000.

Ensign Eaton searched for a week but failed to locate the missing publication. The chief yeoman requested him to submit his quarterly report of registered publications, and finally the executive officer ordered him to get it in immediately. Ensign Eaton typed up a RPS destruction report for the missing publication and predated it to a date before the last day of the quarter. He then told Ensign Slack that he now remembered having burned the publication by mistake and persuaded Slack to sign the destruction report as a witness. The destruction and inventory reports were then turned over to the captain's office for signature.

About a week later, the foreman of the Yard Radio Material Office came on board and asked to see the captain. After being seated in the captain's office, Mr. Duff, the foreman, pulled the missing copy of CSP 000 from his coat pocket and handed it to the captain. One of his men had found it stuffed in the cabinet of the HF/DF that had been removed from the ship.

PROBLEMS:

1. What incorrect actions are indicated in this case?
2. What action would you take as commanding officer against Ensigns Eaton and Slack?

Situation 22

Ensign Alfred reported on board the USS *Nimitz* (CVN-68) on 9 July, having graduated from the Naval Academy in May. On 12 August, he was a member of the shore patrol. He came ashore at 1300 and reported to the senior patrol officer at his office in the city police station, two blocks from the dock. The senior patrol officer designated him as beachmaster, and Ensign Alfred took his station on the dock. As beachmaster he had the same responsibilities as any other officer on patrol, but his supervision was primarily concerned with the dock, boat schedules, loading liberty parties, etc. He was in full charge of the dock area.

Four men were assigned to Ensign Alfred's detail. He assigned two of them to patrol the dock along with himself, and he ordered the other two to maintain order and to announce boat arrivals in the fleet waiting rooms at the head of the dock.

At 1730 Ensign Alfred directed the two men with him to go uptown for their supper, leaving him alone on the dock with several groups of civilians, who were awaiting transportation to various ships. These civilians consisted mostly of officers' wives and guests who were going on board for dinner.

Shortly after the two patrolmen had departed, four enlisted men came onto the dock. They were all petty officers, one a first-class machinist's mate. This group proceeded to the end of the dock, conversing loudly and obscenely. All were apparently intoxicated, with the first-class machinist's mate being the loudest and most obscene.

Ensign Alfred approached the group and said, "You men go into the waiting room until your ship's boat is announced."

One of the men replied drunkenly, "Aye, aye, Sir," and Ensign Alfred moved away.

Since the group made no move to leave the dock as ordered, Ensign Alfred again approached, and, addressing himself to the first-class machinist's mate, said, "You take these men and go into the waiting room immediately."

The first-class machinist's mate grumbled unintelligibly something that sounded like "Stuff it!" but took no action.

Ensign Alfred then good-naturedly took hold of the machinist's mate's elbow and attempted to steer him in the direction of the waiting room. The man immediately swung on Ensign Alfred, who ducked the blow and struck back. Immediately all four men pounced on the ensign.

The commotion had by this time been noticed in the waiting room, and the two patrolmen assigned there rushed down to the dock to aid Ensign Alfred. They quickly subdued the four enlisted men and placed them under arrest. The men were returned to their ship under guard. As a result of this fracas all four of the men were given general court-martial, and Ensign Alfred received an official letter of reprimand from commander-in-chief, Atlantic Fleet.

PROBLEMS:

1. What mistakes did this young ensign make?
2. How would you have handled the same situation?

Situation 23

Submarine Division Ten, consisting of SSN575, SSN578, and SSN579, has arrived from Coco Solo, Canal Zone, to be placed out of commission. The division commander, with the rank of commander, was aboard the flagship, the SSN578. All submarines were berthed together at the same dock. (The process of laying up the ship for decommissioning requires about ninety days, and the ship's force does the work with the assistance of shipyard facilities.)

Within an hour after the ships were secured to the dock, the commanding officer of the SSN579 went aboard the SSN578 and received permission from the division commander to go to New York to meet his family. The commanding officer of the SSN579 returned on board and told the executive officer, Lieutenant Brown, that he was shoving off for New York for a day or so, and to go ahead with the decommissioning during his absence. He further stated that there were no unexecuted orders to be carried out by the ship.

After his commanding officer had departed, Lieutenant Brown proceeded to the shipyard barracks where the crew was to be berthed. He contacted the lieutenant in charge, who was most cooperative, showing Lieutenant Brown the area laid out for the crew of the three submarines and that portion assigned to the crew of the SSN579. He told Lieutenant Brown that the barracks were ready to receive the crews at any time, and Lieutenant Brown arranged with him for the SSN579 crew to move in at 0800 the next morning. Lieutenant Brown then returned to the ship, called his crew to quarters, and told them that all hands were to pack their gear for moving immediately after

0730 quarters the next morning; that a truck would be provided at 0800; that ship's work for decommissioning would start immediately after the move had been completed; and that all hands except the duty section had liberty from after this quarters until 0730 quarters the next morning. He then dismissed the crew.

After 0730 quarters the next morning, the move to the barracks went off as scheduled. By 0930, the barracks area assigned to the crew of the SSN579 was ready for inspection (bunks having been made and lockers stowed), and all hands were back on board at work. (When a ship is laid up, all equipment is stripped down to nuts and bolts, repaired as found necessary, cleaned and preserved with special compounds, and then reassembled. In addition, all electrical gear is sealed by wrapping and taping.)

At 1045 the division commander sent for Lieutenant Brown and asked him why the 579 had moved into the barracks in violation of his orders. Lieutenant Brown stated that he had not received direct orders from the division commander in this matter, but had proceeded on his own responsibility. The division commander then told Lieutenant Brown that the day before he had issued orders to all ships that all crews would move into the barracks with the other submarine crews at 1300. Lieutenant Brown remonstrated as strongly as he felt he could without bringing serious reprimand from the division commander, and finally left with an "Aye, aye, Sir."

Lieutenant Brown went back on board the SSN579 and called the crew back for quarters.

PROBLEMS:

1. What would you, as Lieutenant Brown, say to the crew at this point?
2. What principles of leadership should be used in this talk?

Situation 24

Rudder was a reliable, truthful, and efficient coxswain attached to the USS *Valdez*. His division officer, a lieutenant (junior grade), had been serving on board with Rudder for over a year. Each had the greatest respect for the other.

One morning after quarters, Rudder approached his division officer and asked permission to consult him, as a personal friend and counselor, concerning a matter on which he needed advice. The division officer, feeling perfectly secure, told Rudder that he would be very glad to hear his story as a friend and to give him whatever advice he could.

It turned out that Rudder had a friend, a seaman apprentice, now living with him at his house in Philadelphia, who was a deserter from the USS *Saratoga* (CV-60) on the West Coast. The deserter had been to a party in San Pedro, had become intoxicated, perhaps doped, and had not regained normalcy until two days later. The knowledge that he was over leave caused him to panic, and he ran away, and it was not until some days later that he came to his senses and realized that he was a deserter from the U.S. Navy and guilty of a very serious offense. He immediately thought of his old friend Rudder and decided to go to him for protection and advice. It took him nearly six weeks to work his way from the West Coast to Philadelphia. Rudder had taken him in on condition that he would do what Rudder told him to do after he, Rudder, had consulted with his division officer, in whom he had the utmost trust and confidence. Rudder explained to the division officer that the seaman was still in a quandary as to his course of action and was unable to decide whether he should turn himself in or continue in his desertion. Rudder explained to the division officer that he was sure that the seaman never really intended to desert; that he liked the navy and wanted it as his career, but that he didn't want to turn himself in to be imprisoned and subsequently be dishonorably discharged. The seaman was perfectly willing to suffer a penalty for the offense as long as he would be allowed to remain in the navy and rectify his mistake.

PROBLEM:

As the division officer in this case, what would you do?

Situation 25

You are the division officer of one of the six deck divisions aboard the USS *Arkansas* (CGN-41). Each of the divisions, except your own, has a boatswain's mate first class as the leading petty officer. The ship has been one short in complement in this category for over a year, and your leading petty officer has been a boatswain's mate second class, with six years' service, who has done an excellent job.

An extra boatswain's mate second class is ordered to the ship as a substitute for the missing boatswain's matc first class in the ship's complement and is assigned to your division. He has five years' service to his credit and is, therefore, placed in a secondary position to your second-class boatswain's mate. Four weeks later the new boatswain's mate second class is promoted to boatswain's mate first class.

PROBLEM:

Would you accept this situation, or would you attempt to initiate some transfers within the ship to prevent any difficulties that might arise? What factors would influence your decision?

Situation 26

You are an ensign attached to the USS *Texas* (CGN-39), and you are on shore leave on the Fourth of July in a port that is not a regular navy port of call and where large groups of navy liberty parties have never been ashore. You are dining in a restaurant with two civilian couples when two of the enlisted men in your division enter with two middle-aged, prosperous-appearing civilian men who are evidently showing them the town. You know the two enlisted men as young, inexperienced seamen with above-average ability and good conduct records. It is obvious that they have had more to drink than they should.

They and their civilian companions order drinks and become increasingly noisy. As all the attention in the restaurant becomes focused on this group, the proprietor comes to you and requests you to quiet them down. He explains that the civilians, although they are influential in the community, are not as important to him as the reputation of his restaurant.

PROBLEMS:

1. What action would you take at this time?
2. What additional action, if any, would you take on return to the ship?

Situation 27

You are the assistant plotting room officer and the operator of the main battery rangekeeper. You are in the main battery plotting room during captain's inspection. The gunnery officer is accompanying the captain, and, because of the latter's interest in the operation of the plotting room, the gunnery officer quickly describes some of the details of the operation of the stable element and trunnion tilt corrector. During this description the gunnery officer makes a technical error.

PROBLEM:

Do you correct the gunnery officer, or keep quiet? Why?

Later you are the junior officer of the watch, entering port, and you overhear the captain tell the executive officer to have his gig alongside the starboard gangway immediately on anchoring. A few minutes later you overhear the executive officer tell the boat coxswain (out of hearing of the captain) to bring the gig alongside the port gangway as soon as the ship is anchored.

PROBLEM:

Do you correct the executive officer in this case, or keep quiet? Why?

Situation 28

You have just been assigned as a division officer aboard ship. Your leading chief, a chief boilerman, reports to you that the morale of the division is very low, and that in the last captain's inspection the division received an unsatisfactory mark in both personnel and material inspection of division spaces. He cites to you the following, which he feels are the causes for the present situation: First, the food is poor, and it is a well-known fact that the commissary officer (a lieutenant) is trying to get a good fitness report by skimping on ration money and wants to impress the captain by returning ration money to the bureau. Second, the men have to stand engineering watches, and when going off watch they have to change into the uniform of the day before eating. Third, the chief master-at-arms insists that all hands must turn out at reveille, including the mid-watch standers. Anyone who does not is summarily placed on report. Fourth, the ship uses a cafeteria-style of feeding, and the petty officers are disgruntled because they are not permitted to go to the head of the line. Finally, the entire division has been restricted from liberty by the executive officer on several occasions when he has been dissatisfied with the appearance of division spaces.

The chief goes on to say that these complaints have all been brought to the attention of the previous division officers, but apparently nothing was ever done about them because the division was never told anything at quarters—and, besides, nothing has changed.

PROBLEM:

As the division officer, how would you proceed to improve the morale of your division?

Situation 29

You have taken over as a division officer in the gunnery department. Shortly thereafter one of your men goes AWOL and stays away

48 hours. In reviewing his record for Captain's Mast, you are surprised to see that he has been on report three times within the past six months, twice for AWOL, once for insubordination to a petty officer. You also find that the man had a very high mark on his General Classification Test, and that he is a high school graduate.

When you bring the division leading chief (a chief gunner's mate) in to discuss the man, he tells you that the man has only been in the division a month, and that when he reported to the division, it was obvious from his record that he was a troublemaker. While in the division he has been assigned as a compartment cleaner and has had to be "chewed out" several times for not cleaning the division compartment properly. The man is always wanting to know how to put in for a school, but he has been told that it is useless to apply because of his bad record.

PROBLEM:

As division officer, what course of action would you take in this case?

Situation 30

You are the flight deck officer aboard an aircraft carrier. During flight operations, a new plane handler starts to walk in front of the jet intake of an aircraft that is turning up full power in a deck spot position. In violation of flight deck regulations, the jet intake is not fitted with a jet intake safety screen, and in all probability the man will be seriously injured or killed if he is drawn into the jet intake. The excessive noise on the flight deck prevents anyone giving a verbal warning to the man. As you decide it is certain that the man will be drawn into the intake, another plane handler, observing the situation, bodily knocks the man from in front of the jet intake and thus prevents a serious flight deck injury.

PROBLEMS:

1. Conduct an interview in which you commend the man for his alert action.

2. Write up a sample letter to the commanding officer recommending the man for Meritorious Mast.

Situation 31

You are a division officer, and one of your men submits a request to be permitted to take the examination for entrance to the U.S. Naval Academy.

PROBLEM:

Conduct an interview with the man to evaluate his potentialities as a naval officer.

Situation 32

You, Lieutenant Smith, are a division officer aboard ship. The following occurred at morning quarters prior to captain's inspection.

Ensign Williams, your junior division officer, while making an inspection of the division, observes that Seaman Easton has on a dirty and wrinkled uniform and is not freshly shaven. Ensign Williams, in an angry tone, severely reprimands Seaman Easton and says, "I can't understand why our chief permits you to appear this way at inspection. Clean yourself up at once, and report to me personally." Chief Boatswain's Mate Chandler, the leading chief, is accompanying Ensign Williams during the inspection, but Ensign Williams makes no comment to the leading chief.

Ensign Williams is a recently commissioned officer, excitable by nature. He lacks confidence in himself and often reflects this through an overbearing attitude toward his men.

Chief Boatswain's Mate Chandler is an old-timer who knows his rights and his duties. He is contemptuous of inexperienced officers and is sensitive about his prerogatives. His attitude is that, if they think they know it all, then let them go ahead and suffer the consequences.

Lieutenant Smith is a friendly type, with a personality that permits him to talk informally with the junior officers without becoming overly familiar.

PROBLEM:

As division officer, how would you correct the above situation and attempt to establish a good working relationship between the leading chief and the junior division officer?

Situation 33

You are a division officer and find that the personnel in your division are apparently not interested in taking the training courses for advancement in rating.

PROBLEM:

What steps would you take to develop their interests?

Situation 34

Because there has been a shortage of help in the galley, Seaman Jones has been ordered to duty as assistant to the cook. The job involves considerable dirty work, and Jones thoroughly dislikes most of it. It is necessary, however, that he be trained to perform the functions of a cook because he is the most eligible man from the point of view of background and previous experience as well as availability. Jones presented himself to his division officer with the complaint that he definitely wants a change of duty. He states that he does not like the job of cook, and that although he would like very much to become a petty officer, he never thought much of cooks.

PROBLEM:

You are the division officer. What action would you take in this case?

Situation 35

New fire-fighting gear is to be installed on your ship. The work involved is very dirty and disagreeable, and the men are hesitant about starting. The junior officer in charge of the group, although he is a commissioned officer, removes his coat and begins to work, asking the men to follow him. You are this junior officer's senior.

PROBLEM:

What is your reaction to his behavior, and what action would you take, if any, toward him?

Situation 36

Seaman Jones, thoroughly familiar with the customs and courtesies of his ship, deliberately passes through officers' country.

PROBLEM:

What action would you, as Seaman Jones's division officer, take when this is reported to you?

Situation 37

A fireman first class has just come aboard a destroyer from shore duty. His records show that he has been an unusually fine man. Aboard the destroyer, however, he becomes very seasick on his first tour of duty. As soon as the ship touches port, he jumps ship and is picked up by the shore patrol. When they ask him why he jumped ship, he says he just couldn't stand it any longer.

PROBLEM:

If you are this man's division officer and have the power to decide what to do in his case, what do you recommend?

Situation 38

You have overheard your enlisted personnel criticizing and ridiculing one of your fellow officers. To some extent the officer is to blame for the unpopularity with the enlisted personnel.

PROBLEM:

Would you say anything to your fellow officer about it, and what action would you take with the enlisted personnel?

Situation 39

A seaman, a combat veteran of many battles, has come to you and said that he would rather go to the brig than hear another gun go off.

PROBLEM:

How would you, the division officer, handle this situation?

Situation 40

You are ensign and have been given the duty of assistant gunnery officer. Your senior officer has presented you to your men.

PROBLEM:

Just what would you say to your men on your first meeting?

Situation 41

You are a division officer, and because Seaman Frantz has done extra work for you, you have recommended him for special liberty. Five of your personnel now present themselves to you and ask for special liberty on the grounds that you gave it to Frantz.

PROBLEM:

Explain how you would solve this situation and point out, if you can, what might have been wrong with your approach when you recommended the liberty for Frantz.

Situation 42

The deck hands over whom you have supervision have developed a serious dislike for the executive officer. One of the deck hands has come to you and has told you that he is going over the hill.

PROBLEM:

What action would you, as the division officer, take to prevent this from happening?

Situation 43

Seaman Johnson has been employed as a signalman aboard a destroyer and has been doing an excellent job. He is now being replaced by a signalman third class who has nowhere near the ability or the skill of Johnson. Johnson is seriously discouraged and goes about his duties in an indifferent, sullen manner. He feels that he should have been rated as a signalman third class and kept on the job.

PROBLEM:

You are Johnson's division officer. What can you do to improve Johnson's morale?

Situation 44

You are a platoon commander, 1st Bn, 6th Marine. You find that your requests for emergency leave have increased so that the number of them is out of proportion to the number of personnel under your command.

PROBLEM:

What, if anything, might be wrong in this situation?

Situation 45

You are a division officer aboard a ship that has been involved in routine duty for a considerable length of time. The men have become indifferent to training and have completely lost their snap.

PROBLEM:

Analyze the situation and describe just what actions you might take to improve morale.

Situation 46

You are a junior officer aboard an escort destroyer. Your senior officer has bypassed you and gone directly to your men to order them to do a certain job.

PROBLEM:

What action, if any, would you take?

Situation 47

A junior officer has a practice of addressing his men individually as "Mac" and in a group as "Mates." His men are apparently doing an excellent job and seem to be quite loyal to him.

PROBLEM:

If you were his senior officer, how would you regard this practice? What would you do about it, if anything?

Situation 48

A junior officer has a senior officer over her who sometimes seems to have a "better way" of doing the job. She constantly interrupts the junior officer's subordinates while they are working on a job, correcting them and indicating to them that there is a better way of doing the work. The subordinates, under these circumstances, have become very confused and resentful.

PROBLEM:

Is there any action that the junior officer can take to remedy this situation?

Situation 49

Your senior officer has ordered you to reprimand one of your personnel for failing to salute him. You know that the failure to salute was unintentional.

PROBLEM:

What action would you take?

Situation 50

You are a division officer. Another division officer is deliberately performing duties that are rightfully yours.

PROBLEM:

What would you do about it?

Situation 51

One of your fellow officers has not been able to obtain high morale in his division because he is too arbitrary with his men. You know you can help him.

PROBLEM:

Would you say anything to this officer? If so, just what would you say?

Situation 52

Your senior officer calls you by your first name.

PROBLEM:

In a social situation, is it ever permissible to address him by his first name? In a military situation, is it ever permissible? Explain your opinions.

Situation 53

Conversation in the wardroom has drifted to personalities of known senior officers and has become rather heated.

PROBLEM:

You are the senior officer present. What would you do in such a situation?

Situation 54

You have been given an assignment by your senior officer. It involves knowledge about fire control that you do not have. You know you cannot carry through this assignment.

PROBLEM:

Just how would you explain this to your senior officer, assuming that you have just reported aboard and that he does not know you?

Situation 55

You have been given an assignment by the executive officer. The captain unknowingly gives you another assignment.

PROBLEM:

What would you do?

Notes on the Sources

Much of the material in this edition of *Fundamentals of Naval Leadership* appeared in the first edition of the book, which was published by the U.S. Naval Institute in 1949. The passage of time has not altered the principles of sound leadership, but it has made locating the sources of quotes difficult. The following notes on the sources, while necessarily incomplete, contain the information available to the authors regarding sources used in the earlier editions and printings. Memorandums, directives, and instruction pamphlets from government agencies, while not cited specifically here, were used widely in the preparation of this material.

Chapter 1. The definition of leadership is adapted from *Naval Leadership* (Annapolis: U.S. Naval Institute, 1939), p. 1, and Frederick Ellsworth Wolf, A.M., *Leadership in the New Age* (Annapolis: U.S. Naval Institute, 1946), p. 3.

Chapter 7. The quotes attributed to Admiral Arleigh A. Burke are from NAVPERS 15890, *Moral Leadership*, and "Naval Leadership in Action," in *Selected Readings in Leadership* (Annapolis: U.S. Naval Institute, 1957).

Chapter 8. Admiral William V. Pratt's ideas appeared in *Selected Readings in Leadership*, p. 1. The material on naval customs, usage, ceremony, and traditions was adapted from the pamphlet entitled *Leadership and Administration*, from the Naval Line School. The meeting between Lee and Grant at Appamatox was described by Bruce Catton in *This Hallowed Ground* (copyright 1955, 1956, by Bruce Catton; reprinted by permission of Doubleday & Co., Inc.).

Chapter 9. Admiral Arleigh A. Burke's outline of leadership qualities appeared in "Naval Leadership in Action," pp 11–16.

Chapter 12. The principles referred to in the chapter's closing sentence can be found in *Selected Readings in Leadership*, p. 114.

Chapter 14. Admiral Arleigh A. Burke's description of a well-disciplined organization appeared in *Selected Readings in Leadership*, p. 104. Human limitations are outlined in pp. 102–5 of the same book.

Chapter 16. The principles of organization are adapted from *Principles of Administration*, vol. 4: *Economics of National Security*.